THE LION OF WALL STREET

THE TWO LIVES OF JACK DREYFUS

The Lion of Wall Street

Author of *A Remarkable Medicine Has Been Overlooked*

Jack Dreyfus

REGNERY PUBLISHING
Washington, D.C.

Library of Congress Cataloging-in Publication Data

Dreyfus, Jack, 1913-
    The lion of Wall Street : the two lives of Jack J. Dreyfus.
    p.   cm.
    Includes bibliographical references.
    ISBN 0-89526-461-7
    1. Dreyfus, Jack, 1913-   . 2. Capitalists and financiers--United
States--Biography. 3. Dreyfus, Jack, 1913-   --Health.
    4. Depression, Mental--Patients--United States--Biography.
    5. Phenytoin. I. Title.
    HG172.D75D74   1995
    332' .092--dc20   95-37523
    [B]   CIP

Published in the United States by Regnery Publishing, Inc.
An Eagle Publishing Company
422 First Street, SE, Suite 300, Washington, DC 20003

Distributed to the trade by National Book Network
4720-A Boston Way, Lanham, MD 20706

Printed on acid-free paper.
Manufactured in the United States of America
Designed by REM Studio, Inc.

1 3 5 7 9 10 8 6 4 2

Books are available in quantity for promotional or premium use.
Write to Director of Special Sales, Regnery Publishing, Inc.,
422 First Street, SE, Suite 300, Washington, DC 20003,
for information on discounts and terms or call (202) 546-5005.

PTB

This book is dedicated to
Mark Twain, to Helen Raudonat,
to Joan Personette, and to Johnny.

CONTENTS

AUTOBIOGRAPHY

A REMARKABLE MEDICINE HAS BEEN OVERLOOKED

PREFACE

This is called Preface because of its location. It wasn't written until I had almost finished this book.

To write an autobiography one has to look back at one's life. I looked back at my life. Then I looked again—this time more closely—and was astounded. I've never known of any life, so diversified, with such a high degree of success. It's embarrassing to say something like that about one's own life, but it's the truth. It's a sure thing I didn't do all those things on my own.

Let me explain.

A few months ago I had thoroughly exhausted myself trying to get help from someone in the U.S. government. I was so worn out I was almost too tired to take a vacation. I selected a place where no one would know me, Blackberry Inn in the hills of Tennessee. I planned to do nothing and plenty of it.

When I arrived at the Inn I noted it was attractively furnished, and everybody there was extremely nice. I'd made a lucky selection.

There were 1,100 acres of wooded property and one could drive a golf cart around it. I'd brought two books with me: *In*

Search of the Miraculous by P. D. Ouspensky and *The Complete Essays of Mark Twain.* In the morning I would take the golf cart down to a beautiful little stream with a few chairs scattered near it. Each day I would sit in a different place and read.

I started with *In Search of the Miraculous,* which I'd read years ago. It's a story of Ouspensky's meetings with Georges Gurdjieff, a superbrilliant man, extraordinary in many ways. Some called him a mystic. The book is deep. I skipped around in reading it. On the third day I read (Mr. Gurdjieff talking to Mr. Ouspensky):

> "Man is a machine. All his deeds, actions, words, thoughts, feelings, convictions, opinions, and habits are the results of external influences, external impressions. Out of himself a man cannot produce a single thought, a single action.... It all happens."

That stirred a memory of Mark Twain's "What Is Man?" which by coincidence, probably not by coincidence, was in the other book I had with me. In it, The Old Man talking to The Young Man says:

> "Personally you did not create even the smallest microscopic fragment of the materials out of which your opinion is made; and personally you cannot claim even the slender merit of putting the borrowed materials together. That was done automatically—by your mental machinery, in strict accordance with the law of that machinery's construction."

Mr. Gurdjieff and Mark Twain don't need my concurrence, but they have it.

I'd like to go further. If something happens in an individual's life that can be of great importance to the rest of the creatures on this earth, it may not be that it "just happened." It is almost a sure thing that the life was influenced from above.

Most of my life I have been an agnostic. I'm not now.

Ida Lewis Dreyfus
Section, Earth
Heaven

Dear Ida:

This is the year of your one-hundredth birthday. It is custom at this time for you to receive a report on the activities of your eldest child—in this case, your son Jack.

In 1939 your son was married to Joan Personette, a fine artist. They had a son, John. Although Joan and Jack have been divorced for forty-seven years, the love between them and John goes three ways.

A brief summary follows:

ATHLETICS

Golf—Before he was twenty, your son won the City Golf Championship of Montgomery, Alabama, twice. He has won eighteen club championships, at four different country clubs.

Jack qualified for the National Amateur Golf Championship on each of the three occasions he tried.

Tennis—When he was sixty-two, your son won the U.S. Open (Open means professionals and amateurs) Doubles Lawn Tennis Championship for 60s-and-over. Ten years later, in Australia, he won the World's Open Doubles Lawn Tennis Championship, for 70s-and-over.

CARD PLAYING

Jack qualified for the Masters Bridge Tournament when he was twenty-eight. When he was thirty he devised a scientific method of playing gin rummy and beat the best players.

For thirty years the *Encyclopedia of Bridge* said Jack was reputed to be the best gin rummy player in the United States.

HORSE RACING

Your son established Hobeau Farm, a thoroughbred breeding farm, in Ocala, Florida. The first horse he bred was a champion. Twice, Hobeau Farm won the New York Turf Writers' Award for Outstanding Breeder of the Year.

Jack was head of the Horsemen's Benevolent and Protective Association and received the Fitzsimmons Award, "One Who Contributed Most to Racing."

On two occasions your son was Chairman of the Board of Trustees of the New York Racing Association. He received the Eclipse Award, "Man Who Did Most for Racing."

BUSINESS

Your son became senior partner of a New York Stock Exchange firm when he was thirty-three.

Business was poor, and it was decided to advertise. The budget was so small that Jack, who had no experience in advertising, had to write the ads. His firm received the first Standard & Poor's Gold Trophy for Excellence in Wall Street Advertising.

Business improved, and a mutual fund was started. Your son was head of research for the Fund. For the twelve years he directed the research the Fund outperformed all other mutual funds by a large margin.

Your son wrote the prospectus and created the advertising for the Fund. He received an unusual award, one of the five best marketing persons of the 1960–1970 decade.

An article in *Life* magazine about your son was titled, "Maverick Wizard Behind the Wall Street Lion." In it was said, "He has been called an upstart, an interloper and a genius. Yet he is, without doubt, the most singular and effective personality to appear in Wall Street since the days of Joseph Kennedy and Bernard Baruch."

When he retired from Wall Street your son was one of the wealthiest men in the United States.

Your son received Honorary Doctor of Law Degrees from the University of Lehigh and from the University of Alabama, medical branch.

MEDICAL RESEARCH

In 1958 your son had a depression, called endogenous (coming from within). The intense part of the depression lasted for about a year, but it persisted for more than five years. He saw a neuropsychiatrist six days a week.

One weekend, he had thoughts about the effects of electricity in his body. As a result, he asked his physician to let him try a medicine not generally known to be useful for his symptoms. To the surprise of them both he promptly returned to good health. [*Note:* For a patient to be correct in selecting for himself one drug, from a pharmacopoeia of thousands, is believed to be without precedent.]

When your son saw six other persons, with symptoms similar to his own, have prompt recoveries with the medicine, he realized he had an obligation to investigate further. After unsuccessful attempts to get studies done by members of the medical profession, he established a charitable medical foundation and retired from business to work full time in it.

Your son participated in research studies. Then it was discovered that physicians around the world had published thousands of studies reporting the medicine useful for a broad range of disorders. The foundation painstakingly gathered this information and condensed it into bibliographies. On three occasions, bibliographies were sent to all the physicians in the United States.

Your son has spent many years trying to get officials in the U.S. Government to do something about this vital matter. But he found Government too busy with problems to have time for solutions.

Your son was not an author, and it took him six years to write a book, *A Remarkable Medicine Has Been Overlooked*. Written for the physician, the U.S. Government, and the public, all at the same time, it received excellent reviews.

The bibliographies and your son's book have been translated into many languages, and understanding of the medicine is increasing around the world. But the lack of understanding is still great, and much needless suffering exists. Your son must continue his efforts.

Ida, I have seen many reports. Permit me to observe that your son's is unlike any other I have seen.

With kindest regards,

The Reporting Angel

A self-addressed envelope is enclosed, if you care to use it.

Ida Lewis Dreyfus
Section, Earth
Heaven, June 14

The Reporting Angel
Department of Records
Heaven

Dear Reporting Angel:

Thank you for your kind letter and the spirit behind it.

I must tell you that a terrible mistake has been made—it's only fair to the mothers of the other boys whose records have been mixed in with my son's.

The part about golf and cards sounds like Jack. But you can see for yourself that for him to win National Tennis Championships doesn't make any sense at all.

One thing I can tell you, for my son to have become one of the wealthiest men in the United States is impossible—if I knew a stronger word I would use it. Before I left, Jack had had three different jobs, at fifteen dollars a week, and hadn't made a go of any of them. It was no secret in the family that he would have a hard time making a living. He was a nice boy, but lazy, and had no ambition at all. Once he told me, in confidence, if he ever made $100,000 he would retire and live on the income—but he knew he never would.

As far as the medical part you speak of, Jack knew nothing about medicine and had no interest in it. Apparently things got mixed up in the celestial computer. Could people from the U.S. Government be involved here?

Again, I'd like you to know how deeply I appreciate your thoughtfulness.

With warmest regards,

Ida Lewis Dreyfus

Ida Lewis Dreyfus
Section, Earth
Heaven

Dear Ida:

My sending you a self-addressed envelope was unusual, in fact it required special permission. But I thought you might be dissatisfied with my letter—the opposite of its purpose.

Your comment that U.S. government people might be involved with my Computer requires no response.

As to your letter, I will explain.

The facts in my letter to you are correct. But you are also correct. It would not have been possible for your son to have done all those things, not on his own. He had to have a great amount of instruction, assistance, and direct aid from Departments up here.

Let me go back to 1908. At that time, the High Command, foreseeing the expanding use of electricity and radiation and the development of the nuclear bomb, decided it was necessary to give the human being a drug that would work against excessive anger and fear, by correcting inappropriate electrical activity in the body. In so doing, this drug would help against a host of symptoms and disorders, since almost all of the body's functions are electrically motivated. It would not affect normal function, sedate, or be habit-forming.

To achieve this our Pharmaceutical Department synthesized a medicine and our Messengers put it in the hands of Heinrich Biltz, a German chemist, who naturally thought he synthesized it himself. When our Messengers saw that Heinrich had sold the medicine to a drug company, they assumed that within a reasonable period of time the facts about the drug would become known. Then they left

Earth. As you know, we are busy with more important places in the Cosmos.

Our Messengers checked back fifty years later and were astonished, no—nothing the human being does astonishes—they were dismayed to find that the medicine was almost exclusively thought of as an anticonvulsant. A miracle was not applicable here, but something had to be done. And it had to be done in a way that the human being would consider perfectly natural.

Your son was selected for a difficult assignment from among many candidates. One requirement was a good sense of probabilities, an aptitude that comes with the baby. Your son had that. And he had two other aptitudes—I should say disaptitudes—that made him an excellent candidate. His sense of direction was in backwards, and along with this came a faulty copying device. As you know, humans learn by copying and Jack can't learn that way. It is usually a disadvantage, but not for our purposes. Since he couldn't copy, he had to figure things out for himself. In addition, as you have said, he had no ambition. This was also an asset. We didn't have to struggle with any personal desires.

For our purposes it was necessary for your son to have a great deal of money. It was decided he should make it in Wall Street. While he was making the money there, we could accomplish other things. He could be trained in research, and his ability to communicate could be enhanced. These abilities would be needed later.

I am not at liberty to say more.

Be happy always,

The Reporting Angel

You will hear from me in a hundred years.

Mother

EARLIEST RECOLLECTION

My earliest recollection is of a debate I had with my mother. I was almost two years old and in my high chair.

Mother had brought me supper, which included a carefully mashed sweet potato. There was also an unpeeled sweet potato on the tray. I said I wanted that one. My mother said the mashed potato was for me. I said I wanted the whole one. Mother said I must eat the mashed potato. Then, appealing to my better instincts, she said the whole potato was for her, without it she wouldn't have any supper. My better instincts were small. I said I wanted the whole potato and got it.

That was about seventy-five years ago. I doubt if one remembers things that far back on a straight line. I thought of that potato every five or ten years, always with a sense of guilt. I was thirty-five or forty before I woke up and realized that Mother could have eaten my potato. Since then I've felt better.

Before going any further I should say that I think my mother was the sweetest person in the world. If she wasn't, at least she was tied for first place.

A story illustrates Mother's sweetness. She and her sister Bertha were driving from New York to Montgomery, Alabama. After about 150 miles they stopped at a roadside restaurant for lunch. Mother had to walk around the front of the car. As she passed the grille, she saw the usual gnats and moths to be expected there, and exclaimed, "My goodness, Bertha, can't you be more careful."

When Aunt Bertha told us this story we laughed at the idea of her driving down the highway dodging moths and other bugs. Years later it occurred to me that it showed how sweet my mother was. She even worried about little bugs.

Mother loved me, which wasn't always easy; I loved her, which was always easy.

AT THE BEGINNING

If you want to write an autobiography, you have to be born. I was, in St. Margaret's Hospital in Montgomery, Alabama, on August 28, 1913. This event was not attended by Halley's Comet, as was the case with Mark Twain.

After I had been sufficiently born I was brought to 307 Mildred Street, the home of my parents, in the Penick (pronounced Peenick) Apartments. The Penick Apartments were small brick houses, but called apartments because they were glued together by common walls. These walls must have been pretty thick because we never heard the neighbors.

There were four apartments on Mildred Street, and four, at right angles, on Mulberry Street. This semi-square was squared off in the backyard by a tall board fence. There were a couple of empty, optimistic garages if any of us got affluent. There were also eight large chicken coops—one for each apartment. Chickens were executed by our janitor, Reuben. When I was a little boy this didn't bother me. Now it would bother me a lot.

When I was four my father's business (he sold candy) was not good, and we moved to my mother's house in Newark,

N.J., for a year or so. My mother's father had a large house on Shanley Avenue. He had established the I. Lewis Cigar Manufacturing Company, a successful business. I don't remember my grandfather well, but I liked him.

I have a few memories from Newark. I remember falling off the porch, and my Uncle Donald digging me out of four feet of snow. And I remember a Galapagos tortoise in the backyard. He was so big, and I was so small, I could sit on his back.

Across the street from our house was an empty lot. There I used to play marbles, for keeps, with a little kid from down the block. One day I bankrupted him—won all his marbles and ten cents besides. Apparently I was born with a gambling instinct. Fortunately, it came with a good sense of probabilities. My advice to the unborn is, don't be born with a gambling instinct unless you have a good sense of probabilities.

In the field where we played marbles, there were lots of weeds. That summer they got pretty high and dry. I considered what lighting a match to them would do. I tried it, and the effect was better than expected. It started a roaring fire. I departed the scene early, and before the fire was discovered was a couple of blocks away. I was suspected but had such an innocent look that nobody could be sure.

The fire was picturesque and also dangerous. It could have lapped over to the houses. Fortunately, it didn't. As the reader can see, I was rotten from the beginning. Later, my father's hairbrush didn't knock it all out of me.

■ ■ ■

When I was five we left Newark to return to the Penick Apartments in Montgomery. The one we returned to was 308 Mildred Street. It had two advantages over our previous apartment. It was an end apartment, with windows that gave us a side view. Also it had a small tree on the lawn. I loved to climb that tree.

On Mildred Street—my first horse

At the corner of Mildred and Mulberry Streets, there was a big old house. On its lawn was a great magnolia tree with white blossoms, the shape of melons. They smelled wonderful. That was the nice part of the house. The other part of the house was two kids, six and seven years old, named Sam and Charlie Gordon. They were tough cookies.

I was six when Sam was six. One day I got in a fight with him, or rather Sam started a fight. Some of my friends were around so although I was scared to fight, I was more scared not to fight. So I fought. Apparently, it was a draw because Sam stopped. I was complimented by my friends, but I was not happy about the situation.

A few weeks later I found myself, fortunately, in front of my own house—at least I thought it was fortunate—in a debate with Charlie, who was a tougher cookie than Sam. We exchanged comments that could not be mistaken for flattery. The name of the game was to look tough. I saw my mother peeking out the window, and I thought, "Oh, thank goodness, she's going to get me out of this," but she had more wisdom than that. I was shaking in my boots, although barefoot, but somehow I bluffed my way through, and Charlie went away. I went inside and asked Mother why she hadn't helped me. She said that would have made things worse, he'd have caught me the next day.

Except for the fight with Sam Gordon I don't think I've ever had an actual fight. I used to wrestle in the fourth grade, at recess, with my friend Willie Winkenhopper, but that was for fun. And nobody ever won. I love the name Willie Winkenhopper. I'm not making it up.

When I was eleven or twelve, in the summer, a friend, Cooper Griel, and I used to get up early and go out to the Woodley Country Club. We'd play tennis when nobody was around until about noon, and we never seemed to get tired. We got up around seven o'clock in the morning—without waking our parents—with a toe-pull alarm I invented. It consisted of a string, tied around the big toe, and dropped out the window. Cooper and I would put the strings on before we went to bed. When Cooper pulled my string, I woke up—promptly. This alarm clock has two advantages. It's cheap—and it will wake up the dead. Cooper always woke up first, so I never had the pleasure.

When I got dressed, Cooper and I would walk up to Hull Street and take the streetcar which went out to the Woodley Club. There was a man on the streetcar who used to make change. I was very impressed with him. He had a little belt around his stomach, and he would press a button and eject nickels, dimes, and quarters. That's the job I wanted to have when I grew up. It was my only ambition. As fate would have it, streetcars were abolished so I never got to be what I wanted to be.

Cooper Griel was a nice boy and unusual in several ways. I've never heard of anybody else whose first name was Cooper. And he had a great Russian wolfhound named Zaree. And Cooper was a Griel. In Montgomery there was a small Jewish community. The leading family, the aristocracy so to speak, was named Weil. They were big in the cotton manufacturing business. The next best-known family was the Griels. There was an expression around Montgomery, "the Weils, the Griels, and the schlemiels." I never felt like I was one of the latter, but probably I was.

On the subject of religion, my parents were Jewish, by descent, but they never made any issue of it with me. Anyway, it never took. I'm neutral on the subject of which religion. As I see it, it's the question of whether or not there's a God. That's up to everybody. How He wants you to conduct yourself, as I see it, is between you and Him. I don't think anybody's got a lock on the right way, so to speak. So I've been neutral. The few times I think about it, it does seem that if people would deemphasize the religious thing and stop feeling they've got the only right way, we could spend more time being nice to each other. It really doesn't make much sense. There are a thousand religions, and everyone thinks theirs is the right one. This is probably not correct.

My father was born in Montgomery, and so were his brothers. He had an older brother, Morris, and three other brothers and a sister. I remember Grandpa Dreyfus. He lived to be eighty-seven and used to drink a quart of corn liquor every day. Grandpa and I used to play dominoes when I was about five. I beat him sometimes. He wasn't happy about that.

Grandpa Dreyfus was called "Major." I don't remember why. I think it was some sort of honorary title. I heard in the family that he was a cousin of Alfred Dreyfus of the famous Dreyfus case. My grandmother's name was Emma. I never saw much of her because she died when I was a few years old.

Apparently Grandpa hadn't been a businessman and my Uncle Morris had been the breadwinner for the family. When he was thirteen he had a little store, and from what I gather, that had supported the family. When he became older, Morris, with his brother Dave, started a company called The Dreyfus Brothers Candy Manufac-turing Company, a very successful business. Their best seller was a huge peppermint cane that sold for a nickel.

Uncle Morris retired when he was forty-nine. Unlike some retired people it wasn't a drag on him—he found plenty of things to do. From a business point of view, he invested his money in mortgages with the people around town. I never heard of him foreclosing; I think he was lenient that way.

Uncle Morris had a little house which he bought for $10,000–in those days that was a lot of money. There was a bit of ground around the house and Uncle Morris became a gardener–planted all sorts of flowers. He loved to work in the garden. So between shopping and gardening and a little business activity, he was fully busy. He was a happy man and enjoyed his retirement. He lived with his wife, my Aunt Helen, and her mother. Living with your mother-in-law is not always a pleasure, but Uncle Morris took it in good spirits.

I'd never heard Uncle Morris say a cuss word. I sort of assumed he didn't know any, and I hadn't had any thought of teaching him.

Uncle Morris drove a middle-aged Buick and was an indifferent driver—that's a fancy word for lousy. One day, we were going up Hull Street, and he was driving. From the left a gentleman ignored the stop sign and flew right across Hull Street, while we were crossing the intersection. Uncle Morris deftly, for him or for anybody for that matter, pulled our car to the right. We went up on a sidewalk, up on a neighbor's lawn, around a neighbor's tree, down onto the sidewalk, past a telephone pole, and back onto Hull Street. No harm was done. However this released a new vocabulary from Uncle Morris. My surmise that he didn't know any cuss words had been wrong. He knew some. In fact, he knew some I'd never heard. Altogether it was a memorable experience.

I was told that my father went somewhere in Kentucky to bet on the horse races. He did well for a while but then went broke and wired Uncle Morris for money. Uncle Morris replied that he'd send him some, along with candy samples, so that Dad could work his way back, by visiting "jobbers," the name for candy wholesalers in the South. That's how my father became a candy salesman. Dad used to be away from home almost six months a year, visiting jobbers.

When I was twenty, Dad got the idea of not working with jobbers, but working with the large chain stores, of which there were about eight or ten, like Woolworth, Kress, and McCrory. A sale to one of them would be the equivalent of fifty sales to a jobber. It was a good idea, except it caused us to move to New York City.

I had two sisters, Lorraine and Joan. Lorraine was born about four years after I was. There was a great deal of fuss about Lorraine, and I didn't like it. I tried to swap her for a billygoat, but the transaction fell through. As we grew older I preferred Lorraine to a billygoat. Really, I loved her very much. Unfortunately, she died about ten years ago.

My sister Joan is still in good shape and bothering me regularly, and I love her very much. However, if someone would offer me two billygoats... Joan lives in Boston, the Hub—of the Universe I suppose.

Sunday mornings, Lorraine and Joan would come into my bed with me and I would read the funny papers. All week long we looked forward to Sunday. The funnies were so good that they were a section by themselves. I remember Maggie and Jiggs, Mutt and Jeff, Bringing Up Father, The Katzenjammer Kids, and Little Orphan Annie.

Lorraine had great faith in me. I had a BB gun when I was about seven years old. She would put a BB on her shoe and let me shoot it off, from two or three feet. I promised her I would give her a Kewpie doll for this. And I kept my word—on her fiftieth birthday I gave her one. This was a squarer deal than Mark Twain made with his brother, Henry. To secure favors, Mark promised to give Henry the first fifty-cent piece he found floating down the river on an anvil.

When I was six years old, I had to go to school.

GRAMMAR SCHOOL

I was six when I went to grammar school in Montgomery. I'd had the great fortune to miss kindergarten. One day, in the first grade, Mrs. Barclay, a sweet, blond, elderly woman of about thirty-eight, was playing the piano. The children were in back of her, singing, and she turned around and said, "Who is that singing like an angel?" I looked around for an angel and saw that all the children were pointing at me. That's the last time I have been confused with an angel.

After first grade comes second grade. Here I had another elderly teacher, Miss P., not nearly as sweet as Mrs. Barclay. In fact I think she was a witch. At that time, when we came to school, each class lined up in front of the school. There was to be an award for promptness among the different classes. One day I got there a few minutes late and Miss P. was not delighted. I had injured our chances, and she told me that, at recess the next day, she was going to have me "bumped." I didn't know what "bumped" meant but the way she said it made me think I wouldn't care for it.

Miss P. was mistaken about the next day because the next day I wasn't in school. I had a sore throat which my mother couldn't exactly put her finger on. Anyhow it persisted the following day. By the third day my mother thought my sore throat might do just as well in school, so I dragged myself back to second grade. Sure enough, Miss P. hadn't forgotten, and at recess she took me back to a fence and had four large boys—two holding my hands and two holding my feet—swing me back and forth and bump me against the fence. Well, it wasn't as bad as I had thought it might be, but, gosh, the anguish I went through before the bumping.

One day, before recess, I acquired, or obtained improperly— it's hard when you're talking about yourself to say stole—a ham sandwich from the lunch shelf. My parents didn't give me school lunches because they fed me pretty well and I was on the plump side. Anyhow, I did this deed, and the little girl who was the owner of the sandwich apprehended me in the backyard and brought Miss P. into the matter. I whipped out a lie, and said my parents had guests over for bridge the night before and had served baked ham. It was logical that I would have a ham sand-wich. It was a close call, but perhaps Miss P., having had the pleasure of bumping me, thought, well, let him get away with this one. Now if you want to say that I was only seven and it was all right for me to steal and that I didn't know any better, you're wrong. I did know better. And this was an early lesson in the value of constructive lying. I'd gotten off to a good start.

When my father's business took a turn for the better he sent me to a private school called Barnes University School. I don't know what University had to do with it. I guess it just sounded good. It had a little over a hundred boys in it. We had to buy mil-itary uniforms which we wore on special occasions, not every day, thank goodness. It was a nice school. I remember a few things about it—playing touch football in a big back yard, and wrestling at recess.

Professor Barnes was a music buff, although I doubt if there was such a word in those days. He had a choir of eighteen boys. They sang for a half an hour every day. He also had a special, special choir of four boys, and I was in it. One day Professor Barnes said, "Dreyfus, could you sing like that by yourself?" I said, "Sure." So he asked everybody to hold it, and the piano started up. I couldn't open my mouth. Pure 100 percent stage fright. It's nice to remember that he had picked me as a soloist from the special, special choir. Right next to me was Frank Tennille. Frank became an outstanding pop singer.

One other memory from Barnes University School sticks in my mind. Many years later I read Mark Twain's "What Is Man?" In it he talks of the "flash of wit" and how it really is a flash. You don't have time to think.

It was such a flash that got me into trouble at Barnes. I was eight years old at the time. We were in Mr. Henderson's class, a kind man who wanted to do something nice for one of us—give us a little gift. Mr. Henderson asked Tommy Curtis to choose-up, to see who would get the present. In those days the custom was to say "eenie, meenie, minie, mo, catch a gentleman by the toe." It's gone out of style. Tommy started out in a way none of us had ever heard. He said, "eenie, meenie, dixie, deanie." And I said, "catch a doggie by his weenie," before he could finish. There was an uproar. Mr. Henderson admonished me on the spot and arranged a private meeting with Professor Barnes. After some stern comments from Professor Barnes I was let go, but I think I saw crinkles around his eyes.

I repeat this story because it's worth thinking about. Here's a little eight-year-old boy, minding his own business, and something like that pops out of his mouth. It sort of confirms Mark Twain's point.

I went from Barnes University School, which was nice, to Starke University School, which was, to say the least, rigorous. Starke's made a big deal about military issues. We had to wear uniforms daily, with a stiff two-inch collar. Some genius figured out if you have a stiff two-inch collar, you'll hold your head up right. I'd like to have gotten hold of his head.

We went through all the motions of a military school, including drilling with heavy guns. And we had guard duty, as a punishment. You'd get it in clumps of three hours, with a rifle that felt like a ton, and you'd have to walk back and forth for three hours. We drilled every day. I have a mixed-up sense of direction; when I pivoted on the wrong foot, Mr. Cochran who was drilling us would say, "Stick Dreyfus." Ouch, three hours guard duty.

Professor Starke was a bugger for the truth and had a little contraption called a hickory switch which he used on us when we were caught lying. I still remember the formal expression, "Hold out your hand, sir," and then the hickory.

Another pleasantry was called columns. One column was a word written fifteen times. Ten columns (150 words) was not too tough if the word was cat or dog. But if it was interdenominationalisticism or paraminobenzoldiethyminoethynol, it was suffering.

I remember getting ten columns of interdenominationalisticism on a technicality. I used to kick my friend Hart Lyon in Mr. Meyers' class. One day Mr. Meyers said, "Dreyfus, if you kick Hart once more in class, I am going to give you ten columns of interdenominationalisticism." I heeded. But when Hart went out of the room, once he was over the doorstep, I kicked him and Mr. Meyers said, "Okay, Dreyfus, ten columns." "But," I said, "Mr. Meyers, Hart wasn't in class." I thought I had him on a technicality. But it didn't work.

One day Bolling Starke, Professor Starke's son, was asking the students some questions. I don't remember what they were about, but he gave me a compliment. He said, "Dreyfus, you're not so dumb." I was amazed because I thought I was, or I wouldn't have remembered it to this day.

Professor Starke was an unusual character. By the way, I never knew what his first name was, we always called him Fessor Starke. One day he told us how he'd made a mistake on his income tax and shortchanged the United States government by eighty cents. But he thought it unfair to send them a check for eighty cents and put them to all that trouble. So he came up with an idea he was proud of. He bought eighty cents worth of

Mother, sisters Joan and Lorraine, and me in my Starke uniform

postage stamps, and burned them. He told this to the class as an example of integrity at its peak.

There was another time when Professor Starke, in a grandiloquent mood, decided he was going to award three hours guard duty, free, to the person who solved what he called a riddle. He said there was a little boy and a few girls at a picnic. The girls were chatting along. The little boy was shy but felt he should contribute. Finally, he said, "Have you ever worked an enema?" Professor Starke said the boy had misspoken and said, "If you can guess what he meant to say, I'll give you three hours of guard duty, free." Please don't strain your brain. The boy had meant to say, "Have you ever worked an enigma?"

All the older boys took a shot at this, but nothing was right. As time was running out my friend Hart Lyon, feeling you shouldn't blow an opportunity like this without a try, held up his hand. Professor Starke said, "What did the little boy mean, Hart, when he said, 'Have you ever worked an enema?'" Hart said, "He meant to say, 'Has an enema ever worked you?'" I never heard such a spontaneous roar. Even the Fessor almost smiled.

I should mention part of the education at Starke's which was good, a course called Mental Arithmetic. It consisted of problems that we had to solve orally, standing up in class. I can still remember some of them.

Here's one. A man paid $35 for a bookcase. Three-sevenths of the cost of the bookcase was four-fifths of what he paid for a bureau, and three-fourths of the cost of the bureau was five-fourths of what he paid for a table. What did he pay for the bureau and for the table?

You stood up in class and said, "One-seventh of $35 is $5, and three times $5 are $15. Fifteen dollars is 4/5ths of what he paid for the bureau. One-fifth of what he paid for the bureau is 1/4th of $15.00 or 15/4ths of a dollar and..." I won't go further, you can't buy furniture that cheap nowadays.

Fessor Starke jumped on us if we said two times four is eight. Two times four are eight. I'll never forget that one times something carries an "is," and two or more carries an "are."

Now that I think about it, that was the best course I had in school. It got me to know fractions pretty well. To tell the truth, I wouldn't give you a nickel for percentages. I can understand them if I have to, but I hate those 0.1 things.

Play

I may have given the impression that during my grammar school days it was all work and no play. Not so, or I would be a duller boy. There was plenty of play—on weekends and those long wonderful days called summer vacation.

The first "play" I recall was when I was six years old. On weekends I would wake up at six, bounce out of bed, put on my overalls, and head for the bathroom. When duties were completed, I would glance at my toothbrush—I didn't have time to use it—and rush out to the backyard to play with my dog Scott. Usually my pal Rose Morris was there, and some of the other children, but that wasn't necessary. The juices of play were in me.

One morning I was in a hurry to get to the other side of the fence. I could have walked thirty yards and gone around it. Instead, I scrambled over the fence, and caught the top of my right foot on a protruding nail. The gash made a white mark on the top of my foot that lasted thirty years. It also settled a running argument with my mother, as to whether I should wear shoes.

About two blocks from my house there was a big lot. In the summer many children, fifty or sixty or more, came there every day. We ranged in age from six to fourteen and assorted ourselves accordingly. The older boys played softball, and at the end of the summer switched to touch football. The rest of us played anything—tag, hide-and-seek, mumbly-peg, and kitty-o-cat. For the uneducated—when four or more boys and a baseball and bat were present, someone would yell "first bat kitty-o-cat," and the others had a moral obligation to play. There was a pitcher, a batter, a catcher, and at least one fielder. The batter had to get to first base and back to home plate. Not too difficult due to the scarcity of fielders.

Those summer days were pure joy. I thought back to them about fifteen years ago when I was in Central Park, trying to write *A Remarkable Medicine Has Been Overlooked*. Each day around noon about a hundred children were let out of school. They came running into the park, yelling, jumping, skipping, and chasing each other. There was no semblance of a game. I said to myself, they have the juices of youth in them. Then I looked fifty yards away and saw the elderly sitting on the benches, quietly staring ahead, and thought, they have the juices of old age. This could be studied. There might be chemicals in the young that could be safely given to the aged, with benefit.

After I had gone to Starke University School for two years, my parents sent me to Sidney Lanier High, a public school. Maybe my father thought I'd learned how to tell the truth. More likely, my mother was tired of guard duty and the hickory stick. I was grateful for the change, but I must say that Starke's made a lasting impression.

HIGH SCHOOL

Sidney Lanier High School was not named after Napoleon Bonaparte. A piece of information that floated around the school was that Sidney Lanier (a renowned poet) had ordered the first shot to be fired at Fort Sumter that started the Civil War. We took pride in that. I don't know why.

Sidney Lanier was a great deal different from my previous four years of school. There wasn't that strict attitude—and there were lots of pretty girls. Barnes' and Starke's had been for boys only.

I don't remember much about high school, I was so absorbed with playing golf at that time. I played after school, weekends, and of course summer vacations. But I remember a few things.

My grades were average. The only course I remember was one I flunked. It was first-year Latin. I'd flunked it at Starke's, and I flunked it again at Lanier. The third time I took no chances. I studied hard—carried Miss Caldwell's tray at lunch—and passed.

Any possibility that I might have had a singing career came to an end at Lanier. I was singing in a large group. The teacher stopped us and said, "Dreyfus, you're off key." (My voice was changing and I didn't realize it.) Several of the students who knew my singing background said, "Mrs. Simpson, Jack's a wonderful singer." Mrs. Simpson was not impressed. She insisted I was doing the music no good. Since that put-down I've never sung, except to mumble "Happy Birthday." Mrs. Simpson may have cost us another Elvis, or even an Enrico.*

At school there was a big, quiet boy named Johnny Caine. He played on the football team, later went to the University of Alabama and made All American. He was extraordinary on kickoff, could consistently kick the ball out of the end zone. Wallace Wade, coach at Alabama, made a profit on this. He had Johnny line up on the right side of the field, and angle the ball to the opposite corner. Often the other team was stopped on the 5- or 10-yard line. I'm still proud of Johnny.

I was shy with the girls at school. I didn't realize how shy— you don't know how other people are. But I got objective evidence. In my senior year I sat across the aisle from a pretty girl named Jurelle. She sometimes sat with her dress a little above her rolled stockings. I noticed, but never when she was looking.

A few years later I met Jurelle. She told me that in our senior year she had bet three girls, twenty-five cents each, she could get me to look at her—and lost the bet. Imagine how shy I must have been for four girls to bet on the subject?

After high school comes college, for some people. As I've said, my grades were average, and colleges were not vying for my attendance.

Before going to college, let me talk about golf, an important factor in my life.

*Caruso, for recent arrivals.

GOLF—A PLEASURE

When Cooper Griel and I played tennis at the Woodley Country Club, we were only fifty yards from the golf course. I loved the look of that green expanse, and yearned to get on the course—there was a strong tug. But the Woodley Club had a rule you couldn't play until you were thirteen. On my thirteenth birthday I started, and didn't pick up a tennis racket for another thirty-five years.

My first rounds were with my mother and my Aunt Helen. They were not good, and bounced the ball along the ground about a hundred yards. I did the same. One day I made a spectacular shot—on a 170-yard par-three my drive trickled onto the green. Mother and Aunt Helen were ecstatic; I was a little puffed up myself. After a few more rounds with them I started playing alone.

Now the first thing you do when you play golf is grab hold of the club. This is called a grip. I had been taught a grip by Mr. Morris of the Penick Apartments, and it wasn't a good grip. It was what you would call a strong grip, with the right hand too much under and the left hand too far over. My powers of observation are impoverished so I didn't notice that other people's grips were different. I started with Mr. Morris' grip, and used it till I was twenty-one. The grip had a major disadvantage, it made you hook the ball.

It never occurred to me to change the grip—when I started to hook, I changed something else. I brought the club back well on the inside, and then moved my body ahead fast, to get the blade open so that it would be square at impact. It was not easy but, with plenty of practice, I got to do it quite well. And it had one advantage. For my weight, less than 130 pounds, I hit the ball a long way, almost as far as Florian Straussberger and Dr. Blue Harris, the long hitters in Montgomery.

There was a place between the fifth green and the sixth tee, a little plateau of grass that I used to practice from. It was a spot where divots were not apt to bother anybody. I used to hit a bag of balls and my caddy, Perry, I'll tell you about him later, would bring them back and I'd hit them again, for hours.

In those days there was no such thing as a practice green at the Woodley Club. I pitched and putted for hours on the greens themselves. They were Bermuda greens, slow and tough, and nobody minded.

Pretty soon I was shooting in the high forties. One day I got a forty-three. That was my best score for a while. Then I had a thirty-nine—such a big drop that nobody in the clubhouse believed it. That was the beginning of my playing well.

By the time I was fifteen I got to the finals of the Woodley Country Club Championship, and almost won it. When I was sixteen I did win it, and won it the next three years.

There were two golf clubs in Montgomery, the Montgomery Country Club and the Woodley Country Club. The Montgomery Club was an eighteen-hole course and the Woodley a nine-hole course. Both were good golf courses. By coincidence, the Montgomery Country Club didn't have any Jewish members, and by coincidence the members of the Woodley Country Club were all Jewish. That was just the way it was. I wasn't aware of prejudice in either direction.

Once a year the champion of the Montgomery Club and the champion of the Woodley Club would play a match, considered the City Championship, since there weren't any other golf courses. I won this twice, from Files Crenshaw at the Woodley Club, and from Dr. Blue Harris at the Montgomery Club. I felt at home at the Montgomery Country Club, and played there many times with my good friends Files Crenshaw, Dr. Blue Harris, Charlie Ball, and the fine pro, Bill Damon.

It was at the Montgomery Country Club that my name was changed. Charlie Ball noted that the barber put a saucer on my head and cut around it. He called me Saucer Head. It must have fit because everybody called me that. My close friends called me Saucer. For the next twenty years, in Montgomery, I was still Saucer Head.

I have some special golf memories from Montgomery.

When I was seventeen I was full of excitement, a week in advance. It had been arranged for me to play a match with Sam Byrd. He was successor to the great Babe Ruth, and I was in awe of him. Sam was an excellent golfer. He had par thirty-six on the first nine, and was six down to my thirty. Sam was astonished. So was I.

Selma, Ala., is fifty miles from Montgomery. In Selma there were two brothers, Glen and Otis Crisman, both outstanding golfers. Glen won the Alabama State Championship. Later Otey became a pro, and a manufacturer of fine golf clubs. Otey used to drive over to Montgomery to play matches with me, for money. Each of us thought he had the best of it.

In our last match, my putting, or rather my putter, received an unusual compliment. I sank a long putt on the fifteenth hole, the third of the day, and Otey asked if he could see my putter. I handed him my old wooden putter. He examined it carefully— then broke it over his knee.

That was sixty years ago. I don't bear grudges. I forgave Otey last week.

■ ■ ■

Before leaving Montgomery, let me tell you about my caddie, Perry Jones. Perry was my constant companion on the golf course in Montgomery. I didn't fully appreciate then what a wonderful relationship we had. We never talked about it, and I never thought about it—but it was there. Perry was a tall, lanky black man, in his thirties. He wasn't "black" in those days, he was "colored." If you called a man "black," it was an insult. "Colored" was the nice word, the polite word.

Perry was always there when I arrived at the country club. He didn't take other bags, he always waited for me. I wasn't a good tipper because I didn't have much money to tip with. So he must have liked me, and I liked him. Perry had good golf sense. The only arguments we ever had were about which club I should use. Sometimes I would drive to the Montgomery Country Club, and Perry would ride in the front seat. This was not considered proper. People called it to my attention, but that didn't bother me.

When I was fourteen, Perry helped me win the second flight of the City Championship, played at the Montgomery Country Club. On the last hole of the finals I had a 30-foot putt. Perry, who knew the course better than I, gave me the line. I stroked the ball too hard, but it hit the center of the cup, popped up about three inches, and fell in. On the way back to the clubhouse we overheard my opponent say to his caddie, "Luckiest little S.O.B. I ever saw." Perry reminded me of this from time to time.

When I think back, Perry Jones was one of the best friends I've ever had.

This is a tragic, unbelievable story. One spring I went to Century Country Club in White Plains, N.Y., and found that George Garvin, a young black man who had been assistant caddie master at the Montgomery Country Club, was now assistant caddie master at Century. George and I were happy to see each other. After we had exchanged remembrances, George said, "Did you hear what happened to Perry?" I said, "What happened?" His tone scared me. He said, "He was killed in a knife fight." My heart sank. That night I called my Uncle Morris and said, "Perry was killed in a knife fight, wasn't he?" Uncle Morris replied, "I don't think so, he caddied for me today." A tremendous relief.

Three months later Perry was killed in a knife fight. I can't explain this.

■ ■ ■

When I finished college, my father's business required that the family move to New York. I went along because I liked to eat. The thought was expressed by my parents that I should get a job. This didn't appeal to me, but I didn't say so. I was lazy and loved to play bridge for money. But my ears perked up when Dad suggested selling insurance—he thought my golf might be an asset.

I told Dad that with my grip, my golf game wouldn't hold up without a lot of practice. I talked him into letting me go back to Montgomery for six months, to work on my swing with Bill Damon, the pro at the Montgomery Country Club. At the same time I could study the insurance business. It was partly a con job, but I don't think I fooled my father. I think he was being nice.

I moved back to Montgomery and lived with my Aunt Helen and Uncle Morris. Bill Damon corrected my grip and worked patiently on my game, daily. It took what seemed forever to break my bad habits. Near the end, to test my new swing, I played in the Valparaiso Invitational. My new swing held up, and I got to the finals. So back to New York.

The first tournament I played in, in New York, was the Metropolitan Amateur, at Metropolis Country Club, in White Plains. In the qualifying, I had a 78 on the first eighteen. In the afternoon I was one over par coming to the third hole, a dog-leg. I tried to shorten the hole by going over some trees. We weren't

sure I was successful so I played a provisional ball. When we got around the bend, my first ball was in a good position.

A member of our threesome threw my provisional ball to me. I didn't see it coming. It hit me on the left temple and lowered me to the grass for a few seconds. Then I continued. I had a 68, the best score of the day. There was a theory that I was unconscious. A headline in the *Herald Tribune* said, "Beaned by Ball, Shoots Sensational Round."

Soon after that I became a member of Metropolis, later a member of Century Country Club also in White Plains, and then Mountain Ridge in Montclair, N.J., where my mother's relatives played. Altogether, I won fourteen club championships at these three clubs. I also qualified for the National Amateur each of the three times I tried. Since only sixty-four in the country qualified, that was good.

I made a great golf shot once. A great shot is more than a perfect shot. If you make a perfect shot and twenty enemies at the same time, that's a great shot.

There was a yearly two-ball tournament at Winged Foot Country Club, the Anderson Memorial Invitational Tournament. One year Howard Bergman and I were partners. We almost qualified. We were in a play-off for two positions, with ten other teams. We started out on the eleventh hole, twenty-two of us. When you think about it, that's five-and-a-half four-somes—quite a crowd.

On the eleventh hole all the teams got pars. The twelfth hole was a par-three. Howard shot first and hit his ball over the green, near a tree. With the chips down, I hit into the right-hand trap. Many of the players were on the green.

Howard's second shot didn't get on the green. We were in big trouble. When I found my ball, we were in bigger trouble. The trap was so deep that my caddy had to hold the flag up high for me to see it. What was worse, my ball was so close to the back ledge of the trap there was almost no room for a backswing.

Paul Runyan, the outstanding pro at Metropolis, had a great short game. His method for playing trap shots was unique. Paul would lift his wedge almost straight up, bring it down so the flange landed in back of the ball, bring his arms forward and up, and the ball would rise, with plenty of backspin. Paul had shown this to me and I'd tried it a few times, but hadn't adopted it. Now I had no choice.

Howard was up on the green watching—with his fingers crossed. Seven or eight other players were with him—just waiting for me to get it over with. I took the club almost straight up and made the Runyan move. The ball bounced out towards the flag, with a nice feeling of backspin. I couldn't see what happened. All of a sudden Howard was jumping up and down. I thought I must be close to the flag. Then I looked at the other players. I've never gotten so many dirty looks—I can't blame them. My ball had landed a few feet past the hole and spun back in.

Howard and I won three matches and were beaten in a close match in the semifinals by Dick Chapman, amateur champion, and his partner.

A last story. I was again playing in the Anderson Memorial, scheduled to tee off at 10 A.M. Winged Foot is a forty-five minute drive from my house. My driver, Lee Robinson, wasn't exactly sure how to get there, so we left at 8:15. Even if it took an hour, I'd have time to change clothes and hit some practice shots.

At 9:30 we were still looking for Winged Foot, and I was in the back of the car, changing. We arrived at Winged Foot eight minutes past tee-off time. I grabbed my clubs and rushed to the first tee.

Two starters were on the tee. I apologized for being late, explained I'd gotten lost, and said, "I hope I'm not disqualified." One of them said, "Probably not, the tournament doesn't start till tomorrow."

Golf was a special part of my life.

TENNIS

I'm a little embarrassed to write about my tennis.

In my late forties I stopped playing golf and played a little tennis when I was on vacation at the Roney Plaza Hotel in Miami Beach. I played with the pros there, Marse Fink and Sol Goldman. I didn't play all year round, just two or three weeks a year. It was fun. Marse and Sol used to give me, and the bum they stuck me with, big handicaps and they beat us almost all the time. We played for "tickers," $50 (that was all Marse's heart could handle according to Sol). One day they paid me an unusual compliment. They said I was ranked third on the International Sucker List (behind a Frenchman in Monte Carlo and a Greek in Philadelphia). I didn't let this go to my head.

My game improved a bit. Of course, all my strokes were terrible because I couldn't copy what others did. My forehand is just a chop shot and my backhand is not believable. I turn my wrist around and use the opposite side of the racket—I wasn't trying to be different, I thought I was copying others.

I was reasonably athletic and played sufficiently well to enjoy myself. One year Marse suggested that I play in New York when I got back, play all year round. I took his advice, and joined a club, and played about an hour a day. I met Tony Vincent who had been a great player, ranked in the first twenty in the world when he was young. Tony gave me the only good lesson I can remember. He told me, when at net, to move my left leg forward when the ball was coming to my forehand, and my right leg forward when the ball was coming to my backhand. That way I would get the ball sooner, and when it was higher over the net.

I let Gardnar hold the cup

This helped me become a fairly decent net player.

When I was fifty-six, I met Gardnar Mulloy in Miami. We had a match for money, as usual, against another pro and a bum like me. I don't remember who won the match, but I remember something else. There was a large black bug crawling on our court and Gardnar ran over to it and I yelled, "Don't step on it, Gar." Gar said, "I wasn't going to," and picked the bug up with his handkerchief and took it over to a grassy spot where the bug was happy. I was surprised, and gave Gardnar a good mark. Later I learned that he had a Pet Rescue Organization.

A few years later, when I was sixty-one, I bribed Gardnar, by contributing to the Pet Rescue Organization, to play with me in the National Doubles Lawn Tennis Championship, for 60s-and-over, at the Rockaway Hunt Club. To my surprise we got to the semifinals. When I was sixty-two, to my amazement, we won it.

Ten years later, Gardnar and his wife, Madeleine, and I went to Australia, and Gar and I won the World's Doubles Lawn Tennis Championship for 70s-and-over. I went into that event hoping to do well, my purpose being to show that Dilantin* was helpful with stamina and reflexes. I didn't expect to win the tournament.

When I tell friends that Dilantin won this tournament, they say, "But you can do anything you set your mind to." I have a stock answer. I say, "Next year I'm going to take up Sumo wrestling."

My good friend Eddie Dibbs, who was ranked in the first five in the world for five years, and was second to Jimmy Connors in the United States, said my winning the World's Double Tennis Championship for 70s-and-over shouldn't just be in Ripley's, it should be on the first page of Ripley's.

I hope it doesn't seem like bragging but I think I'm the worst tennis player ever to win a World's Championship—thank you, Gardnar.

*The subject of *A Remarkable Medicine Has Been Overlooked.*

MY PARENTS

I doubt if we are given a choice of parents. If we are, and I'd known what I know now about human beings, I'd probably have been an elephant. You say elephants are an endangered species, but believe me, human beings are an endangered species.

However, if I'd been given a choice of parents, and assigned to the human race, I'd have chosen Ida Lewis and Jonas Dreyfus. I might not have said that when my father's hairbrush was being applied to my bottom, when I was young. But looking at the whole record, he was the best.

My mother had a lovely face, and beautiful red hair, the sort called auburn. She let it grow long, but wore it in a bun in back of her head. Everybody commented on it. I've told you how sweet she was. My sisters Lorraine and Joan and I vied for her attention. And we all got an equal amount of love.

There was a fourth contender for Mother's attention. Her name was Trixy, a toy fox terrier, white with black spots. (There was a law in those days that all small female dogs be named Trixy.) Trixy liked my sisters and me, but she loved Mother. Whenever she had a choice, she was with her.

When Dad was out of town visiting candy jobbers, Trixy slept with Mother. Otherwise she alternated between my sisters' bed and mine. Even when Dad was in town, Trixy got use out of Mother's bed. As soon as Dad left for the candy factory, Trixy would be in the bed, a little lump under the covers. Mother didn't mind, she made the bed up later.

During school days my sisters came home for lunch between twelve and one. Mother would pick them up in our Buick—our family was sold on Buicks. Trixy made the trip—Mother wouldn't think of going anywhere without her. The first couple of times she had to wake up Trixy. From then on, just when Mother was ready to leave, Trixy would come out of the covers, in a rush.

Mother couldn't understand this. How did Trixy know when to come out? Finally she caught on. Just before leaving, Mother would pick up the car key, on the key ring. There would be a tinkle—and Trixy.

■ ■ ■

When I was young my father was strict with me. I wouldn't say he was a disciplinarian, but of the school that said "children should be seen and not heard." His mother was German and Grandpa Dreyfus was from Alsace-Lorraine, German or French, depending on who won the last war. I was told that the Germans were stricter than most. Perhaps that influenced Dad's attitude although he was born in Montgomery.

As I have said, Dad went to Starke's University School and got the pernicious idea that lies were terrible. I quickly learned to avoid lies, unless absolutely necessary. For instance, sometimes you get into a spot where if you tell the truth you're going to get a licking—you have nothing to lose with a lie—occasionally it works.

Dad's procedure in giving me a licking was formal. We visited the bathroom together. He'd sit on the toilet seat and ask me to hand him the hair brush. Then I'd lie over his lap, and the brush would be applied to my behind. When I had received a certain amount of whacks, I would start to yell and my mother would rush into the bathroom and take the brush out of Dad's hand. He never argued with her—even when I wised up and started to yell before the first whack arrived.

Of course, that old "it hurts me more than it hurts you" was stated. The "but not in the same place" I kept to myself.

Dad used to correct me a lot, particularly at the dinner table. I began to think that good table manners were a sure way to Heaven. I like the song, "Mable, Mable, sweet and able, keep your elbows off the table." Elbows on the table were my biggest weakness. Sometimes my feelings would get hurt. I would cry, and leave the table without finishing dinner.

Recently I told this to my former wife, Joan, who didn't have corrective parents at all. In fact, I think she corrected them. She told me that sometimes her feelings got hurt at the table and she would leave, but she always took her plate with her.

Parents can love their children and bring them up differently. Mine, particularly Dad, were the corrective type. Joan's parents thought the best way was to let her figure it out for herself. I got a laugh out of her recently when I said, "If your parents saw you walking on the edge of the Grand Canyon, they would have said, 'Gee, I hope she doesn't slip.' "

I've always had a small ego. I am sure the psychologists would say that it was because of my father. But maybe my ego isn't small, just realistic, and is small by comparison with others that aren't realistic.

The main thing is that Dad loved me and was doing what he thought best. He did many things that gave me pleasure. I'll never forget when I was in my early twenties and had lost a lot of money gambling, I asked Dad if I could borrow $10,000. He lent it to me without even asking what it was for.

My mother died when she was forty-nine, of a stroke. It was a shock, and I didn't get over it for a long time. When Mother left she was convinced I'd never make a living.

Dad lived to be eighty-eight, and he was happy in his last ten years. We lived only a block apart in New York. I would visit him once or twice a week and spend an hour or two with him, and we both enjoyed it.

When Dreyfus & Co. started to be successful and our advertising campaign was going well, Dad eased up on "constructive criticism." When we did really well, my secretary, Helen, told me that every once in a while Dad would chuckle, and say, "We never thought Jack would amount to a hill of beans."

■ ■ ■

Recently I was listening to the beautiful music of Don McLean, in a plane 40,000 feet in the air. A thought came that brought tears to my eyes. President Nixon had just sent me his insightful book, *In the Arena*. It was autographed to "My favorite genius."

The thought that brought the tears was, "What if my mother and father could know that a president of the United States had written this to their little boy."

FAMILY LIFE

This book is not about my family life. That would be a book in itself. But a few words. . .

I was married to a beautiful girl, Joan Personette, in 1939. I didn't know it at the time but Joan had won a Joan Crawford look-alike contest. I think Joan Crawford got the better of it. In addition to being beautiful, Joan was a fine artist. I didn't realize how fine at the time.*

Joan and I were legally separated after four years. Not Joan's fault at all. I guess marriage was not for me because I never got married again or even considered it. After eighteen years of separation, Joan went to Reno for a divorce. She went with great reluctance—she associated Reno with divorce and gambling. Once Joan got there, she found the country so

---

*Joan was a costume designer for the Roxy Theater for many years—she did magnificent costume sketches, exquisite in form and color, in my opinion the best ever done. Joan has become a wonderful painter. She's very modest, and never tried to sell her paintings. Recently her work came to the attention of The National Museum of Women in the Arts in Washington, D.C. This fine museum liked it so much that they recently held an exhibit of Joan's work in the important months of October, November and December—and it was extended for an extra month.

beautiful she loved it, and decided to stay. There she met Bryce Rhodes, a fine gentlemen. Joan and Bryce have lived together for more than twenty years. Bryce and I are good friends.

Joan and I had a son, Johnny. When we became separated, Johnny was two years old and I didn't see him again until he was almost eight. Freud suggests that these young years are very important for a little boy's old man to be around. It's the greatest regret of my life that I wasn't. When Johnny was eight I visited him every Saturday and Sunday in Purchase, N.Y., and we'd play games. A stroke of luck, and a little help from me, brought Bill Damon, the fine golf teacher from Montgomery, to nearby Century Country Club as golf pro. Bill gave Johnny hundreds of golf lessons, while I watched. Soon Johnny became an excellent golfer, won the Club Championship a few times, had a 66 at Westchester Country Club, also qualified for the British Amateur. Johnny worked at Dreyfus & Co. until I retired. Since then he has done a great deal of volunteer hospital work, which he enjoys.

Six years ago Johnny went out to Reno to see why his mother liked it so much. He found out and bought a house on a street with a lovely name, Mark Twain Avenue, and has lived there ever since. We visit each other a few times a year, and talk on the phone several times a week. Sometimes we have arguments— we're both right, of course. A few years ago I told Johnny if my life were in peril and I was given the choice of one person to come to my rescue, I would pick him. He said I was right, but only after he'd had breakfast. I love Johnny very much. And I still love Joan.

Dad & Uncle Morris

Me and Hart Lyon

*Joan, in her Roxy
Theater studio*

*Johnny and
Nellie von Hoensheim*

With Clemens and
Ling Ling

Joan with Buffy

*Three generations—taken when Dreyfus Corp. first traded
on New York Stock Exchange*

*Stuart Little, me, and hibachi to keep warm, while writing
"A Remarkable Medicine Has Been Overlooked"*

Author's Note

This being my only autobiography, I'd assumed it could be written chronologically. Well, much of it can. But my life has been so diversified that some of it doesn't fit conveniently into the story. Take the chapter on golf. I played golf from the ages of thirteen to forty-five, but I couldn't interrupt the narrative every few pages with golf stories.

It's the same with card playing, horse racing, and a chapter titled "Experiences and Thoughts." They are separate chapters and I'll place them where I think they will interfere least with the chronology.

Following the chapter on "Wall Street," there will be a book I wrote about sixteen years ago, *A Remarkable Medicine Has Been Overlooked*. It's about the most important subject I know.

CARD PLAYING

I don't know how people learn to play bridge. Some take lessons I suppose, but most just pick it up.

When I was nine years old, my parents let me watch their bridge games with the neighbors. I sat behind Dad, by command. I was usually sent to bed before the conclusion. I don't know where my parents learned the game, but they were fair players and did well—except against the Gassenheimers, who were good players.

My father used to subscribe to some bridge pamphlet that he got weekly. There was always a double dummy hand by Emile Werk. Dad would Werk on it, pardon, for a while, and then tell me it was unsolvable. That would get my competitive juices going, and I would solve it. This would annoy Dad, and please him at the same time (he had such a smart son).

When I was twelve I started playing with other children in the neighborhood for a twentieth of a cent a point—two dollars if you were unlucky. I don't know where I got the money.

When I was about sixteen, I started playing against the best players in Montgomery, Julian and Hilda Slager—tournament players. They became close friends of mine. My partner against the Slagers was another friend, Perry Hewitt. These games were fun, and I have good memories. One memory isn't bridge.

Perry asked me to meet him at a restaurant one night. We could discuss bridge while he had dinner—then he would drive me to the Slagers. I got to the restaurant just as Perry's steak arrived. He started talking bridge. I said, "Perry, eat your steak while it's hot." He said he couldn't until he got his coffee. I said, "Oh," and talked bridge. Minutes later Perry's coffee arrived. He poured the whole cup of coffee over the steak, and started to eat. This was a first, and a last for me. It is not recommended as a health hint—but we beat the Slagers that night.

■ ■ ■

As I said elsewhere, I deteriorated to New York City. There I played at a bridge club. There were plenty of games, and a reasonable card fee. At the club I met Morrie Elis, one of the best player of the cards there ever was (not just my opinion). Morrie was not a great bidder.

I should say that the game of bridge has changed since I was a boy. It had been Auction bridge, now it's Contract. In Contract bridge the bidding is of great importance. You only get credit, or grief, for what you bid. In Auction bridge you get credit for what you make, whether you bid it or not.

Contract bridge has the advantage of giving players more to yell about. They can call each other names for the bidding, as well as for the play. In some games the words "idiot" and "stupid" are heard as often as "diamonds" and "clubs."

I started playing in bridge tournaments with Morrie Elis, and we did well. In one tournament, playing with Morrie, one of the most important things in my life occurred. We had just finished two hands against P. Hal Sims, a great player, author of the Sims System, and his partner Eddie van Vleck. We had gotten good scores. As we were leaving, Hal was making some pointed comments about Eddie's bidding. I noticed Eddie's neck getting red with what seemed suffused anger. Morrie and I were at the next table when there was a commotion. Eddie was on the floor having an epileptic attack, as I was told. The convulsions looked to me like a series of electrical shocks. Years later I remembered this. If I hadn't seen it, *A Remarkable Medicine Has Been Overlooked* wouldn't have been written.

At one of the tournaments I met Eddie Hymes, a member of the Cavendish Club. Eddie suggested that I join the Cavendish. He proposed me, and I became a member. At the Cavendish, the smallest game was for a half a cent a point. I played in that, and Eddie took half my game. A quarter of a cent was all I could afford.

I hadn't been a member long before Eddie Hymes started calling me "Baby Face." I supposed it was because of my looks. I couldn't be sure because there was a famous outlaw named "Baby Face" Nelson. Baby Face caught on, and I was called that at the Cavendish for decades.

At the Cavendish Club there were great players. There was a famous team, the Four Aces, which won more tournaments than anyone in those days. Strangely, there were five Four Aces, Oswald Jacoby, Howard Schenken, Jimmy Maier, David Burnstine, and Michael Gottlieb. And there were Johnny Crawford and Baron von Zedtwitz.

At another club nearby, Crockford's, Ely and Josephine Culbertson were members. Ely had invented Contract bridge, and deserves a lot of credit for it.

At the Cavendish, when I was playing with these outstanding players, I was always trying to bid as I thought they wanted me to bid. That's not a good way to play bridge. You've got to have your own personality, your own style, and let your partner cooperate with you on an equal basis. So I didn't do as well with those players as I should have.

When I was thirty I devised a scientific method of playing gin rummy, and used it against Oswald Jacoby and Johnny Crawford, the best players, and beat them regularly. Indirectly this helped my bridge. I got respect. Now I could bid my hand as I thought I should, rather than as I thought they thought I should.

Baron Waldemar von Zedtwitz—we called him Waldy—was an unusual person. In the first place, he was a multimillionaire. In the second place, he looked different from anyone I've ever seen. He was about six feet tall, very thin, almost nothing but bones.

Waldy was nice, but extremely serious. He liked to play with me as a partner because I bid psychics (bids meant to fool the opponents, but sometimes they fooled partner). Waldy was good at picking up psychics.

Waldy was renowned for guessing Queens. If a Queen could be finessed either way, he was great at guessing who had it. He told me he worked on vibes.

One afternoon the Baron and Harold Vanderbilt, the yachtsman, we called him Mike, were playing at Crockford's. They were playing Josephine and Ely Culbertson for large stakes—not to Mike or Waldy, but to me. I was the only kibitzer, behind Waldy.

There was a hand Waldy played in four hearts. To make his contract he had to guess which of the Culbertsons had the queen of hearts. The opening lead gave no indication. I was sitting in back of the Baron, enjoying the situation. I think he was aware of my thoughts.

Waldy played a couple of side suits. Then he went into his act. He brought his right arm up over his head, and started kneading his left earlobe with his finger tips. He did this for a while. Then he reversed the procedure, and kneaded his right earlobe with his left hand. Then he went all out. He put his cards on the table and put both arms over his head, and kneaded both ears.

The strain on the opponents had gotten intolerable. Ely had the queen, and was looking innocent. Josephine was looking slightly guilty. Ely, to be casual, decided to rearrange his cards. Something went wrong, a card popped out of his hand and arched slowly to the floor to the right of Waldy—face up. It was the queen of hearts. The Baron "guessed" it.

Oswald Jacoby, captain of the Four Aces, and a brilliant bridge player, was a good friend of mine. Ozzie had an aptitude for probabilities, an essential in a job he'd had as insurance actuary. He quit the job because he preferred to gamble for a living. He won money at bridge, poker, gin rummy, and would bet on anything. When I began to make money, he told me he was glad he wasn't rich, it would take the fun out of gambling—a profound thought.

Next to gambling Ozzie's favorite sport was eating. Frequently, after an afternoon session at the Cavendish, we would go to a nearby Longchamps restaurant. In the restaurant there was a large table with a variety of desserts. As we went in, Ozzie would pick up a strawberry tart or apple strudel and bring it to our table. He'd eat that as an appetizer. Then he'd have a shrimp cocktail, meal, and dessert.

Ozzie and I were guests at Baron von Zedtwitz's home in Miami Beach one year. Frequently we played golf at Biscayne Golf Course. Ozzie was a poor golfer, the Baron was a threat to shoot 78. One day, on the tee of the seventeenth hole, an easy par-four with a little brook in front of the green, Ozzie said, "Waldy, what odds will you give me that you can get a five on this hole?" Waldy knew Ozzie thought he might hit his second shot into the brook. He was too cagey for that and said, "I'll give you three-to-one." Ozzie said, "I'll take it for a hundred."

Waldy hit his drive, the usual 200 yards down the fairway. He wasn't going to risk going into the water, so he played his second shot short—a little shorter than necessary. He hit his third shot a trifle too firmly, and it trickled over the green. We found it under a bush, with a little branch slightly in back of the ball. That was bad news.

The Baron was a great competitor. He waggled his club back and forth, back and forth. Then he swung, hit the branch, and the ball didn't move. The Baron showed no sign of defeat. He waggled again, waggled again, swung, and hit the branch again.

The need for being a great competitor was over. The Baron grabbed the little branch, and broke it off. Holding it like an ear of corn, he gnashed his teeth at it, and little growls came out of him.

Golf etiquette had required silence until after the Baron's fifth shot. It no longer applied. Ozzie wrapped his arms around his stomach, fell on the green and rolled back and forth with laughter. I would have joined him but I wanted to be invited back to the Baron's.

I qualified for the Masters Bridge Championship when I was twenty-eight, and played in tournaments. But, as business got some of my attention, I gave up tournaments and just played rubber bridge. Later, when the Dreyfus Fund and Dreyfus & Co. occupied so much of my time, I gave the game up entirely, for about twenty-five years, and came back to it twenty years ago. I play at the Regency and the Cavendish now.

Bridge players are funny characters. When they're playing, the game is the only thing. They could have a view of Niagara Falls, but wouldn't care if the drapes were drawn. And don't try to tell a joke at a bridge table. You wouldn't be heard over the arguments about the last hand.

When I was sixty-two, I miraculously won the United States Open Doubles Lawn Tennis Championship for 60s-and-over, at the Rockaway Hunt Club, with Gardnar Mulloy. It was Sunday afternoon, and I went to the Cavendish Club to play bridge. I cut into a game with three of my friends, including Ace Greenberg, senior partner of Bear, Stearns.

Braggarts give me a pain, but this was too good to hold in. I said, "You fellows will be pleased to know you're playing with the U.S. National Lawn Tennis Doubles Champion." There was silence. While they were searching for compliments, I was thinking of modest responses. Fifteen seconds went by. Then Ace said, "Deal." I dealt.

Come to think of it, fifteen seconds of pure silence, from bridge players, is an accolade.

■ ■ ■

I've had some bridge hands published in the *New York Times*. I'll include only this one. I'll tell you why, later.

```
                        North
                        ♠  K   Q   J   10   x
                        ♥  9   8   x   x
                        ♦  K   6
                        ♣  7   6
West                                                    East
♠  x   x                                                ♠  x   x   x
♥  K   x   x                                            ♥  J   10   x
♦  J   10  9   x   x                                    ♦  x   x
♣  Q   9   x                                            ♣  A   J   x   x   x
                        South (my hand)
                        ♠  A   6   x
                        ♥  A   Q   7
                        ♦  A   Q   7
                        ♣  K   10  8   x
```

My partner (North) was an elderly gentleman, a good player, but sometimes he overlooked a card. He passed. East passed. I bid a club. West passed. My partner made the surprising bid of two spades, which suggested that he wanted to get to game even if I had a very weak hand. I thought he must have overlooked something, but temporized by bidding two no trump. He bid three no trump, and I made the optimistic bid of six no trump.

Partner put down his hand: five spades to the K, Q, J, 10, four hearts to the 9-8, and the K and one diamond. I knew he must have something in clubs. I preferred the Q, J to the A, but he put down the 7, 6.

I looked at dummy and wanted to say, "What the heck kind of bid is that?" Instead I looked as though I was thinking. But the hand was really impossible. I had five spade tricks, three diamond tricks, maybe three heart tricks, if the hearts broke well, but I had to lose a heart trick and, of course, the ace of clubs. But I thought I might make three heart tricks and the king of clubs if I did it in an unusual fashion. If I lost a heart trick and then led up to the king of clubs, I'd lose to the ace no matter who had it. So I tried a maneuver.

I took the opening lead with the diamond king, calmly led a club from dummy, a small club came from the hand on my right, and I put up the king. It held. I led a small spade to the king. Then a small heart and put on the seven, losing to the king of hearts. Under the circumstances, West couldn't think of leading a club, so he continued in diamonds. I took five spades, three hearts, three diamonds, and one club, making six no trump.

I enjoyed this hand particularly because my friend Tobias Stone, co-author of *Bridge is a Partnership Game*, called Baron von Zedtwitz (in retirement in Hawaii) and told him about it. The Baron told Stoney this was the best swindle he'd ever seen. Being called a swindler in real life is not considered a compliment. In bridge it is.

▪ ▪ ▪

If you're not a gin player, you should skip this. If you are, it might help you put your children through college.

Lesson in Gin Rummy

The *Encyclopedia of Bridge* says I am "reputed to be the best American player of gin rummy." This compliment stemmed from a method of play that I discovered, by chance, many years ago.

I had finished playing bridge at the old Cavendish Club and sat down to watch George Rapee, a good friend, playing a hand of gin rummy. George's only prospect was in "filling" the five-three of diamonds. His opponent discarded the diamond four and I said to myself, "The lucky stiff, he got hit in the middle." Being "hit in the middle" at the time was thought of as the luckiest thing that could happen. I thought, "Only one card in the deck, and George got it." Somehow that started a train of thoughts and I realized that getting hit in the middle was no more difficult than drawing the jack of hearts to the king, queen—again only one card would do.

One thought led to another. I will skip detail. But it was apparent that a king can be used with four separate combinations: three combinations of kings—the king of spades can be used with the king of hearts, the king of diamonds, and the king of clubs—and in a run with the queen-jack. A jack down through a three can be used in six combinations. In addition to three of a kind, a jack can be used in a run with the king-queen, queen-ten, and ten-nine.

This was helpful because it made things exact, but most gin players have an idea of these probabilities.

One day the thought popped into my head that, at the beginning of a hand, a player rarely splits pairs. If, for example, my opponent discarded the nine of hearts, I could hypothetically eliminate the nine of spades from his hand. With the nine of spades eliminated, the eight of spades could be used only one way in a run, with the seven and six.

Also, since players don't split nine-eight combinations at the beginning of a hand, the play of the nine of hearts eliminates the eight of hearts. With the eight of hearts eliminated, the eight of spades could be used in only one combination of three of a kind, eight of diamonds and eight of clubs.

Therefore, when an opponent plays a card at the start of a hand, a touching card in a *different* suit becomes, hypothetically, a two-way player, twice as safe as a king, and three times as safe as a jack.

Example:
    You've drawn and hold the following:

♠	♥	♦	♣
K	Q	J	8
6	3	3	3
	2	2	2

Your opponent's first discard was the seven of diamonds, and it's your play. The six of spades and the eight of clubs are by far the safest discards.

I won't go further. If you think about this, it will be a great help in making safe discards at the beginning of a hand, the most important part of the game.

Be lucky.

LEHIGH UNIVERSITY

Although my parents weren't wealthy, they decided to send me to college. The University of Alabama naturally came to mind. But a cousin, Monroe Lewis, was going to Lehigh University, and recommended it highly.

My father thought my getting out of the state might have a broadening effect on me (whatever that is). My grades were not up to Lehigh standards but I applied. Perhaps because I was from so far away they decided to take a chance. Lehigh was a nice university, and I wouldn't have wanted to go anywhere else.

■ ■ ■

I got to Lehigh, in Bethlehem, Pa., about a week before school started. It was like a new world. It was a time when freshmen were interviewed by fraternities, and fraternities were interviewed by freshmen. Some of the boys didn't want to join fraternities at all. My problem was simplified because my cousin Monroe was a member of Pi Lambda Phi. By mutual agreement, I joined.

The fraternity was in a large old house, a few blocks from the campus. It had about fifteen rooms, and we were paired up, two in a room. Being with so many boys was completely new, and we talked endlessly about nothing—that's called bull sessions.

There was a paper that published the names of all the freshmen. Mine was included. Instead of saying I was from Montgomery, it said I was from Montz, Ala. Nobody knew about Saucer Head, so for four years, at Lehigh, everybody called me Montz.

When you are a freshman they have a wonderful thing called hazing. You get your bottom slapped with a paddle, and there are other attractions. During hazing week you were constructively employed. As an example, I had to go out one night and come back with a live duck.

One task we all had was to go across the Bethlehem River to a cemetery, at night, find the grave of someone whose name we were given, and come back with the complete inscription. The night we were assigned to the grave hunt was very cold, about ten above zero. Eleven of us freshmen headed towards the Bethlehem River. There was a toll bridge across it that cost a penny. When we reached the river we found ourselves near a trestle that freight trains were supposed to use. We'd never seen a train on it and the other side of the trestle was near the cemetery—the toll bridge was half a mile away.

Si Miller made the sound suggestion that we walk across the trestle. The others agreed. I was the only one who was chicken. I said I would take the toll bridge and meet them there. Apparently there were other chickens in the group, so we headed for the toll bridge. We hadn't gone far when a freight train went over the trestle. We could imagine ourselves hanging from those icy rails, over the Bethlehem River. Cowardice has its uses.

I tried to get good grades, but I didn't kill myself. I must be on the dumb side because I got straight Cs at Lehigh, with one exception. I got an A in Music Appreciation.

Professor Shields was playing César Franck's "Symphony in D Minor" in class. I was taking a light nap, hoping it would be mistaken for music appreciation. At one point Professor Shields stopped the music and said, "Dreyfus, what do you think of this music?" I woke up and said, "It's inexorable." I'd never used that word before or since, and I don't know where it came from. It probably wasn't in Professor Shields' immediate vocabulary either, because he gave me an A. Ever since then César Franck's *Symphony in D Minor* has been a favorite of mine. I recommend it for your listening.

Lehigh was an engineering school. I have a mechanical IQ of eight—some say seven. Taking an engineering course would have been ridiculous for me. I took a Bachelor of Arts course, majored in Latin, of all things, and then in Economics because it was an easy course. We didn't have to do anything except listen to Professor Caruthers, who was very interesting. I remember him saying an economist is a fellow who learns more and more about less and less. I don't remember the rest.

The only course in school that was useful to me was called Psychology. It was a "snap" course, and I took it for credits. I remember a paragraph on rationalization, the meaning of which I hadn't known. It explained that it was wish-thinking, that we see things from our own point of view, and we always give ourselves the best of it. When I got out into the real world—boy, was that true. There's a valuable thought in wish-thinking.

I took a course in Geology. All I remember is the word fault—I knew that already.

I think the main reason for going to college, unless you are going to be a specialist, is to say you are a college graduate, and for the feeling that you are educated. There are so many people that finish college and say, "Now I'm educated," and don't study anything else the rest of their lives that college may have been a hindrance.

My former wife, Joan Personette, knows she is ignorant. She didn't go to college and has been trying to catch up for the last fifty some odd years. Joan is better educated than almost anyone I know.

When I was graduated—you see if I hadn't gone to college I would have said "when I graduated"—I had a nightmare for over a year that they took my diploma back. Recently the Dreyfus Corp. ran an advertisement with my diploma in it—with Lehigh's permission. I feel they can't take it back anymore.

In college, I learned about girls. That is what they were called in those days. I have been a bachelor most of my life and have had adventures with the prettier sex, but that won't be part of this book. But don't despair. I may run for president, and the media will tell you everything.

Dates were usually double dates, and we usually visited bars. I didn't drink. A fellow named Joe Loeb, in Montgomery, had bet me five dollars I'd have a drink before I was twenty-one and I wasn't going to blow that money. I ate an awful lot of cracked ice.

There are some nice memories. There was a fellow in the fraternity house—I won't mention his name—who had a passion for Ravel's *Bolero*. He had it on records, numbered from one to eight, and played them all the time. At first I liked it a lot, then I liked it, then I felt I could do without it. The *Bolero* has a tiny bit of repetition in it. By the time my dreams were accompanied by the *Bolero*, I decided to make a move. In the dead of night I got hold of those records and scratched out the numbers. I think Ravel would have had a hard time re-numbering them. Anyhow, the music stopped and everybody in the fraternity house was grateful, except one. This has been a secret till now.

I'd been told so often by my father that I was lazy that I'd gotten to believe it. That's not fair to Dad, he just reminded me. I really was lazy. My only ambition, other than to be the man who makes change on a streetcar, was to be a hobo. Evidence for this was seen later when I named my horse farm Hobeau Farm, after my first stallion, Beau Gar, and my ambition.

The notion that I was lazy was so strong in me that I made an appointment with Professor Hughes of the Psychology Department. I asked Professor Hughes why I was lazy. He asked me if there was anything I liked to do. I said, "Yes, play golf." He asked me if I practiced. I said, "Sure, sometimes five hours at a time." Professor Hughes said I wasn't lazy, if the job was something that interested me. I didn't argue with him, although I thought golf was not a job, but he made me feel better.

At this late date, I'd like to thank Professor Hughes. Up There, I hope.

I was on the golf team at Lehigh, captain the last two years. Being captain doesn't mean anything, you just show up like the rest of the players. Saucon Valley Country Club was our home course. We alternated with schools in playing at home and away. The place that made the deepest impression was West Point, Army if you prefer. We had lunch with the cadets, and the uniforms reminded me of Starke's University School.

The first match we played after I became captain was against the University of Pennsylvania, at the Merion Cricket Club. On the first hole I was the only one of the foursome on the green in two, and enjoying my captainship. I had a twenty-foot putt. Being brought up on Bermuda greens, I stroked the ball firmly. The greens at Merion were slick as glass. The ball rolled past the hole, and into a trap. The only one on the green in two, the only one in a trap in three.

Fraternities are supposed to have heads. There must be a reason but I don't remember what it was. Anyhow, the head of our fraternity had the modest title of Rex. I preferred the English version, King. But Rex it was.

In my senior year I was nominated for Rex. On the opposite ticket was Si Miller. Si got twelve votes, and I had eleven. The one vote outstanding belonged to the fellow with the *Bolero* records. He disliked me, and he disliked Si, but he wasn't going to waste his vote. He disliked Brooklyn more than he disliked Montgomery, so he voted for me.

Twelve to twelve. We flipped a coin and it came up in my favor. I considered this a mandate.

Just as I was writing this, by coincidence or ESP, Si, whom I hadn't spoken to for thirty years, called me. He was laughing and said he just remembered the time he and I had balanced some shoes and books on top of Joel Rothenberg's door. They crashed down on Joel's head, and scared him half to death. We had nothing against Joel, except he was Rex and we were freshmen.

Si's call reminded me of something that happened after Lehigh. We'd been out of college for about fifteen years. Si was a member of the medical profession and I was a member of Century Country Club. One afternoon, we played a round of golf. A good friend, Leon Fletcher, walked around with us. After golf we drove to Roosevelt Raceway, to see the trotters. I was in the front car with Dr. Miller, Leon followed. When we got to the Bronx Whitestone Bridge, Leon was right in back of us. Si gave the toll attendant a dollar and told him to use the other fifty cents for the car behind us.

At the track we got seats and programs and had started handicapping, when Leon said, "Funny thing happened to me at the bridge. The man wouldn't let me pay." I keep a supply of lies handy and said, "We didn't pay either." Then I said, "I saw an article in the paper a couple of weeks ago about the bridge having amortized its cost down to forty-five cents a car. It was impractical to charge that, so for two hours a day, at random, they let people go through free." Leon looked at Dr. Miller for a second opinion, and got a nod.

A week later Leon came to the City Athletic Club to watch the gin game. Two friends of mine, Monroe Mayer and Ben Sokolow, had been primed. The four of us discussed the stock market for a few minutes when Monroe said, "A funny thing happened to me yesterday. I went over the Bronx Whitestone Bridge and they wouldn't let me pay." Ben said, "That's a lot of rubbish. What do you mean they wouldn't let you pay?" Leon came to Monroe's defense and said, "I had the same thing happen. The bridge has been amortized down to forty-five cents a trip. But it's impractical to charge that, so for two hours a day, at random, people are allowed to go through free." Sokolow said, "That is the worst bull I ever heard— ridiculous." Leon's reply took me by surprise. He said, "I read it in the newspaper." (There must be a moral in this—Leon was reasonably honest.) A heated argument followed, resulting in a $50 bet. Monroe, Ben, and I split the fifty bucks. I think we gave it back to Leon. If we didn't, I owe Dr. Miller $12.50, plus accrued interest.

In my senior year at Lehigh, my roommate was Matthew Suvalsky, possibly Polish. Matt was first-string guard on the football team. One night I came out of the bathroom with a toothbrush and toothpaste, and a tube of Barbasol, a brushless shave cream. Matt didn't see the toothpaste and said, "Do you brush your teeth with Barbasol?" I said, "Sure, everybody does." Matt said, "I think I'll try it." I gave him the Barbasol. A few minutes later Matt came out of the bathroom and I asked, "How was it?" He said, "It tastes good, but it makes my teeth feel awfully slippery."

In 1934 I was graduated from Lehigh—Summa Cum Ordinary. Now you're supposed to get a job.

GETTING A JOB

The purpose of getting a job, most of the time, is to make money. I didn't even know what money was for until I was ten. At that age the laws of Montgomery permitted me to go to the movies.

Saturday mornings my father would give me a dime and I'd go to the Strand Theatre to see a movie, preferably Tom Mix and his horse Tony, and Pathé news—sometimes twice. After the movies, if I had a surplus nickel given me by an uncle or my aunt, I would go to Franco's and get a hot dog, on a large roll with sauerkraut and red sauce. My mother told me these were poisonous, but that didn't stop me. Recently I've started to feel the effects.

The subject of making a living came up for the first time when I was fifteen. I was playing golf with a boy my age, Alan Rice. We stopped for a drink at the seventh hole water fountain. Alan told me that one day he was going to make $100,000 and retire on the income (invest it in sound mortgages that yielded $5,000 a year). I knew I'd never make that much money but, if I did, there would be two retirees.

∎ ∎ ∎

When I left Montgomery the second time, with the sounder golf swing (as discussed earlier), I was in the insurance business. I played golf a dozen times with a wealthy gentleman who couldn't play at all. Finally, I got up the nerve to try to sell him an annuity. He didn't buy it. I went outside his office and cried real tears. That was the end of my insurance career.

My father thought I might be helpful to him in the candy business. I had little option, having no other suggestion. It was decided that I get my training in a candy factory that Dad was associated with, Edgar P. Lewis & Sons located in Malden, Massachusetts.

I liked making candy and for six months worked on the marmalade slab, making imitation orange slices, and struggling to lift 100-pound bags of sugar into a boiling cauldron. After work I'd go back to my boarding house and take a nap before dinner. Those were solid naps. When I woke up, I didn't know where I was, or who I was.

My salary at Edgar P. Lewis was $15 a week, and I had to live on it. Room and board was $10.50, lunch excluded. I had one luxury, an old Buick my father loaned me. Garage used up a buck a week. That left $2.50 for lunches and other frivolities. When I was on double dates with my old college friend Matt Suvalsky, Matt had to split the gas with me. A happy period in my life.

After six months my father felt that I had eaten enough candy, and was ready for sales training with him. My chore was to drive the car and carry the samples. I would listen while my father talked with the candy buyer. I remember the first meeting I attended. While candy was being discussed I toyed with a fountain pen on the buyer's desk. When we got to the street my hand went into my pocket and, to my surprise, came out with the fountain pen. My father was not elated.

We did this for a few months, but things don't always work out with father and son, and I guess selling wasn't my racket. Dad had always impressed on me how important the other man's time was, and I think he overdid it. So I retired from the candy business and still needed a job.

We hear about those people who, while still playing with their rattles, know exactly what they want to do in life. Well, I was twenty-two and didn't have any idea what I wanted to do. Naturally I got into the doldrums. My parents were patient and didn't push me. I lay around the apartment on West 88th Street, played bridge in the afternoon and evening, and fell asleep around 3 A.M. listening to Clyde McCoy playing *Sugar Blues* on the radio.

My father thought I should see a psychiatrist. And I did, twice a week. I used to lie on his couch. Whatever talking there was came from me.

An uncle got me a job with an industrial designer. Salary $18 a week—getting up there. The designer insisted I wear a hat, a Homburg, no less. That ate up my excess profits. I accompanied my employer to different stores, with the thought that I would catch on to the business. I wasn't a quick learner. However, before I could get fired, the designer offered to raise my salary to $50 a week if I stopped seeing the psychiatrist. He proposed we take a trip to Florida. I sensed an ulterior motive, and resigned.

Insurance, candy, and industrial design—two strikes and a foul tip. Back to bridge, and Clyde McCoy. My parents weren't surprised. My father always expected I'd have trouble making a living. I had no discernible useful aptitude, and Dad had a suspicion I was lazy. Privately, I agreed with him.

Around this time I had a creative idea. John D. Rockefeller was overloaded with money, but was too old to enjoy it. I thought I'd ask him to give me a million dollars. I could play golf, chase girls, travel around the world, and he could enjoy this, secondhand. I never got around to asking him. If I had, my whole life might have been changed. I'm sure he would have given me the million.

Anyhow, I didn't have a job. One night, at the bridge club, one of the players who knew I was indigent said I might like the brokerage business. Wall Street was the last place I'd thought of trying, and reluctantly kept an appointment he made. My father went with me to the garment district branch of Cohen, Simondson & Co., Members, New York Stock Exchange. I was interviewed by a registered representative, Mr. Roy. He needed an assistant to answer phones and keep his charts. I got the job, $25 a week. I thought I got it on my good looks. Years later, I learned that Dad had paid twenty weeks of my salary in advance.

This time I took an interest in a job. The fluctuating prices and the gamble of the stock market struck one of my aptitudes. And it wasn't hard to look at the pretty models in the garment district. In a week I felt so much better that I tendered my resignation to the psychiatrist.

The most important part of my first Wall Street job was posting weekly charts, on a daily basis. I could have gotten a hundred jobs that didn't have this requirement. It was pure luck because I developed an affinity for weekly charts, and put a large emphasis on them throughout my career.

After I had been at Cohen, Simondson for six months, I passed a stock exchange test, and became a junior customer's broker. Although I liked the business, I was not good at approaching people for commissions—it was selling again. But I got a modest amount of business from relatives.

■ ■ ■

After several years with Cohen, Simondson, I applied for a job as a full customer's broker at Bache & Co.—and got turned down. Then I went to E. A. Pierce & Co., later to become Merrill Lynch, Pierce, Fenner & Bean. Jim Schwartz, in charge of customer's brokers, looked me over carelessly, and gave me a job at $75 a week, a fortune. I wasn't worth it, and didn't earn it for a long time.

The E. A. Pierce office was spacious. There were tickers, an order room, and about thirty customer's brokers. I was assigned to a desk next to John Behrens, who later became a partner of mine. Everybody in that office was nice, including Mr. Pierce.

On the day I arrived, there was a memo on all our desks from Lawrence Dennis, the firm's economist. It was titled "The Third Great Boom." I'm sure Lawrence was right more times than wrong, but not this time. That was the first day of the bear market of 1938. My weekly charts kept me out of trouble. In fact, my uncles made some money on the short side.

When the market got through going down, business dried up. We had time on our behinds. When you have almost nothing to do, you think of something.

John Behrens had a customer, Mollie Snyder. Occasionally Mollie would come into the office to discuss investments with John, for an hour or so. I didn't want her to get the impression that she was John's only customer, which she was. From time to time I would bring John, from the order room, an execution of a fictitious order—Mr. Livingston bought 75 Coca Cola; Mrs. Browning bought 200 U.S. Steel, etc. Mollie was impressed. John started getting a little cocky himself.

I'd noticed that people have sending machines and receiving machines. Many don't have their receiving machines turned on very often. You'll have noticed it when you are trying to make a point with someone. They're restless to tell their side of the story and you know they're not listening. This observation helped me win a bet. I bet a friend five dollars that I could say to Pop

Melcher, one of the customer's brokers, "My grandmother was eaten by the cannibals," and not get a reaction. My friend wanted to bet more.

A few days later Pop buttonholed me, and started what seemed like a long story. I motioned my friend over. After a few moments Pop paused to take a breath and I said in a normal tone, "My grandmother was eaten by the cannibals." Pop nodded, and picked up his story where he'd left off.

There was a customer's broker, Ralph Kershaw, who used to trade in commodities. His customers followed Lawrence Dennis' recommendations. One week Lawrence recommended the purchase of corn, four days in a row. Each day it went down three or four cents and Ralph's customers were taking a beating. When a substantial loss had accumulated, I got a back office friend to make up a memo from Lawrence saying, "Would take profits in corn." When Ralph was out to lunch, I put the memo on his desk. Several of us were in on this.

Ralph returned from lunch, started to sit down, and saw the memo. Halfway down, he straightened up, and his face got red. Then, memo in hand, he marched stiffly to Mr. Pierce's office. We never heard what happened.

My Uncle Dave had sent me some stock certificates of bankrupt companies to see if they had any value. The certificates were impressive-looking but, as they say, not worth the paper they were printed on. One day I found a use for them.

Pop Melcher was to become a partner of the new firm, Merrill Lynch, Pierce, Fenner & Bean, to be headed by Charlie Merrill. One day Pop came in with an overnight bag and told us he was spending the night at the home of Mr. Merrill. I got my back office friend to make up an envelope, addressed to Robert Ruark, the firm's best customer, with "Insured for $250,000" stamped on it. We put Uncle Dave's certificates in the envelope, and made a hole so they would show through. I stuck it in Pop's overnight bag.

Later, Pop told us he talked with Charlie Merrill until about ten o'clock. Then he went to his room and took a shower. When he went for his pajamas he saw the envelope with the securities. This had to be reported. Pop brought the envelope to Mr. Merrill, who'd been sleeping soundly.

Now that I look back on it, I don't know how I got out of that office unscathed.

■ ■ ■

A few years after I'd joined the firm, the offices of Merrill Lynch, Pierce, Fenner & Bean were moved to 70 Pine Street. There were many different people in it, and a new manager, Victor Cook. Almar Shatford, eighty years old, and a partner, had an important effect on my life.

Coming from Montgomery, I felt frozen in the winter and wore heavy overcoats and gloves. I also got the flu, it was called *la grippe* in those days, at least twice a year. Mr. Shatford told me to stop that nonsense of heavy clothing and let my body get used to the climate, and I wouldn't have all those maladies.

The first year I tried it with just a topcoat, and got the flu only once. The next year I got rid of the topcoat and didn't get sick at all. And there was an extra benefit. I tried to get to the office at five minutes to ten. Sometimes I misgauged and was a little late. On those occasions, our office manager, Victor Cook, would give me an unkind glance, or a few words. Now, without a coat, Victor was stuck. He couldn't be sure if I was late, or just coming back from the men's room.

In those days the market opened at ten o'clock and closed at three. The hours were good for me. At 3:01 I was on my way to my real enjoyment, bridge at the Cavendish Club. I was never any good as a customer's broker, who is supposed to bring in commissions. At my peak, my salary was $12,000 a year. In market judgment I was above average. I kept my own weekly charts, and they were a big help.

Making $12,000 a year must have unsettled my brain. Although classified 4-F, I felt I should try to help win the war, and volunteered for the Coast Guard.

THE U.S. COAST GUARD

Naturally, with my college education, and my fine job on Wall Street, I was invited to take an exam for the Coast Guard Officers' Training School. My mechanical IQ enabled me to flunk it. I was awarded a job as apprentice seaman, equivalent to buck private in the Army. The Coast Guard base I was stationed at was called Manhattan Beach, located at Sheepshead Bay, N.Y.

Getting up for the opening ceremonies at 5 A.M. was not a pleasure to a fellow used to getting up at 9 A.M. "Hit the deck, Mate," is not one of my favorite expressions. But I got used to it, by going to bed at 9 P.M.

The first day, we were issued clothing—white suits, blue suits, and other stuff. A crowd of us were cramped together on the floor of a large room, and instructed to stencil our names on the clothing. I was given a stencil which spelled Jack Dreyfus, and a large bottle of ink.

The space each of us had was small, little more than a yard in diameter. We went to work. My hand and my brain are not too well connected. I spilled the bottle of ink three times (a record at the time). As you know, ink doesn't respect boundaries. After the second bottle was spilled there were growls from my neighbors. After the third, I got threats.

We had a contraption called a seabag. It was about four-and-a-half feet long and twelve inches in diameter. You were supposed to roll your clothing up and tie it with

Apprentice seaman, U.S. Coast Guard

pieces of rope so that, when packed, the circular seabag would have a squared appearance. Only a fiend could have thought of this. But that's not the worst of it. The only entrance to the seabag was from the top. Naturally, you put everything you wanted to be handy near the top. But sometimes you made a mistake. Then you had to empty the whole damned thing— excuse me, I had decided not to cuss in this book—to get the things at the bottom, and then repack the seabag. But perhaps I've been unfair. Maybe the seabag was designed by a genius, to keep us occupied.

The Coast Guard felt, with my college education, I would probably be competent to collect garbage. So I was assigned to a garbage truck. I was third in charge, although I had the highest position, on top of the truck. Garbage cans would be handed me by the second in charge, and I would empty them.

At night I could tell how good business had been. When I took my clothes off there would be a brown line around my stomach or my chest, depending on the haul.

It was while I had this fine position that I learned the difference between garbage and slop. The difference is simple. Slop is slop. Garbage is slop—with coffee grounds added. You can't have garbage without the aroma of coffee grounds. This information should make you glad you bought this book.

Never leaving the base became an awful bore. I would have given anything just to walk through a grocery store. Some of the fellows were beginning to say dumb things, like they wished they could get into the fighting. But one day I got off the base. The three of us had a good load of garbage and were ordered to bring it to the Mineola garbage dump.

Not far from Mineola people started waving wildly at us. We thought, "How wonderful." We'd heard how much people appreciated the uniform, but had never experienced it. The people waved, and we waved back, and felt patriotic. We were enjoying this when a car, with the words Fire Chief on it, pulled alongside. The driver gesticulated for us to stop. We stopped—in the center of Mineola. Then we noticed we had a load of burning garbage. The chief ordered us to dump it, and we did. Firemen came, put out the fire, and shoveled the remains back into our truck, and we took it to the dumps. On the way back to the base nobody waved at us.

Going from garbage to psychology, we all have observed that we don't like to be caught without knowledge. There's no use admitting you don't know something, if you can get away with it. I have noticed this in the medical profession. Dr. Green will say to Dr. Brown, "As you know, Hempleworth and Snodgrass, in 1924, showed that eels have more cholesterol than sardines." Dr. Brown may never have heard of that paper, but he's not apt to let on. This is human. I saw it in the Coast Guard.

The canteen, where you bought everything from candy bars to clothing, was oblong and almost the size of a football field. At the entrance there were many telephone booths, so you could make phone calls. Then you went through a door into the canteen. Once you got into the canteen, you were not allowed to go back through that door.

One day it was raining hard. I was inside the canteen when I remembered a phone call I'd forgotten to make. I didn't want to go outside and make that long trip in the rain to get back to the phones. So I tried a maneuver—I don't know where I got the nerve. I approached the guard at the entrance door and started to go through. He said, "Where do you think you're going, Mate?" I said, "It's okay, I'm a furth burner." He said, "Oh," and I went through.

That was fun. I did it a few times when it wasn't raining, just to keep my spirits up. One day a guard was at the door who was less ashamed to show his ignorance. When I said, "It's okay, I'm a furth burner," he said, "What's a furth burner?" I said, "Where do you think they get the hydrocarbon in the canteen?" That was different, and I went through.

I had a temporary job teaching a course called "Captain of the Port." One of the subjects I was supposed to teach was the workings of the Chrysler Pump. I didn't even know how to plug it in. In class, I read my mates stories from *Reader's Digest*.

■ ■ ■

At Manhattan Beach the beds were double-deckers. I had an upper berth. There was a rule that all windows had to be cracked three inches from the top. It didn't matter if it was 45° or 6° above zero. After being in a steady draft of icy air for many nights, I developed back pains. I could sleep for an hour but then

I would have to get up and walk around for half an hour, to loosen up my back. This continued for weeks, and I didn't get much sleep. Also I found, although I could drill all right, standing at attention for more than a few minutes was extremely painful.

I reported to the infirmary and they were skeptical. Back pains were high on the list for goldbricks. Fortunately, they took my sedimentation rate. It was 56. Normal is 0 to 15, I'm told. This confirmed that I did have a problem, and I was sent to the hospital at Sheepshead Bay.

My doctor was the most handsome man I'd ever seen, straight as a ramrod, six foot two, and a fine face. You would never guess what his name was. It was Twaddle. It was Dr. Twaddle who awarded me malaria (a mild case). There was a theory that the fever from malaria might cure my back. It didn't, but I can tell you about malaria. You start with a chill, I mean really a chill. You're so cold your teeth chatter, and the whole bed shakes. You are happy when the fever comes. Even a 104° fever is better than the chills.

After a couple of months, I was released from the hospital and found myself in what was called Convalescent Camp. In Convalescent Camp there isn't much to do but convalesce. To help me convalesce, I was given a long stick with a nail in the end of it. With this equipment I was supposed to pick up cigarette butts. I did this for a few days, but business was poor. I had a feeling that we could win the war without me and my stick.

There were some huge rocks, on an incline, that protected us from the bay. I climbed down them one day and made a wonderful discovery. There was a cave, just the right size for me. I spent February and March in that cave, accompanied by a book from the library, and a couple of candy bars from the canteen. When the sun was out, even if it was 10° above zero, I could take off all my clothes and get a suntan. I remember one day an ensign said to me, "What the hell's going on here, Dreyfus, you got a sun lamp on the base?"

Well, all good things have to come to an end. Because of my back, I was given a medical discharge. We won the war anyway.

HORSE RACING

There had been no horse races in Alabama. I was introduced to them in an unusual way.

P. Hal Sims, the famous bridge player, and T. Suffern Tailer (Tommy), and I played golf one day—I forget where. Hal was a good golfer, and a better bettor. Tommy had a one handicap. I don't remember the golf, but I remember what followed.

Hal and Tommy suggested we stop at Jamaica Race Track on the way home. I was outvoted, two-to-one. We got to Jamaica before the fifth race. There was a buzz around the track about a jockey named Alfred Robertson, who had won three of the first four races.

With my wealth of handicapping skills, I decided to bet on Robertson's horse in the fifth race. It won. I bet on his horse in the sixth race. It won. Robertson had tied the record of most races won in one day. In the seventh race Tommy gave me some sound advice, and told me Robertson's horse had almost no chance. I bet on him anyway, and he paid a big price.* There

---

* Robertson winning six races in the seven-race card is still a record.

were only seven races, so I had to give up this good thing for the moment.

■ ■ ■

Well, I started to go to the races whenever I got a chance and used a system of betting given me by a friend. Later I read some books on handicapping and started figuring things out for myself.

Going to the races and betting became a great pleasure to me. Every day that I could get loose I went to the track. In my informal attire, I always visited the grandstands where I became friends with lots of the regulars.

There was a period when I was too busy with business to go to the afternoon races so I went to the trotters at night. They're called trotters although they're mostly pacers. I used to go at 6:30 and watch the early workouts. During the races I would mark my program as to which horses went wide. I must have been one of the best handicappers because I learned that when people gave the guard at the $50 window $5 for the "hot" horse he usually gave them my selection.

While watching the thoroughbreds, I observed a two-year-old filly named Bellesoeur and thought she was great. She was second to Bewitch in the Experimental Handicap that year. Bellesoeur didn't race at three and was bred to Count Fleet, who had just retired. Count Fleet was a great horse—not nearly as great as a stallion—but that wasn't known at the time. I wanted part of that first foal. At the time, I couldn't think of buying all of him.

A friend at the City Athletic Club was a friend of Laudy Lawrence, owner of Bellesoeur. He arranged for me to buy half of the foal, named Beau Gar, for $14,000. A friend of my father bought one-quarter. I could barely afford my $7,000 purchase.

Before Beau Gar's first race, let me tell a story. I was going with a girl whose roommate had been robbed and was in financial straits. I offered to give her roommate $50, but my friend said

Handicapping at Hialeah

she wouldn't take it. I asked if she'd mind if I bet $10 on a horse that won, and gave her the money that way? My friend said, "What horse?" I said, "Beau Gar." She agreed, and I gave her $52, wanting it to look realistic. Three weeks later Beau Gar had his first race. He won and paid $10.40—exactly $52 for the $10 bet. Some handicapping.

Beau Gar raced under Laudy Lawrence's name and won a few more races. He had to be retired because of an injury to his back. I still had faith in him. A few years later, and a few bucks richer, I bought the other three-quarters of him, at the original price.

Beau Gar had shown plenty of speed before his injury, and Maje Odom, his trainer, thought well of him. I loved his breeding and decided to take the long shot of trying to make him a successful stallion. Of course, no one else wanted to breed to Beau Gar and I didn't have any mares, or a lot of money.

If you have a mare and want a foal, you buy a service to a

Bill Boland, Beau Purple
after winning the Man O'War

stallion. As you know I do things backwards. I had a stallion and wanted foals, so I leased mares, six of them for a year. I don't know if it's been done before or since, but it turned out well.

I bought one mare, Water Queen. Bred to Beau Gar, she produced Beau Purple, a great horse. Beau Purple won the Kentucky Derby Trial, but in it he fractured a bone in his leg and had to be retired for over a year. When he came back, he was sensational. He established five track records in a period of eight months, from seven-eighths of a mile, to a mile-and-a-half on the grass. Kelso was Horse of the Year five times in a row. Beau Purple beat him three times out of the six times they raced. He also beat Carry Back, Kentucky Derby winner, three times.

Beau Purple was the result of breeding my first horse, Beau Gar, to my first mare, Water Queen. In *Sports Illustrated*, I was quoted as having said, "It was 110% luck, the rest was skill."

■ ■ ■

For the first few years, Maje Odom was my trainer. Later, when my stable got larger, it wasn't convenient for him to handle it exclusively. I met up with Allen Jerkens, an exceptionally fine trainer, and to this day he trains for Hobeau Farm. Allen and I are the closest friends. He's a bit of a nut, quite like me, so we understand each other thoroughly.

Beau Gar initially stood at Henry White's Plum Lane Farm in Lexington, Kentucky. A few years later I got the impression that a higher percentage of good horses than would be expected, considering the quality of the breeding, were coming from Ocala, Florida. When I noticed Rosemere Farm was for sale, I went to Ocala and met Elmer Heubeck, who had been manager there for seventeen years.

Elmer and I liked each other from the beginning. He told me there was a cattle farm that he knew well, about fifteen miles outside of the city, that had plenty of limestone and beautiful oak trees. He thought it ideal for a horse farm, and it was for sale. Elmer recommended I buy it instead of Rosemere, and I did.

Elmer built the farm. We named it Hobeau Farm. Elmer and his wife, Harriet, built it with every thought from the horses' point of view. My former wife, Joan, made creative architectural suggestions, which were followed. And the fences are a lovely blue. Elmer built a first-class one-mile track. At that time, it was one of the few private one-mile tracks in the country. After a few years Elmer became a partner in Hobeau Farm. He and Harriet did a wonderful job, and I can't thank them enough.

■ ■ ■

For years I was a member of the Board of Trustees of the Horsemen's Benevolent and Protective Association (HBPA), a group of horse owners who defend the rights of the horse owners. On one occasion the president of the HBPA was absent for three months, and I found myself temporary president. It happened at a critical time. The owners were justifiably upset about the small end of the track profits they were getting. They were furnishing the entertainment, the horses, and felt they were not being paid properly.

The directors wanted to boycott the races, but accepted my suggestion to try discussion. I made arrangements to see Governor Nelson Rockefeller. He was gracious, listened to the story, and recognized that it was valid. The governor said he would make arrangements for us to get an extra half percent of the handle. The horse owners had wanted more, but they agreed.

About a week before we were supposed to get the half percent we found out that some members of the legislature had blocked the governor's proposal. At that point it was felt necessary to have the boycott. (For reasons best known to lawyers, we couldn't call it a strike.)

I found myself the equivalent of a labor leader of the HBPA. It was a lot of responsibility, and not a lot of fun. The New York Racing Association (NYRA) made it especially tough by saying that if only one horse was entered in a race, he'd get the purse. Somehow we held together for a week, and there weren't any races.

That was a tough week. I got two phone calls, with sinister overtones, from an alleged friend of one of the legislators. I pretended not to understand, but I did, and was worried. The weekend was particularly trying. I decided that on Monday I'd call Governor Rockefeller and get together with him again. When I got to my office I found the governor had called me. It had been arranged for us to get the half percent. That was my first and last experience as a labor leader. The HBPA graciously presented me with its annual award, in memory of Sunny Jim Fitzsimmons, "One Who Contributed Most to the Best Interests of Racing."

This event brought me to the attention of James Brady, who had been, for six or seven years, head of the New York Racing Association. His little boy, Nicholas, recently was Secretary of the Treasury. Jim asked me if I would like to join the Board of the NYRA. I was surprised because I was from the grandstand side. But it was nice, and I accepted. Jim went a step further and said, "In a year or so I'm going to retire and maybe you'd like to take my job." That was flattering, but I took it with a grain of salt.

A year later, in 1970, Mr. Brady asked me if I would take the job as chairman, that he'd had it long enough, and would like a little rest. This happened at a particularly convenient time. The Dreyfus Medical Foundation had just sent a bibliography, *The Broad Range of Use of Phenytoin,* to all the physicians in the United States. With the world literature sent to the physicians and the government, I felt I'd done what I could, and others would take over. So I accepted Mr. Brady's proposal.

I thoroughly enjoyed the job. Everyone was wonderful to me. My secretary, Terry Troglio, helped me more than could be believed.

■ ■ ■

In those days, the backyard of Aqueduct was spacious, but occupied by cement and wire fences. My experience in the grandstand helped me understand the need for change. We had the backyard grassed over, and benches and chairs were added. They got so much use that a tote board was installed.

Races are run every half hour. Between races many of the less sophisticated handicappers are bored. We arranged for bands to play music at Aqueduct and Belmont. The public seemed to like this a great deal. My favorite band was one we got from New Orleans, the Preservation Hall Band.

After I had been chairman of the NYRA for a year I had to

resign to spend full time in the medical field. Much new information had been published on phenytoin, and I had to assist in preparing a supplementary bibliography. This work was completed in 1975. By coincidence, I was again offered the position of chairman of the NYRA. I accepted again.

The second time I became chairman, I did it with the reservation that I might not be able to keep the position long, and suggested we have an assistant chairman. Dinsmore (Dinny) Phipps took the job. It was a pleasure working with him and we have been the best of friends ever since. When, a year later, I felt obliged to spend more time in the medical field, Dinny became chairman and did a splendid job.

The second time I was chairman I had some fun stirring up the advertising for the track. A series of ads was done on the race horse as the fastest animal in the world. He is not as fast as the cheetah for a hundred yards, but for a mile, he's the fastest animal (I think). Other ads were done on taking a half-day vacation from the city by going to the track. There was a noticeable improvement in attendance following these ads.

■ ■ ■

Hobeau Farm won the Turf Writers' Award for best breeder, twice. This was a tribute to Allen Jerkens' training. One year we won nineteen races at Saratoga, a twenty-four-day meet—a record at the time.

In 1977 I received the Eclipse Award, Man Who Did the Most for Racing, which I deeply appreciated. The award was given in Los Angeles.

On the way to Los Angeles a nice thing happened. I had my own plane but it couldn't go that far in one hop, so we stopped in Phoenix, Arizona. President Nixon had told me he thought the Arizona Biltmore was the finest hotel in the world. I figured his opinion would be pretty good, he'd been around a little. So I stopped at the Biltmore, getting there around eleven o'clock in the morning. It was too early for lunch and too late for breakfast, but I was hungry.

There was a large menu in my room. On it was continental breakfast. I don't go for formality. If I wanted that, I'd ask for coffee, rolls, and jelly. But what the heck, in Rome do as the Romans do. So I dialed the number. A nice female voice said, "How may I help you?" I said, "This is Room 346. Could I have a continental breakfast, please?" The nice voice said, "Which continent would you like it from? This is the overseas operator." What a wonderful put-down.

I'm still on the Board of the New York Racing Association. I miss a few of the meetings because of medical research. Every once in a while I make a speech about how crazy it is for the state to charge the bettors 17 percent per race. It's ruined the business. Anybody but government would change it to 10 percent. Now I've said it in writing, and gotten it off my chest—again.

I'd like to finish this chapter with a story for my friend Gloria Steinem, of Women's Lib renown.

Robyn Smith was one of the earliest female jockeys. My trainer Allen recognized her talent and was one of the first to give her mounts. Much later Robyn was married to Fred Astaire.

One day I got to Aqueduct too late to make a bet on the first race. It was winter, the grandstand was enclosed with glass, and I hurried to the front window to see the race. There were a lot of people in back of me. Robyn was riding a seven-to-two shot. As the race started, I heard a distinctive voice yell, "Come on, Robyn." Robyn's horse broke second to the favorite. As it pursued the favorite up the back stretch, the voice urged, "Come on, Robyn. Come on, Robyn." When the horses came into the stretch, Robyn's horse started gaining on the leader. The voice became more intimate and said, "Come on, Honey. Come on, Honey." As Robyn's horse went over the finish line, the winner, the voice lowered and said, "Okay, bitch."

Now that wasn't nice.

Before leaving this chapter I should say I've thoroughly enjoyed my association with the members of the Board of the NYRA. As a group, and as individuals, they have been a pleasure to be with.

EXPERIENCES AND THOUGHTS

In this chapter I'll discuss aptitudes, my personality, extrasensory perception, Mark Twain, and a suggestion for Congress.

Aptitudes

In the chapter on Probabilities in *A Remarkable Medicine Has Been Overlooked,* which follows, I discuss aptitudes at some length, so I'll be brief here.

Some of my aptitudes or disaptitudes, you might call them, I got from my father.

Aptitudes as I see it are gadgets in the brain that come with the baby. I can't prove it by pictures of the brain. But think of the homing pigeon and his perfect sense of direction, and the bird dog and his aptitude for smelling.

One aptitude we all have, a strong one, is an aptitude not to die. If we didn't have that aptitude our manufacturer would be wasting His time. Another aptitude that most of us have is what we call a conscience. It's really a judge in the brain. When He decides we've done something good, He makes us feel better with a little happy juice. When He decides we've done something bad, He punishes us with a little unhappy juice. The neurotic has a tough judge.

I lack many aptitudes. My sense of direction is in backwards. My copying device is faulty. My ability to remember names is so bad it's embarrassing. And I have a mechanical I.Q. of about seven. One good aptitude I was born with is a sense of probabilities.

My aptitudes to forget names and get lost I inherited directly from my father. Let me illustrate Dad's ability to forget names:

Dad and my wife Joan and I were taking a train to Ocala, Florida. Hobeau Farm was being built by my farm manager and friend, Elmer Heubeck, and his lovely wife Harriet. On the train we drilled Dad. Every couple of hours we'd have him repeat Elmer and Harriet, Elmer and Harriet. We arrived at Hobeau Farm and went to a trailer to have lunch. Dad walked in and said, "Hello, Elmer. Hello, Harriet." And Joan and I were proud.

Harriet has a pet name for Elmer. She calls him Abbie. During lunch she would say, "Abbie, may I have some coffee." "Abbie, please pass the butter." Abbie this, Abbie that. Dad couldn't stand it any longer. He said, "I know this is Elmer. I know this is Harriet. But why does she keep calling him Chuck?"

I could give you illustrations of my father's ability to get lost, but why pick on Dad. I'll tell you a story that demonstrates my own talent:

One day I was at the races at Aqueduct and didn't have my car. An apprentice jockey, Terry Drawdy, had just come to New

York and had won the last race on a horse of mine. I was wondering how I could get a ride home when my trainer, Allen, said Terry would drive me, if I would show him the way. That was no problem, I'd been to Aqueduct at least 2000 times.

We had the bad luck to leave on the wrong road, and the first thing I knew we were on Atlantic Avenue, heading for Brooklyn. I was unperturbed and asked a gas station attendant how to get to New York. He said, "No problem. Just follow this road till you come to the Manhattan Bridge, take that and you'll be there." We followed instructions and went over the bridge. Now we were supposed to be in Manhattan, but I knew Manhattan was loaded with street numbers, 10, 11, 12 and so forth, and we couldn't find any. We drove around and around, looking for street numbers. I thought, this is peculiar. Finally we came to a familiar sign, Holland Tunnel. Now I knew where we were. Years earlier at Lehigh, Monroe Lewis used to drive me to New York and we always went through the Holland Tunnel.

So we went through the Holland Tunnel—and came out in New Jersey. I'd overlooked the possibility that the Holland Tunnel went both ways. No problem, we went up the Jersey side to the Lincoln Tunnel, through that, and up to 75th and Madison, where I live. It took us three hours and twenty minutes to make a forty-minute trip. I've been told this is the only time anybody went from Aqueduct to 75th Street by way of New Jersey.

I could tell endless stories about my getting lost but it'll seem like I'm bragging, because in *A Tramp Abroad,* my friend Mark Twain said, "For me, East is West, and West is East."

■ ■ ■

Personality

I prefer not to be called Mr. Dreyfus, and try to get everybody to call me Jack. A few won't, they say it doesn't show proper respect. But believe me, you can disrespect a person and still call him Mister.

They say, clothes make the man. I don't think that's all of it. I wear good clothes but never a tie and collar, if I can get away with it. Take Donald Trump for instance. People wouldn't mistake Mr. Trump for an unsuccessful person, even without a tie and collar. He has a presence. Apparently I have an absence, and I project it.

A few illustrative experiences follow, some with ladies. That's what I call them, being raised in Alabama. I'd have to be reincarnated before I'd call them guys.

After watching the horses train at Hialeah, Maje Odom and I went to a diner for breakfast. On the way to our table there was a lady with a tiny baby. To be friendly, I said, "They're making them awful small these days." She said, "I'll have a coke, please."

While I was in my bathing suit on the beach at the Roney Plaza Hotel in Miami, a lady strode up to me and said, indignantly, "I'd like to report that the toilet in the ladies' room isn't working." I apologized—and passed the word along.

I was sitting on a bench in Miami Beach, waiting to be picked up, when a lady came up to me and asked, "What time does the bus leave?" An empty bus was about fifty yards to the left. I said, "I don't know, Ma'am." She said, "You don't know? Aren't you the bus driver?" I demurred.

At Tropical Park, my horse, Beau Purple was entered in a Stake race, which he subsequently won. I went into the paddock with my close friend Bill Rogers, Secretary of State, who was dressed as a Secretary of State should be dressed. I was in my usual attire. We hadn't gone far when a guard jumped in front of me and said, "Where do you think you're going?" I said, "Into the paddock." He said, "What would you be doing in the paddock?" I said, "I have a horse there." He said, "*You* have a horse there?" I said, "Yes." He said, "What horse?" I said, "Beau Purple." He said, "*You* own Beau Purple?" I said, "Yes." He said, "Let me see your owner's license." Luckily, I found it in my wallet. He looked at it and repeated, "You own Beau Purple?" I said, "Somebody's got to own the horse." I wouldn't have remembered saying that, but years later Bill reminded me. Of course he could have saved me the aggravation, but he was enjoying it.

Now to the height of my career.

For several years I ate lunch at a small restaurant on 62nd Street, called Truffles. It had two window tables, a small one in the corner and a narrow one parallel to the window. One day I sat at the small table, facing the interior of the restaurant.

I'd ordered my usual sandwich, cheese and tomato on a toasted roll, when two young ladies came in and sat at the other table. They hadn't been there long when the one whose back was close to me turned around and started searching the floor. I said, "Did you lose something, Miss?" She said, "Yes, my wallet." I looked around on the floor and said, "I don't see anything." She turned back to her companion and a moment later they had a heated discussion.

My sandwich had arrived when the young lady turned around and glared at me. At first I didn't get it, but when she continued to glare, I said, "My goodness, Miss, I don't have your wallet." She said, "You're the only one who could. It was in my bag on the back of my chair."

At that point the ladies got up and started to leave. I got up too and my new acquaintance said, in a loud voice, "I don't mind the money but please leave my wallet, it has papers in it I need."

They marched out of the restaurant. I went after them. The one whose wallet I had "stolen" was about five paces in front of her friend. I happened to have $5,000 in new bills I had just gotten from the bank. I showed it to the friend and asked, "Does it look like I have to pick pockets?" She said, "Put that away. Somebody will steal it." Apparently they had stealing on their minds.

I went back into the restaurant and sat at my table, facing all the other guests. The lady nearest me seemed to shrink together with all her possessions. Everyone was staring at me. Understandable. It's not often you can enjoy lunch, and look at a pickpocket at the same time.

I counseled myself, "Now, cool it, don't get upset. You haven't done anything to be upset about. Don't let this bother you. Eat your sandwich. Chew well," and similar thoughts.

After about ten minutes my friend came back. I stood up and she said, "I'm awfully sorry, I found my wallet in my car." I could have given her a blast. But I said, "You've got a lot of guts to come back, and I appreciate it."

Let me conclude with a nice story.

I have been to Milan, Italy, twice—both times for medical conferences. The second time, I was staying at a lovely hotel, Principe di Savoia. I was to be picked up at 8:45 A.M. I had breakfast and went out front a little early. In the seven days I was in Milan, I saw the sun only once, but the air was always nice, compatible with my body's electricity.

When I got outside, I saw a little pussycat. It wasn't that it was so little, it was so skinny it looked little. I hurried back to the breakfast room and bought some ham and turkey. When I came out the kitty was still there and I gave him the food. He didn't eat it, he just inhaled it. I've never seen food disappear so quickly, and I realized I hadn't given him enough.

Now I had a problem. I had a few hundred dollar bills, but no small change. So I went to the desk to get change. The desk had a piece of plastic on top of the nice wood that made it difficult to talk over. I waved to the young man who had shown me to my room. He spoke a fair amount of English. He came over, and I handed him a hundred dollar bill over the plastic and said, "Could I get change for this, please?" He said, "Oh, thank you *so* much, Mr. Dreyfus, this is so nice. I really appreciate this. You don't know how much this means to me!" Well I remembered what Jesus said, "It's better to give than to receive," but this was a borderline case. I decided that I would go along with the thought, and smiled at him. I think I smiled—it felt more like a wince. Then I went back into the restaurant, negotiated a loan, and got more ham and turkey for the pussycat. This time it was eaten rapidly, but not inhaled, so I felt it was enough for the time being.

I was picked up and taken to the meeting, and came back around 3:45. I was tired and went to my room, washed up a bit, and went out to enjoy the nice Milan air.

Across the street from the hotel was a tiny park, the shape of an ellipse. As I got to the park I saw two elderly people sitting on a bench. Their clothes looked more elderly than they. I was about to offer them some money, but decided against it—their feelings might have been hurt. I went to the other side of the park, sat on a bench, and enjoyed the air. It was so relaxing I lay down. Pretty soon I was asleep.

I was wakened by a tap on my shoulder. I sat up and there was a well-dressed serious-looking lady holding out a ten-lire note. I couldn't take the money, of course. But remembering my thought from the other side of the park, I took the note from the lady and thanked her very much. As she left there was a little smile on her face, proving that Jesus was right. And I had a feeling that in taking the note I'd given something myself, and felt happier too. It was a nice day.

■ ■ ■

Extrasensory Perception

Many experiences have convinced me that there really is such a thing as ESP. These are just a few. I could give more, but these seemed clear-cut.

I was sitting in a theater waiting for the curtain to rise. There was the usual whispering and chattering in the audience when I heard a man in back of me say, "It was an awfully long trip," and my mind said, "to Barcelona." I don't know why Barcelona instead of Newark or Philadelphia. The man continued, "from Cannes" (I was a phrase ahead) "to Barcelona." ESP, I think.

One day my secretary, Helen Raudonat, said, "Jack, may I take Thursday off?" Well Helen had been so wonderful to me she could have taken a thousand Thursdays off. Helen is small and I knew she didn't play golf. So, to be a wise guy, I started to say, "To play golf." But, before it came out of my mouth, I embellished it and said, "You want to play in a golf tournament." Helen said, "Who told you?" I said, "Who told me?" and we got into a hassle. ESP, I'm sure.

I was in a bridge game with some tough players, playing the dummy. A good bridge player, Alan Kahn, was sitting near me, jabbering away with a neighbor, and I couldn't concentrate. I said, "Alan, for gosh sakes, be quiet. Why don't you go play Mah-Jongg." I hadn't used the word Mah-Jongg for fifty years. To my amazement, Alan pulled a book on Mah-Jongg from his pocket. A bridge player with a book on Mah-Jongg can't be. That must have been ESP.

There has to be two kinds of ESP—sending and receiving. One can be stronger than the other, but both are necessary. You can't have ESP with a stone. The next story is an illustration of the sending ESP being strong.

I was going to dinner at the Forum of the Twelve Caesars on 46th Street. It was only eight blocks from where I lived, so I decided to walk. In the last few blocks I thought of the TV debate that had taken place the night before between the presidential candidates Kennedy and Nixon, the first of a series. I had decided to vote for Mr. Nixon. I'd seen him on David Susskind's show and thought he'd answered some tough questions about the Russian situation extemely well.

The debates were set up in a formal way. A panel had selected subjects for each debate. I don't remember what the first subject was, but I remember what it wasn't. It wasn't about injustices to the black people. But Mr. Kennedy, the first speaker, started talking about these injustices, and what should be done about them. I was thinking, from Mr. Nixon's point of view, that when I got my turn to talk, I'd have said, "Mr. Kennedy, we had a subject to discuss tonight, but you've talked about something else. I agree with what you've said, but it wasn't tonight's subject. If we're not going to talk about the subject of the debate, let's agree on that and forget about subjects."

I arrived at the restaurant and was standing at the desk from which the head waiter operates. These thoughts were still going through my head when a voice from the side and a little in back of me said, "Mr. Vice President." I turned and saw a white-haired gentlemen coming towards me. He said, "Oh, I'm so sorry. I thought you were Mr. Nixon." At that moment I thought I was.

■ ■ ■

Mark Twain

Of all the people I know, leaving the Bible out of this, I think Mark Twain was the greatest. His sense of humor was so extraordinary that many think of him as a humorist. That was just part of him. And his ability to write was beautiful. That was just part of him. The greatest part of him was his insight into members of the human race. Stories by him, "The War Prayer," "My First Lie and How I Got Out of It," "What Is Man?" and others, have great depth and importance—and I recommend them to you.

There was a time when some black people thought that Mark Twain was prejudiced against them, and suggested barring his books. I'm glad this is in the past because he was anything but prejudiced against black people. In fact he was an outstanding supporter. A quote from "My First Lie" makes that clear:

> "It would not be possible for a humane and intelligent person to invent a rational excuse for slavery."

■ ■ ■

Suggestion for Congress and the American People

Many years ago, when I read that Mark Twain said, "Government is organized imbecility," I thought he was being humorous. I don't think so anymore. For twenty-five years I've been trying to give the United States Government a great present.* But I've found that there's no place in government to receive presents. There are plenty of places to receive problems. However, I don't

*Explained in *A Remarkable Medicine Has Been Overlooked.*

think we should pick on the politicians about this. I think we should pick on ourselves—at least as much as on them.

Congress and the President are supposed to have the most important jobs in the United States—they run our country. And we should pay them top salaries, but we don't even come close. Our Senators get $135,000, plus perks. Let's call it $150,000. The same for Congressmen. Our President gets $200,000, plus perks. For easy figuring, let's call it $300,000.

During the recent baseball strike you read that the average major league baseball player (there are 700 of them) received $1.2 million a year. In other words, the average baseball player earns eight times as much as a Member of Congress, and four times as much as our Chief Executive Officer, the President of the United States.

Here are some annual earnings of recent date:

Top CEOs (in millions): $25.9, 23.8, 16.6, 15.8, 14.7, 14.6, 13.7, 12.4, 12.3, 12.1 —*Business Week*

Top Athletes (in millions): $30.0, 16.7, 14.8, 13.6, 13.5, 13.5, 12.1, 12.0, 11.4, 11.3 —*Forbes*

I won't give you any more figures, you'll find them in the sports pages every day.

Suggestion—Let's pay our Senators $4 million, Members of the House $3 million, the President $7.5 million. If you say they're not worth it, that may be so. But that's just the point. If we pay outstanding salaries in government maybe we'll get outstanding people. Compared to our national debt of $4.9 trillion, this is peanuts.

WALL STREET

When I was discharged from the Coast Guard, the law of gravity required I return to my job as a customer's broker at Merrill Lynch. I found that my best customer, who had been handled by a partner while I was away, did not want to change back to a customer's broker. It wasn't the partner's fault, but it didn't make me happy.

I had been in civilian life a few months when Chester Gaines, a specialist on the floor of the New York Stock Exchange, who played gin rummy with me at the City Athletic Club, told me that judging by my gin game, I would do well trading on the floor of the Exchange. I'd never thought of such a thing. Besides, it needed the purchase of a stock exchange seat. My capital for such a purchase was about 97 percent short.

In those days I used to play golf with a friend, Jerry Ohrbach, at Metropolis Country Club. One day, when we were in the same foursome, I got a seven on the first hole, an easy par-five. I was steaming, and asked Jerry what odds he would give against my getting a 33 on that nine. Par was 35, so that meant I would have to be four under for the next eight holes. Jerry said 1,000-to-1. I said

I'll take a hundred dollars worth of that if you like, and he said okay. He could afford the hundred thousand and I could afford the hundred dollars. Jerry had the best of the odds and I had a shot at my Alan Rice fortune. I made him sweat to the last hole. I needed a birdie there for the thirty-three, but didn't come close.

When Chester Gaines made the suggestion of the stock exchange seat, I spoke to Jerry about it. He told me that the golf bet had scared him so much he would like to be partners with me. By borrowing from my father, one of my uncles, my wife, and adding my own few dollars, I got up 25 percent of the necessary capital. Jerry and his father, Nathan, put up the rest and became limited partners in the small firm, Dreyfus & Co., members of the New York Stock Exchange. And we lived happily ever after. Well, not quite.

We cleared through Bache & Co., the firm that had turned me down for a job as a customer's broker. John Behrens became a partner and handled business in the office.

I was on the floor of the Exchange. I executed orders for Bache, and traded for the firm's account, with a small amount of capital. The first year, we made $14,000 trading. Jerry and his father, Nathan, didn't realize how good that was. It was a bear market, the sort of market in which they say, "not even the liars made money."

Nathan Orbach had wandered into a brokerage firm in 1929 and had gotten the indestructible notion that you couldn't make money trading in the market, and wanted us to get into the brokerage business. One day Jerry introduced me to a partner of Lewisohn & Sons, a stock exchange firm that cleared its own transactions. The story was that the partners of Lewisohn were getting old and wanted to get out of the business. Another reason, which we didn't know at the time, was that the business was in bad shape.

Jerry thought we should take over the firm. I wasn't keen about this, knowing nothing about managing a brokerage firm, but went along with it because three of the partners were going to stay on. To shorten this story, after a year or so those partners were gone and I had to leave the floor, where I was reasonably competent, and start managing a brokerage firm, where I had no experience at all.

Business was bad. I cut my salary to zero, and the Ohrbachs didn't draw interest on their money. We couldn't even go out of business without considerable loss. In this pickle, we decided to try advertising. In those days New York Stock Exchange ads were proper—and dull. But if we wanted to advertise, the natural thing was to go to the agency that handled all the Wall Street advertising. The first and only ad they did for us, I wrote.

In those days the margin requirement for stocks was a ridiculously high 75 percent. I wanted to comment on that and wrote an ad titled "On Returning from the Moon." In the ad it was said, you have just returned from a five-year trip to the moon. Having made a fortune selling Blue Moon Cheese to the natives, you are anxious to invest some of this money. You haven't seen a stock table for five years and you ask your broker for vital statistics on five of your favorite stocks. After getting the statistics, you thought the stocks were reasonably priced and told your broker to buy 100 shares of each. Then the ad went on to say that all the statistics were correct, but the price of the stocks was one-half of what you'd been told. And it was suggested that the stocks were that cheap because of the ridiculously high margins.

Whether the ad had an effect or not, three weeks later the margin requirements were reduced to 50 percent.

It didn't take long for me to learn that the agency that did the Wall Street advertising was set in its ways. I went to a new, imaginative agency, Doyle, Dane & Bernbach. The first ad they wrote for us was different from Wall Street advertising, in appearance and in content. It said you don't have to be old-fashioned to be conservative. I wasn't crazy about that because it suggested that other firms were old-fashioned. When I was told that the agency planned to run this ad quite a few times (our budget, $20,000, was so small they couldn't afford to spend much time on new copy), I decided to try to write the ads myself.

This struck an unexpected aptitude in me. At that time I didn't realize that my copying device was faulty. This can be a hindrance, but in this case it was an advantage. I tried to do ads that would get attention and be enjoyable.

Freddy Dossenbach, our account executive, and I lunched at Schwartz's on Broad Street. Freddy would bring old prints and cartoons. Inspired by liverwurst, Swiss cheese, and iced tea, I would dream up copy to fit them. Our firm had little to brag about, so I just tried to give general advice hoping it would reflect favorably on us. Apparently it did. To my astonishment we won the first Standard & Poor's Gold Trophy for excellence in advertising. Some of the ads follow on the next page.

As a result of the ads some customer's brokers who had decided to leave their firms for one reason or another applied for jobs. When a customer's broker came with us, no matter how small his business, we ran a good-sized ad announcing that Joe Doaks had joined Dreyfus & Co. This ad was expensive, but valuable. Some of Joe Doaks' customers might have been thinking of leaving him, but seeing his name in the business section of the *Times* made a good impression. So it helped him with his customers, and it also helped him with potential customers. There was another benefit that I'm not sure I recognized at first. When customer's brokers considered leaving their firm, and that was always happening in the Street, they considered coming to Dreyfus & Co. because they knew they would see their names in the paper. So the firm grew steadily.

Sizable producers came with us. Some with so much business

"PETS" CAN BE EXPENSIVE

Too often, investors become sentimentally attached to stocks which have done well for them in the past. These "pets" can be expensive if they are allowed to prejudice sound judgment. Be sure that you use unsentimental, clear-headed analysis so that every stock in your portfolio today is there because of present merit.

Dreyfus & Co.

TODAY'S METHODS FOR TODAY'S MARKETS

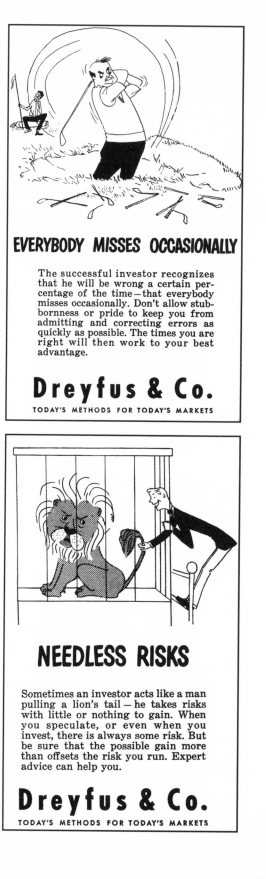

EVERYBODY MISSES OCCASIONALLY

The successful investor recognizes that he will be wrong a certain percentage of the time—that everybody misses occasionally. Don't allow stubbornness or pride to keep you from admitting and correcting errors as quickly as possible. The times you are right will then work to your best advantage.

Dreyfus & Co.

TODAY'S METHODS FOR TODAY'S MARKETS

"WISHING WELL" WON'T WORK

There is no room for wishful thinking in your investment program. Keep in mind the security markets are not concerned with your desires. If you think clearly and unemotionally you are much more likely to get the best results.

Dreyfus & Co.

TODAY'S METHODS FOR TODAY'S MARKETS

NEEDLESS RISKS

Sometimes an investor acts like a man pulling a lion's tail—he takes risks with little or nothing to gain. When you speculate, or even when you invest, there is always some risk. But be sure that the possible gain more than offsets the risk you run. Expert advice can help you.

Dreyfus & Co.

TODAY'S METHODS FOR TODAY'S MARKETS

they insisted on partnerships. At that stage it seemed desirable to take on partners, if they were the right sort. Soon we had enough partners to always have a quorum for an argument.*

■ ■ ■

At the age of thirty-three, without experience, I found myself managing partner of the firm. Most of the customer's brokers were older than I. My only method was to try to work with people as friends. I could never boss people around. Once in a while somebody would call me "boss" and I would jump a foot. I don't like that word.

What I learned at Lehigh about wish-thinking and rationalization was solid. Almost all of the customer brokers felt they weren't being paid enough. Even when they knew they were being paid enough, they worried that a neighbor might be being paid more. (There were two brothers, not with us long, who were the worst. I used to say the Blank brothers were 100 percent honest, Max 60 percent and Arnold 40 percent.) I solved the problem for all by putting the customer's brokers on a sliding scale, the larger the production, the larger the percentage of commission.

I won't bore you, or myself, with the details of the growing of a brokerage firm. Just one illustration of my managerial skill.

One of our customer's brokers, a small producer, was making more errors than he brought us in commissions. English was not his native language. Finally I called Dan into my office, talked firmly to him, and told him he had to be more careful. He listened, and left. I was wondering if I'd done any good when the door opened a little. Dan's face came in, beaming. He said, "Don't worry, Jack, from now on I'll be at my wits' end." Success.

---

*Over the years I've enjoyed partnerships with John Behrens, Samuel Pearson, Samuel Strasbourger, Robert Tulcin, John Cranley, Raymond Schibowski, Thomas Bligh and Duncan Cameron.

The firm continued to grow. The time came when our nice offices at 50 Broadway were too small, and we had to move. A new building was being built at 2 Broadway and, before it was finished, we took the top two floors. While they were being built, my former wife, Joan, made the wonderful suggestion that the window levels be lowered so that we could have a beautiful view of the harbor. It cost us $40,000 but it was well worth it.

When we moved into these offices with the wonderful view, I felt good about them and wanted the public to know about them. But my small ego wouldn't allow me to say it in a straightforward fashion. Finally, after much thinking, we decided on a television ad.

I'd seen some wonderful cartoons on TV. I forget who did them. In them there were a couple of ping-pong players—elderly gentlemen who spoke with a British accent. The table they played on was small. They hit the ball back and forth in the air—it never touched the table.

Our agency designed an ad. A camera takes you through the entrance of a posh club and into a room where two old English gentlemen are playing ping-pong. After a few bats of the ball, one of them says, "Who's your broker, old chap?" The other says, "Broker?" The first one says "Yes, stocks and bonds, that sort of thing." The other says, "Oh, Dreyfus—Dreyfus & Company." The first says, "Why old chap?" Here you expect "a great research department" or something like that. But the response is, "Magnificent view of the harbor, boats and all that."

The ad was a lot of fun, and it got the idea across in the best way. It was popular and we ran it often. I remember when some Germans came over to look at Wall Street advertising they selected our lion (I'll tell about him later) and the ping-pong players for reproduction in German. These old English gentlemen, talking in German, were a sight to hear.

■ ■ ■

One day John Nesbett, a fine gentleman, applied for a position as a customer's broker. John was the president of a small mutual fund, the Nesbett Fund, which he had been trying to develop for three years. The fund had only reached $500,000. With 1/2 percent management fee, John couldn't make a living.

When I had been a customer's broker with E. A. Pierce & Co. I had suggested to Mr. Pierce that a mutual fund would be a good idea, but nothing had happened. I still liked the idea. Unsophisticated investors would have their money handled by professionals, who spend their time studying the market. Also, as a customer's broker I'd noticed that if I had ten customers, seven might do well and three poorly. Not necessarily my fault, the three had an instinct for picking my worst recommendations. But I worried about those three. In a mutual fund, the investments would be the same for all.

An arrangement was made with John for the name of the Nesbett Fund to be changed to the Dreyfus Fund. He and I managed it jointly until he left, two or three years later. It took us nearly five years to get the size of the Dreyfus Fund up to a million dollars (mostly by stock appreciation). During this time, Dreyfus & Co. lost a lot of money on the Fund, and my partners started giving me strange looks. Fortunately the five-year performance of the Fund was so good that it became easier to sell.

Managers of a mutual fund have two chief responsibilities. First, and most important, is the management of the money in the fund. Second, for management to make money, advertising and promotion are necessary. Let me discuss the latter briefly, then the management of the Fund.

When the Fund was still very small, Frank Sweetser, who was with Value Line, suggested we needed a sales department, which we certainly did. Frank offered his services and they were accepted. After Frank had been with us a short while he suggested that our logo be changed from DF to a stylized lion, and we did this. A few years later Frank left us for greener fields, but I thank him for the lion.

One day Freddy Dossenbach and I were having lunch at Schwartz's. Over the Swiss cheese and liverwurst, I broached the subject of a TV advertisement for the Fund, with a live lion. Fred liked the idea and his firm went to work on producing it.

They did a splendid job. The commercial had a majestic lion coming up out of a Wall Street subway, walking casually past a news dealer, into our lobby at 2 Broadway, jumping up on a block of wood, and freezing into the Dreyfus Fund logo. This one-minute commercial was accompanied by the wonderful lion music of Saint-Saens' "Carnival of the Animals." During the lion's walk, an announcer, in a quiet voice, said, "The Dreyfus Fund is a mutual fund in which management hopes to make your money grow, and takes what it considers sensible risks in that direction."

The advertisement was a great success. Nobody got tired of the lion, or the music. That was fortunate because we had to run the same ad thousands of times—shortly after it was approved the SEC put restrictions on TV commercials.

My inability to copy was valuable in the Dreyfus Fund prospectus. Other prospectuses were written by lawyers. Not knowing any better, I wrote the nontechnical part of our prospectus.

I was surprised and delighted when *Barron's National Business and Financial Weekly* made the nice comment: "Dreyfus Fund's latest prospectus is like none we have ever seen. Instead of the usual forbidding makeup with its weighty and legalistic prose, Dreyfus has substituted color and supplied the facts in an attractive manner...Dreyfus is the first fund to acknowledge, in its prospectus, that the average small investor is not a financial lawyer. And this is quite a step forward."

One day Freddy Dossenbach and I were lunching at Schwartz's with a representative from the *New York Times* who made the suggestion that we put the balance sheet of our prospectus in a Sunday *Times* supplement. I enlarged on the idea, and we put the entire prospectus in the Sunday *Times*, as a supplement. It was excellent advertising, and we used the supplement as our official prospectus—a bargain, the *Times* sold us copies for three cents apiece.

■ ■ ■

As to the management of the Fund. I'm keenly aware that today's markets are vastly different from the markets of those days. Today there are options, puts and calls, indexes, and other things. Today 300 million shares a day are ordinary. In those days, the average volume was three to four million shares. But I think certain fundamentals still exist.

The management fee of $2,500 (1/2 percent of $500,000) was so small when we started the Fund that we couldn't afford a research staff. A young man, Alex Rudnicki, and I ran the Fund. Alex was a nice boy, extremely shy—even more shy than I. We were so shy that neither of us had the courage to call an officer of a company and ask how the company was doing. Maybe this was an asset. According to the Arthur Wiesenberger report, during the twelve years Alex and I made the decisions the Dreyfus Fund outperformed all other mutual funds, by a large margin.

Alex was never found without a Standard & Poor's or Moody's booklet in his pocket. Alex was strong on the fundamentals. He had been a student at the Graham Dodd School of Investing. Graham Dodd believed that if a stock had $12 in cash, it was all right to pay $8 for it. I'm exaggerating a little, but the principles were that you had to be very sound. My method, of course, was different. I didn't object to soundness, but I was interested in market timing.

I had used weekly bar charts, posted daily, from my beginning in Wall Street. I found these the best for me. Daily charts gave too many opinions, monthly charts didn't give enough. So weekly charts, posted daily, and *looked at daily*, were what we used. We had six hundred of them made up, on a large scale. I didn't try to squeeze opinions out of the charts. Perhaps 5 percent of the time a chart position formed which, based on my experience, indicated the stock a probable buy or sale (in those days funds were not permitted to sell short). Then we acted. Even then we made enough mistakes to satisfy ourselves. When the stock didn't act as we expected, we took our loss. We didn't want to become what was called "involuntary investors."

In our commercials we said, "We're trying to make your money grow and management takes what it considers sensible risks in that direction." But how did we think of that money? Well, I struck on an idea which we used. We thought of it as our mother's money. The emphasis was on *our*. If it was someone else's mother's money we would be inhibited by what her accountant or her lawyer would think. This was our mother's money. At the same time it was a mother's money, so we were not going to take wild risks.

We always had in mind that the dollar bill was just a piece of paper. It would seem that if you wanted to be careful, you'd just keep the paper. But there were signs of inflation, and keeping the paper wouldn't necessarily keep the purchasing power. You just couldn't buy bonds and be safe, you couldn't buy stocks and be safe. You had to keep thinking.

One of our general rules was to follow the major trend. Markets in those days—not as much now—had major trends. The markets tended to go up as a unit, or down as a unit. If you've got an escalator that's going up, you're better off betting on an individual on that escalator than on an individual on an escalator that's going down. The whole market was like an escalator. In other words, if a company did poorly, a bull market escalator would usually keep it from going down. The opposite was so in a bear market. Of course there were exceptions.

Although it was our mother's money, we had our minimum limits. We didn't often buy "cats and dogs" (that was an expression in those days)—they call them secondary stocks now. Occasionally we did, but I was careful about it. That's where Alex and his Moody's handbook helped.

A fundamental fact of the market was explained, I think by Jeb Stuart or Stonewall Jackson (not General Schwarzkopf), who said, "Get there fustus with the mostus." That meant that you can win a battle, even if you've got a smaller number of people, if you get there first. In the days that I'm talking about, margin accounts swung the whole market. They were a small part of the total investment holdings, but margin traders worked in concert—the investors worked individually. When an investor sold his house, he might invest the proceeds in the stock market. If he wanted to buy a house, or spend money, he would sell stock to do it. But that wasn't in concert with other investors. And the investment accounts managed by the banks and investment funds were not too flexible. In those days there was a little bit of "buy a good stock, put it away, and forget about it."

But the margin accounts were very flexible. They were in constant touch with their brokers. When a piece of news occurred, they responded. Obviously, they had varying opinions. The only time they worked in concert, unfortunately, was when they were overextended. When too many of them were fully margined and the market went down, the brokers had to call the weakest accounts for more money. Many of these accounts didn't have more money and the only way of getting it was by selling stock. This would cause the market to break and then the next group of accounts would come under pressure. This continued until those who were on the most conservative margins had to sell.

There had been a domino effect (I hate the expression). When the margin accounts had been cleaned out there was usually a good deal of pessimism, and the market was usually a buy.

We must keep in mind that being bullish doesn't put the market up. Having purchasing power is what puts the market up. Being bearish doesn't put the market down. Having selling power, being long of stock, can put it down. So, comparatively speaking, a small segment of the investment public, the margin trader, had a lot to do with market swings.

The short interest was an important gauge. It was like a Gallup poll of market sentiment with the margin traders. Most people didn't sell short, but you knew that when the short interest was high, a large percentage of the other margin accounts would be in cash. When the short interest was low, you knew the margin traders were mostly long of stock. That was the most reliable way of knowing what the margin players were doing.

In the management of the Fund, we had certain principles. One of these was to not pound the table when we had an idea. The reason for that was simple. Once you pound the table, you take away some of your flexibility (it's harder to admit you were wrong). And admitting that we were wrong was something that we put high on the list, because taking losses early is a valuable thing when you're speculating in the market. So we never pounded the table.

As I said earlier we tried to follow the major trends. We thought of the money as our mother's money. We tried to be flexible. But the only rule we had, that was an absolute rule, was to keep thinking.

■ ■ ■

There was one stock that was an exception to our flexibility rule. We bought it for long-term investment. The stock was Polaroid. It was by accident that I knew about Polaroid. My brother-in-law, Dr. Elkan Blout, was head of research at the company and told me about the 3-D glasses they were making. Some of you will recall that for a while movies were being made in three-dimensions. It required special glasses to see them.

Once I got interested in Polaroid, because of the glasses, my upside-downness saw the value of the camera. I thought if that had been the first camera invented, you would have had a devil of a time selling an Eastman Kodak camera, even with its larger picture and negative.

The Dreyfus Fund took a large position in Polaroid. Dreyfus & Co., of which I owned about 51 percent, did also. Polaroid was an outstanding growth company.

Dr. Blout introduced me to Hal Booth, Vice President in charge of advertising at Polaroid. I designed a few ads, which Hal ran. I include one here, with a picture of my son Johnny, and my bulldog Henry.

Taken with a Polaroid camera–
enjoyed sixty seconds later.

When I found it necessary to retire from the management of the Fund, for reasons of medical research, I had an important decision to make. Who should take my job as head of the Dreyfus Fund? A fine firm called Head Hunters introduced me to four candidates, one at a time. After each introduction, Howard Stein, in our own organization, began to look better and better. I offered Howard the position and he accepted. One of the best decisions of my life. When Howard took over the management of the Fund it was less than $1 billion. With his creative management the Dreyfus Corporation now manages over $70 billion. Howard is one of my best friends.

To shift to today's markets for a moment. The indexes are not a large part of the investments, but they have a powerful effect. You can buy an interest in hundreds of stocks in an index on less than 10 percent margin. But if you want to buy General Motors or Dupont, you have to put up 50 percent. This is one of the strangest things I have ever seen. It happened when I was looking the other way—not that I care one way or the other. But you have in those indexes a tail that can wag the dog.

It's just possible the market of 1987 was an index market. You don't have bear markets that quickly. While people were looking for the second leg of the bear market to go down, the whole bear market had happened, not just one leg, but a leg, an ankle and a foot.

I don't want the reader to get the impression that markets of today can be approached with the methods of twenty-five years ago. Let me say flatly they can't. Today's markets are no longer dominated by margin traders. The investor's money is largely in the hands of professionals, mutual funds, and other funds. Many of these investors are not on margin. Although these managers are flexible, they don't act in concert.

I'd like to be able to give you a suggestion as to how to manage money now, but I'm not competent to do so. However, I think some general advice is as good now as it was then.

About fifty years ago, Tobias Stone, an excellent bridge player and friend, and I were dining sumptuously at Horn & Hardart's Automat (35 cents apiece). Stoney asked me a hypothetical question, what would I do if I had a million dollars. I asked him what he would do if he found himself on the moon. But his question stimulated a thought. I asked him, if he had a million dollars, would he bet it if someone offered him ten-to-one on the toss of a coin? He said, "Of course. I'd be getting so much the best of the odds." I told him he was nuts. His first million was worth a lot more than the next ten million, so he'd be getting the worst of the odds. That brings us to the general subject of investments.

A young person with $30,000 and a good salary should not be unwilling to put that money in a speculative account. If it's lost, it's not a disaster since most of his capital is his earning power. On the other hand, an older person with a substantial amount of money and not much earning ability, I believe, should put 25-40 percent of his money in very conservative holdings and the rest in the hands of someone who would try to make the money grow. No longer can one keep one's money in dollar bills because of inflation. There's no sure way to be safe and one should split the difference.

One other thing. Unless you have made a study of the market and have time to continue to study it, and have confidence in your judgment, it's well worth a half a percent or one percent to put your money in the hands of professionals. Good professionals will keep up to date on current events and study the many factors that are involved in this complicated market, and earn their money. Of course some professionals are better than others. If one wants, one can diversify by putting his or her money in the hands of more than one professional.

Let us leave Wall Street now.

The last thirty years of my life have been occupied with medical research. It's a different field, but in it objectivity and sense of probabilities are the same.

A Remarkable Medicine Has Been Overlooked, which follows, was written before my autobioghraphy was even thought of. For that reason there will be a slight amount of repetition. Please forgive it. This is an urgent matter. Besides, there may be those who will read *A Remarkable Medicine* without reading the autobiography.

At the end of *A Remarkable Medicine* there will be a new chapter. Following that there will be the first fifteen pages of *The Broad Range of Clinical Use of Phenytoin* including the Table of Contents and the Summary of Thought, Mood and Behavior Disorders.

A REMARKABLE MEDICINE HAS BEEN OVERLOOKED

with a letter to President Reagan

Dear Mr. President

I write you about a matter of such urgency and importance that it requires the attention of your office.

The properties of a remarkable and versatile medicine are being overlooked because of a flaw in our system of bringing medicines to the public. This is to the great detriment of the health of the American public, and millions of people suffer because of it. This tragic condition can be remedied—almost overnight...

When this book was published by Pocket Books in 1982, quotations from the lay and medical press were included. Some are reprinted here.

"'Jack Dreyfus, Maverick Wizard Behind the Wall Street Lion' was the title of a long article in *Life* back in 1966... His book is sure to become a classic."

—HARRY SCHWARTZ
Fortune

"The Foundation's efforts to examine PHT in such extraordinary detail represents the first time in medical history that a single substance has been so thoroughly investigated as a potential remedy for such a variety of aches and ills."

—ALBERT ROSENFELD
Science 81

"How Jack Dreyfus became acquainted with this remarkable medication is a story that's exciting and full of human drama. It should be a best-seller."

—*The Berkshire Eagle*

"As a rule, I'm not much for battle stories. But *A Remarkable Medicine Has Been Overlooked* is an exception. Dreyfus deserves our admiration for his truly heroic efforts."

—RUTH B. SCHWARTZ
The American Council on Science and Health

"Dreyfus, a winning competitor in whatever he attempts...the book contains an exhaustive bibliography and abstracts from 2,140 published references to PHT research."

—*Medical World News*

"A man who cannot be overlooked... Dreyfus tells the story of his experiences with simplicity and humor...."
—*MD Magazine*

"I believe this book is a labor of love by a man who has chosen to take on the established mode of looking at things that often precludes fresh thinking."
—SUSANNE HARVEY
Pharmaceutical Executive

"This successful author is the founder of the Dreyfus Mutual Fund, a power on Wall Street. How he got out of his Wall Street business to establish and work in a charitable medical foundation is a story in itself... a service to physicians."
—BETH HARRIS
Desert Sun

"This remarkable man has sketched in simple and beautiful prose the story of his life..."
—RAY KERRISON
New York Post

"Nobody doubts that Dreyfus has a good deal more than a lick of sense... His message is simple: PHT, best known as the antiepilepsy drug Dilantin, has been shown rigorously to be useful for the treatment of more ailments than any other compound known to medical science."
—WILLIAM HINES
Chicago Sun-Times

"A book with a dramatic and often spellbinding quality—on the side of the angels."
—PETER SCHWED
Turning the Pages

Thanks for their friendship and help is expressed to:

DR. J. ANTONIO ALDRETE

HELEN BARROW

DR. SAMUEL BOGOCH

JAMES H. CAVANAUGH

DR. JOHNATHAN O. COLE

DR. THEODORE COOPER

DR. STUART W. COSGRIFF

DR. CHARLES EDWARDS

DR. JOEL ELKES

HON. JOHN W. GARDNER

DR. PAUL GORDON

DR. LIONEL R. C. HAWARD

DR. RICHARD H. HELFANT

DR. A. D. JONAS

GOV. FRANK KEATING

DR. PAUL L. KORNBLITH

DR. HERBERT L. LEY

DAVID B. LOVELAND

ALBERT Q. MAISEL

VIVIAN J. MCDERMOTT

PROF. RUDOLOFO PAOLETTI

DR. TRACY J. PUTNAM

DR. OSCAR RESNICK

HON. ELLIOT L. RICHARDSON

HON. NELSON A. ROCKEFELLER

ALBERT ROSENFELD

DR. ALEXANDER M. SCHMIDT

DR. MAXIMILLIAN SILBERMANN

DR. BARRY M. SMITH

HOWARD STEIN

DR. ALFRED STEINER

DR. JOSEPH H. STEPHENS

DR. PETER SUCKLING

DR. WILLIAM H. SWEET

DR. WILLIAM R. TKACH

DR. WILLIAM J. TURNER

I would also like to express my deep appreciation to Dr. Natasha Bechtereva and Dr. Sviatoslav Medvedev of Russia; Dr. Liang Derong, Dr. Huang Mingsheng and Dr. Yang Guanghua of China; Lawton Ackah-Yensu of Ghana; Dr. Raul Chapa-Alvarez and Dr. Eduardo Rodriguez-Noriega of Mexico; and Dr. Kanti Jain and Dr. G.N. Menon of India.

I would especially like to thank Stuart Little for his extraordinary patience in helping me write this book.

Prescription Medicine

PHT is a prescription medicine, which means it should be obtained through a physician. Nothing in this book should be mistaken to suggest that it be obtained in any other way.

Terminology

The drug that is the subject of this book is known by two generic names, diphenylhydantoin and phenytoin. Phenytoin (PHT) is used in this book.

CONTENTS

A REMARKABLE MEDICINE HAS BEEN OVERLOOKED

TO THE READER

DEAR READER

In 1963 a great piece of luck led me to ask my physician for a medicine that was not supposed to be useful for the symptoms I had. It took me out of a miserable condition. When I saw six others have similar benefits, I felt I had the responsibility of getting the facts to the medical profession. This was not as easy to do as I thought. I had to retire from two successful Wall Street businesses. A medical foundation was established. Soon it became apparent that the medicine had been overlooked for the widest variety of disorders.

This book begins with a letter to President Reagan in which this matter is outlined and his help is sought.

For eight years, from 1966 through 1973, I did all I could to awaken the federal government to its obvious responsibilities in this matter with little success. By 1975, the Foundation had sent two extensive bibliographies on PHT to all the physicians in the U.S.* When the second bibliography had been sent to physicians, it seemed that all a private foundation could do had been done. And there was progress, but it was slow. Something was wrong.

It's a national pastime to look for culprits. I looked for culprits but I didn't find individual ones. It took me a long

---

* Since this letter was written: In 1988, a third bibliography, containing 3,100 medical references, was sent to all the physicians in the U.S., along with a copy of *A Remarkable Medicine Has Been Overlooked*.

time to realize that the culprit was a flaw in our system of bringing prescription medicines to the public.

The only option left was for me to write about my experiences and explain the flaw in our system for the public, the physician, and health officials, all at the same time. That might get something done.

Nowadays, when you start to read a book, a hand reaches out of the TV set and takes it off your lap. Since this book is about health, you might consider cracking the hand across the knuckles and keep on reading.

Good luck,
JACK DREYFUS

DREYFUS MEDICAL FOUNDATION

NEW YORK, NEW YORK

August 5, 1981

The President
The White House
Washington, D.C.

DEAR MR. PRESIDENT:

I write you about a matter of such urgency and importance that it requires the attention of your office.

The properties of a remarkable and versatile medicine are being overlooked because of a flaw in our system of bringing medicines to the public. This is to the great detriment of the health of the American public, and many millions of people suffer because of it. This tragic condition can be remedied.

This letter is meant as a briefing, Mr. President. Material outlined in it will be expanded on elsewhere.

The medicine is a prescription medicine. Its best known trade name is Dilantin; generic, phenytoin (PHT). The first disorder for which it was found useful was epilepsy. This was in 1938. In those days it was customary to think of a single drug for a single disorder, and PHT promptly got the tag "anticonvulsant."

Since this early discovery, many thousand medical studies have demonstrated PHT to be one of the most widely useful drugs in our pharmacopoeia. Yet today, forty-one years later, PHT's only listed indication-of-use with the Food and Drug Administration is as an anticonvulsant. This description is accurate but tragically misleading and plays a major role in the misunderstanding of PHT by the medical profession.

It should be emphasized that this is not the fault of the FDA.*

---

*Today, in 1996, this statement is not correct.

If you will look at the Table of Contents (pp. 299-304), it will give you an idea of the breadth of use of PHT. It's been reported useful for over 70 symptoms and disorders, in over 300 medical journals throughout the world.*

When we see the number of symptoms and disorders for which PHT has been found therapeutic, our credulity is strained. Nothing could be that good, we say. But then we look closer, and we reevaluate. In number the studies are overwhelming. Not having been sponsored by a drug company they were spontaneous and independent, the authors' only motivation being scientific interest and a desire to help others.

A brief discussion of the basic mechanisms of action of phenytoin will be helpful. A general property of PHT is that it corrects inappropriate electrical activity in the body, even at the level of the single cell. When we consider that most of our bodily functions are electrically regulated, our messages of pain are electrically referred, and our thinking processes are electrically conducted, it makes it easy to understand PHT's breadth of use.

Although PHT corrects inappropriate electrical activity, in therapeutic amounts it does not affect normal function. Thus it can calm without sedation and effect a return of energy without artificial stimulation. PHT is not habit-forming, and its parameters of safety have been established over a forty-year period.**

You may ask, Mr. President, why I haven't brought this matter to the Department of Health or the Food and Drug Administration. Well, that was the first thing I thought of years ago. And for eight years I spent an eternity with officials in government, being shuffled back and forth from one to another with encouragement and even compliments. During this period I saw

*This paragraph has been brought up to date.
**Sixteen more years since this paragraph was written.

three secretaries of HEW, two assistant secretaries of HEW, two commissioners of the FDA, members of the staff of the FDA, a surgeon general, and other officials.

It took me a long time to realize this was the wrong approach. Although everyone agreed that something should be done, no official seemed to think he had the authority or responsibility to get it done. (See "Travels with the Government," p. 207.)

About the flaw in our system for bringing prescription medicines to the public:

Years ago doctors concocted their own remedies, but that's in the past. Today the origination of new drugs is left to the drug companies motivated by that reliable incentive, the desire to make profits. Between the public and the drug company is the FDA.

The FDA was set up to do for many individuals what they could not do for themselves. Although its broad purpose was to improve the health of our citizens, it was set up as a defensive agency, to protect against ineffective drugs and those more dangerous than therapeutic, and was not equipped to reach out for an overlooked drug.

Since 1938 drug companies have been required to seek approval from the FDA as to the safety of new drugs and, since 1962, approval of both safety and effectiveness. When an FDA listing is granted it entitles a company to promote a drug for the purposes for which it has been approved. If the drug sells well the company has a good thing. Patent protection gives up to seventeen years of exclusive use. During this period profit margins are high. When patents expire, the financial incentive to look for a new drug is far greater than it is to study new uses of an old drug.

The process patents on PHT expired in 1963 and much of the incentive to do research on the drug expired at the same time. It should be noted that Parke-Davis, the company that had the patents on PHT, did not synthesize the drug, and physicians outside the company discovered it to be therapeutic. There is reason to believe that Parke-Davis never understood its own product. In addition to no patent incentive, this could be a reason it has not applied to the FDA for new uses.[*]

The public's access to a prescription medicine is through the physician. Physicians get their information about prescription medicines from the drug companies, through advertisements and salesmen, and from the *Physicians' Desk Reference*, which carries only those uses for a drug that are listed with the FDA.

One can see how an FDA listing may carry more weight than is intended. In fact some people think of the lack of FDA approval as the equivalent of FDA disapproval. This is clearly wrong. How could the FDA disapprove a use for a drug if it hasn't even had an application for it?

Let's look at the overall picture. Doctors were taught that PHT is an anticonvulsant. The usual sources that the doctors rely on for prescription medicines only indicate that PHT is an anticonvulsant. Is it any wonder that doctors have PHT out of perspective, and that as far as the public is concerned most of the benefits of PHT might as well not exist?

It is apparent that no drug company is going to apply for new uses of PHT. The clock has run down on that probability. Perhaps the FDA does not have a specific means to reach out for this medicine. But since the FDA's broad purpose is to protect the health of the American public, the neglect of a remarkable drug should be in its province, and a means should be found.

A simple solution would be to put the matter in the hands of those qualified—the 450,000[**] physicians in this country. The FDA could address itself to the basic mechanisms of action of PHT and list it as a substance effective in the stabilization of bioelectrical activity, and refer the physicians to the literature of their colleagues. There are other solutions. The fact is any

[*]One exception, see A Flaw in the System.
[**]Now over 510,000.

official nod from the FDA to the physician would let the light shine from under the bushel, and PHT would find its own level, pragmatically, by its use vis-à-vis other medicines.

Mr. President, this letter is a public one because it is also meant for government officials in health as well as for physicians and the public. The information in this book, for all to see at the same time, should be helpful if you decide to use the influence of your office in this matter. I hope you will. I think you will.

Respectfully,

Jack Dreyfus

Dreyfus Medical Foundation

This letter to President Reagan was in the original book. It has been repeated here because it gives a good outline of the matter.

FROM INSIDE A DEPRESSION

Until I was in my forties, I never really thought about my nerves—a sure symptom of a person with good nerves. I was president of the Dreyfus Fund and a partner in Dreyfus & Co., with responsibilities in research, in sales, and in management. People would ask, "How do you do all the things you do?" "How do you stand the strain?" I hardly understood the question because at the time I felt no strain.

Sometime in my forty-fifth year I became aware of a change in myself. At partners' meetings, which I'd used to enjoy, I began to notice that my patience was shorter and I was anxious for the meetings to end. Occasionally I felt a trembling inside me that I didn't understand. On weekend trips to the country it had been my habit to read or take a nap in the car. These trips had been relaxing, but they weren't anymore. My mind would become occupied with pessimistic and aggravating thoughts, thoughts I couldn't turn off.

In 1958 I had spent a few trying weeks with a problem in the stock market. It was resolved successfully, but I had been under a good deal of pressure and needed a vacation. I went to Miami and stayed at the Roney Plaza, a nice old-fashioned hotel that I had visited many times before. Usually after a day or two, with the sun and salt water, I would unwind and relax. But this time I didn't relax.

Some premonition made me invite a good friend, Howard Stein, to come down and join me. Howard accepted, and the next day he was at the Roney. Two days later my depression started.

■ ■ ■

I awoke at six o'clock in the morning in a state bordering on terror. The early sun was shining, and the birds were singing. In my room at the Roney I was in the safest of surroundings. Yet I was overwhelmed with fear. The fear couldn't have been greater if a tiger had been clawing at the door. I knew there wasn't any tiger, and common sense told me I was safe. But common sense wasn't in charge—fear was. The fear was so great I was afraid to be alone. I called Howard, at that early hour, and asked if he would come to my room. When he got there I told him I knew it didn't make any sense but I was afraid to be alone.

Howard arranged for me to see a doctor, and a few hours later we were in his office. The doctor said, "Miami is the right place for you. Get some sun, go swimming, play a little golf or tennis, and relax." Normally this would have sounded great. But now this advice didn't seem right, and at two o'clock that afternoon I was on a plane back to New York. Although it was a Saturday and I wouldn't see my doctor until Monday, I hoped more familiar surroundings would make me feel better.

I still remember that trip. The plane was half-filled and I had a seat in a row by myself. Even with a dozen or more people in the plane I felt alone, and was afraid. I wanted to ask one of the stewardesses to sit next to me and keep me company, but I didn't because I thought it would be misunderstood. I couldn't tell a stewardess that I was afraid to sit by myself.

My former wife, Joan Personette, one of my closest friends, met me at the plane, and I spent the weekend at her home in Harrison, New York. It was difficult to explain to Joan how frightened I was. My brain was filled with fearful thoughts I couldn't turn off. Saturday night I slept little. Sunday we went out in the cold weather and roasted hot dogs over a fire—something I'd always enjoyed. But this didn't help. The intense fear never left me.

On Monday morning I saw Alfred Steiner, my family physician. He sent me to a neuropsychiatrist, Dr. Maximilian Silbermann. The first question I asked was, "Have I gone crazy?" I'd never had an experience like this intense fear without apparent cause. And my mood was so pessimistic that the worst seemed plausible. Dr. Silbermann assured me that I was sane but said he thought I was depressed. I remember that he said, "When people are insane, they may think others are a little off, but they rarely question their own sanity."

That first day Dr. Silbermann asked me what I liked to do, what I really enjoyed. I told him that going to the racetrack was something I enjoyed a lot. He said, "Well, why don't you go to the races tomorrow? Don't worry about business." He also suggested that I not be alone and have someone spend the night with me in my apartment.

The next day I intended to go to the races. But I didn't. They had no appeal for me, and even seemed a problem. That day, when I saw him for the second time, Dr. Silbermann diagnosed my condition as an endogenous depression. He explained that endogenous meant "coming from within," and he differentiated it from a reactive depression, one with an outside cause. He assured me that this condition was temporary and that I would come out of the depression. He said he didn't know how long it would take; it could be gradual or it could happen suddenly.

Being told this was important to me intellectually, but emotionally I had a hard time believing it.

That was the beginning of a long and close relationship with Dr. Silbermann. For the next few years I was to see him five or six times a week. From the start Dr. Silbermann told me that good sleep was important for my condition and prescribed sleeping medication. With the help of this medicine I slept soundly, and the benefits of sleep carried over. In the morning I was at my best. As the day wore on my mind became busier and busier with worries and fears, and occasional angry thoughts. Frequently around dusk a little depressive cloud would descend upon me; I would tremble and my hands and feet would get cold.

Seeing Dr. Silbermann almost every day was important to me. In his warm office, with his friendliness and willingness to listen, I would unburden my brain of the thoughts that were tormenting me. But intense fear persisted for almost a year. During that period I was afraid to be alone, and I arranged for my housekeeper to spend the night at my apartment.

Of course I had my business responsibilities, and I asked Dr. Silbermann what to do about them. He told me that people misunderstood depressions, and it might be best not to tell anyone about it. He suggested that I leave it vague and say I would be away from the office for a period of time. But this was in conflict with my sense of responsibility, and I didn't feel right about it. Mark Twain advised, "When in doubt, tell the truth." So I told the truth to my partners and asked them to run things without me for a while. Although I was not aware of feeling better, a realistic source of worry was removed.

Dr. Silbermann advised me to try to get out of the house and keep myself occupied, as long as I could do things that were not abrasive to me. I visited museums. One of my main haunts was the Museum of Modern Art and I had many lunches in the cafeteria there. I became friends with the paintings and with the sculptures in the backyard. The attention I gave these pleasing objects was helpful in taking attention off myself. I had similar benefits from the Central Park Zoo where I spent time with the seals, polar bears, and other nice creatures.

I tried to avoid things that would upset me. I found that my mind would magnify the slightest unpleasantness by some large multiple. Newscasts were anathema to me and I couldn't listen to them. If a busload of children overturned in Nevada the news would be dragged fresh and gory to our attention in New York. I quickly learned that the news, with its disaster *du jour*, made things worse. One piece of news I couldn't avoid was the dog in the Sputnik space capsule. I couldn't get it out of my mind, and I suffered with thoughts of that dog for many weeks.

I gave up watching movies on television. There'd be some sad theme or violent incident that would upset me, and the image of it would stick in my head. I had a similar problem with most books. One author I could always read was Mark Twain. I'm sure I missed many of his subtleties but he never dragged me through unpleasantness.

When I'd been in the depression for about six months Dr. Silbermann asked me if I thought it might make me feel better to be in a hospital. I said I didn't know but I was willing to try it. So he got me a room at the Harkness Pavilion of Presbyterian Hospital. In the room I noticed that the windows were discreetly barred, and I asked the nurse about this. She explained that sometimes deeply depressed persons had to be protected from themselves.

Fortunately I was not classified as deeply depressed. I had outpatient privileges and walked in the neighborhood a few hours each day. It was cold and I would have a bowl of hot soup in a nice little corner restaurant. During the walks I had plenty of time to think. The conversation with the nurse reminded me that Dr. Silbermann had once tactfully brought up the subject of suicide. Now I gave it honest thought and realized I'd never considered it. Not that life seemed that desirable. At that time everyone was talking about the next rocket to the moon, the first to carry men. In my mood I thought chances for success were almost nil. But I remember thinking if a high authority told me it was for the good of the country I might be willing to make the trip.

After three days in the hospital, not feeling better or worse, I returned home. Each day Dr. Silbermann and I talked over my, mostly imagined, problems. Part of me knew that some of the worries were not logical, but the rest of me couldn't feel it. Max cautioned me not to make any major business decisions while I was depressed because my perspective would be out of kilter. This was good advice. The Dreyfus Fund was not large at that time, but quite successful, and the only problems it had were the healthy ones connected with growth. Yet on more than one occasion I wished I could give the Fund away.

My apartment was just a few blocks from Dr. Silbermann's office. Often I would leave for my appointment as much as an hour early and kill time by walking. I usually felt cold, and would seek the sunny side of the street. After the appointment, if it was daylight, I would walk in Central Park. I would still try to stay in the sun. As the shadows moved across the park I would walk faster to keep ahead of them.

During these walks I used to think about my condition. I was aware of daily headaches, frequent stomach irregularity, chronic neck pain, and lack of energy. But my dominant symptom was a turned-on mind that never gave me rest and was always occupied with negative thoughts related to anger and fear. And the fear was the worst.

When you have fear in you, you'll find something to be afraid of or to worry about, even if you have to make it up. This happened to me all the time. I'll give two illustrations.

One Sunday, on Madison Avenue, I saw a woman looking at a dress in a small shop. She seemed to be looking at it longingly, as though she wanted it but couldn't afford it. I felt unhappy for her. The dress looked so old-fashioned and unattractive it made me feel even sadder. Now this woman was a complete stranger. For all I knew she might have been able to buy that block of Madison Avenue. But my mood made me decide she couldn't afford the dress. This unhappy picture stuck in my brain and bothered me for days.

Another incident occurred at a cocktail party. One of the guests, a young girl of seventeen, was introduced as the daughter of a famous movie actress. She mentioned that she would have to leave in a little while because she was taking dancing lessons. The girl seemed plain-looking and I felt sad for her. I knew she didn't have a chance to be successful, and was trying to follow in her mother's footsteps because it was the thing to do. When she left, she kissed us all good-bye. She'd even adopted Hollywood ways, and this made me feel even sadder. I worried about this poor girl for many days. It wasn't really necessary—the "poor girl" was Liza Minnelli.

It is almost impossible to convey to a person who has not had a depression what one is like. It's not obvious like a broken arm, or a fever, or a cough; it's beneath the surface. A depressed person suffers a type of anguish which in its own way can be as painful as anything that can happen to a human being. He has varying degrees of fear throughout the day, and a brain that permits him no rest and races with agitated and frightening thoughts. His mood is low, he has little energy, and he can hardly remember what pleasure means. He's in another country, using a different language. When he uses words such as "worry" and "afraid" he may be expressing deep distress. But these words seem mild to the person whose mood is all right.

■ ■ ■

The deepest part of my depression lasted for about a year. Then it lessened gradually and there were periods of improvement. These better periods alternated with periods of mild depression for the next few years. "Mild" depression is plenty unpleasant, but I use the term to distinguish it from severe depression.

It began to look as if chronic depressive periods might be with me for life. Then I had an incredible piece of luck.

AN INCREDIBLE PIECE OF LUCK

Dr. Silbermann and I had numerous discussions about why I was depressed, without reaching any conclusions. There was a theory, proffered by relatives of mine in Boston, that I was neurotic and needed to be psychoanalyzed. Dr. Silbermann didn't agree that psychoanalysis was what I needed, and as a practical matter felt that it would be too arduous while I was depressed.

On my own, as objectively as I could, I considered my relatives' suggestion. I didn't question that I was neurotic. But I didn't see how that could be the answer. Presumably I'd been neurotic before the depression, yet my nerves had been fine.

I began to notice that changes in my mood frequently occurred without apparent environmental or psychological cause. And the same stimulus didn't always evoke the same response. Sometimes, while driving in the country, I would see a dead woodchuck on the side of the road. The sight would hit me like a blow and I couldn't get it out of my mind. But on other occasions I'd see a dead woodchuck and react in what seemed a normal way. The difference in reactions couldn't be caused by my being neurotic; my childhood from one to five hadn't changed. It seemed plausible that these disparate reactions were due to changes in my body.

I discussed this with Dr. Silbermann, and he was inclined to go along with the idea that there might be something wrong in my body "chemistry." But Max said that he didn't really know, and emphasized that when he said "chemistry," he was using the word in quotes.

■ ■ ■

One night, a seemingly insignificant incident started a chain of events that changed my life. A young woman took my hand and massaged my fingers. I was full of tension at the time. As she pressed my fingertips I felt the tension slip away, and I had the feeling that electricity was going out of my body. This didn't make sense to me. I'd never heard of electricity in the body—but the impression was strong. The next day, a Sunday, the impression of electricity was still with me.

It's a misconception, I believe, that we originate ideas. I used to think we did, but I don't anymore. Too often I find my brain does what it wants—it's on automatic pilot most of the time. That was the case this particular Sunday because, without instruction from me, my brain went into its files and came up with three experiences I'd had with electricity. The first went back almost forty years.

One. When I was a little boy I saw a brass plate with a hole in it, in the baseboard. It aroused my curiosity. I stuck my finger in the hole and my curiosity was satisfied. The electric shock I got, and the sudden, intense fear that came with it, were indelibly impressed on my memory. I remember that after the shock I had a flat, metallic taste in my mouth.

Two. I had gone into a garage with my former wife to get the car. I picked up an old vacuum cleaner, to get it out of the way, and received an electrical jolt. I said to Joan, "This damn thing shocked me."

"It always does that," she said quietly.

At this calm appraisal I exploded. "What do you mean, 'It always does that!'" and I took Joan by the shoulders and shook her. This was so unlike me that I felt my explosion of anger had been caused by the electricity.

Three. On two successive nights I'd had the same frightening dream, or was it a dream? Each of these nights, before going to sleep, I had intense feelings of fear. The "dreams" occurred early in the morning. I felt that I was awake and couldn't open my eyes. I tried to reach for the table light but couldn't move—in the dream I felt I was frozen with electricity.

Each of these experiences with electricity was associated with a symptom of my depression. As I reviewed them, side by side so to speak, they seemed to be related. Numbers one and three made a connection between electricity and fear. Number two connected electricity with anger. And number one also made a connection with the metallic taste in my mouth which I associated with fear.

The logic of these connections was not clear then. But the pieces held together well enough for me to say to myself, When I see Max on Monday I am going to bring up the subject of electricity.

That Monday my appointment with Dr. Silbermann was after dinner, around ten o'clock. I had some "problems" that I wanted to talk out. It wasn't until late in the hour that I brought up the subject of electricity. I said to Max, "You know, I think my problem is electricity, and electricity causes some people to get depressed, others to bump themselves off, and others to go crazy." I said this as though I meant it, but actually I had little conviction.

At that moment my brain jumped back twenty years to a bridge tournament. My partner and I had got the best of two hands, and one of our opponents, a famous player, P. Hal Sims, made some pointed remarks to his partner. I noticed the partner's neck getting red. As we moved to the next table there was a commotion, and I turned and saw the man on the floor, having convulsions. Someone said he was having an epileptic attack. Now, as I thought back to the attack, the convulsions looked like they had been caused by a series of electrical shocks.

I continued with my hypothesis and said, "And some people have an electrical explosion which we call epilepsy." Max said, "It's curious that you mention epilepsy. We know from brain wave tests that the epileptic has a problem with his body electricity." This was the first time I'd heard that there was such a thing as body electricity. Also, connecting the epileptic to an electrical problem was a direct hit. When I'd started the discussion I'd thought the odds were 10,000-to-1 against me. But now the odds dropped sharply, and they were realistic enough to make the subject worth pursuing.

I knew a girl who'd had an epileptic attack when she was six. She was now fifteen and seemed to be leading a normal and happy life. She had been given a medicine for her epilepsy and I asked Dr. Silbermann what it was. He told me it was Dilantin.

"Well, why don't I try that?" I asked.

I didn't realize then how crucial Max's answer would be for me. He could easily have said no—and that might have been the end of it. But he said, "You can try it if you like. I don't think it will do you any good, but it won't do you any harm."

That night Max gave me a prescription for Dilantin and told me of an all-night drugstore where I could fill it. He suggested that I take 100 mg before going to bed and skip my sleeping pill. He thought the Dilantin might put me to sleep.

I followed instructions. Around midnight I took 100 mg of Dilantin, and no sleeping pill. Apparently I was dependent on the sleeping medication because when I went to bed I promptly fell awake. Before I finally got to sleep, at four in the morning, I thought, this medicine is a flop. Not until years later did it occur to me that I would not have lain quietly in bed for four hours if I'd had my usual fears. I'd have gotten up and taken the sleeping medicine.

I awoke at eight the next morning and, as Dr. Silbermann had instructed me, took another 100 mg of Dilantin. I had missed half a night's sleep. Sleep was so important that when I saw Max that afternoon, I started to tell him the Dilantin didn't work. But Max said, "You look better than you did yesterday." Then I looked at myself and realized that in spite of the loss of sleep I felt much better. We agreed that I should continue the Dilantin.

The following morning, according to routine, I called Dr. Silbermann. I couldn't make an appointment to see him because I was going to be too busy that day. The next day I was too busy again. The third day, when I was going to make the same excuse, I realized that I wasn't too busy. I was ducking the appointment. It was the first time in five years that I didn't feel a need to see Max.

I saw Dr. Silbermann only three more times in his office. My need for psychotherapy was gone, and we just talked as friends. Max told me he had never heard of Dilantin being used for the purposes I was using it. And he was a close friend of Dr. Houston Merritt, of Putnam and Merritt, who, twenty years earlier, had discovered the first clinical use for Dilantin. So for a while we were waiting for the phenomenon to go away. At least I'm pretty sure Max was. Intellectually I was too. But my feelings told me things were all right.

On my last visit Max gave me a renewable prescription for Dilantin. I haven't seen him as a patient since. We've stayed the closest of friends, and frequently have dinner together to swap lies and trade psychotherapy.

From the day I took Dilantin my major symptoms of distress

disappeared. I noticed fundamental differences. My brain, which had been overactive and filled with negative thoughts, was calmer and functioned as it had before the depression. The headaches, the stomach distress, the neck pain all disappeared. And my patience returned. I enjoyed partners' meetings again and could sit back and observe someone else getting impatient, which was a switch.

Before taking Dilantin I'd been so tired and worn out I just dragged myself around. Although Dilantin had a calming effect on me, to my surprise it didn't slow me down. On the contrary my energy returned full force. It was as though the energy that had been wasted in my overactive brain was made available for healthier purposes.

I didn't realize it right away, but my good health had returned. I was neither tranquil nor ecstatic. I was just all right. For the first time in my life I realized how good you feel when you feel "all right."

NEW EVIDENCE AND
A BROADENING PERSPECTIVE

What had happened to me doesn't happen in real life. You just don't ask your doctor to let you try one drug, out of a pharmacopoeia of tens of thousands, and find that it works. But this did happen. And it happened so casually, in such a matter-of-fact way, that the vast improbability of it didn't occur to me at the time.

Being of the human race, I naturally returned to routine. Much of my new energy went back into the Dreyfus Fund and Dreyfus & Co., as though I were trying to make up for lost time. Still, much of my thinking was on Dilantin and the intriguing puzzle it presented. There were many questions to be answered.

The first question was whether Dilantin had been the cause of my return to health. My body might have been due for a recovery and a coincidence could have occurred. But this question was soon answered in the affirmative because I was able to observe benefits from Dilantin an hour after taking it. A second question, about the safety of the medicine, was answered by Dr. Silbermann. He told me it had side effects but they were rarely serious, and it had been tested by time, millions of people having taken it daily for many years. A question that could not be answered right away was whether the benefits of Dilantin would last. But as months went by, and I continued to feel well, I gained confidence they would last.

The most important question was a broader question. Could Dilantin help others as it had helped me? It seemed highly improbable. How could important uses for a medicine have been overlooked for twenty years? It didn't make sense, it seemed almost impossible. But if it were so, I clearly had an obligation to do something about it. I needed more facts.

In the course of the next year I was to get more facts. During this period I saw six people, in succession, benefit from Dilantin. I wasn't looking for these cases. They just happened in front of my eyes, so to speak. Each of the six cases was impressive. But the first two, because they were the first two, had the most significance and will be described in some detail.

■ ■ ■

The first person I saw benefit from Dilantin was my housekeeper Kathleen Fenyvessy. A month after I had started taking Dilantin I noticed that Kathleen was not her usual self and seemed depressed. Normally she was energetic but now she seemed worn out. Kathleen, who had recently come from Hungary, spoke imperfect English, and I was in the habit of talking slowly to her. Now she would interrupt before I could finish a sentence, saying, "I understand, I understand" and most of the time she didn't. Obviously she was extremely impatient.

I asked her what was wrong. She told me her mind was busy with miserable thoughts and she couldn't stop them. She'd seen several physicians and they'd told her she was having a nervous breakdown. She'd tried a variety of medicines that hadn't helped. I thought of Dilantin. There seemed little to be lost, and much to be gained, by her trying it if Dr. Silbermann agreed. At my suggestion Kathleen visited him. After considering her condition he prescribed 100 mg a day for her.

Since I saw Kathleen at least a few hours every day, I was in a good position to observe the effects of Dilantin. Within a day or two it was apparent that her good disposition had returned. And she was full of energy again. As for patience, she no longer interrupted me in mid-sentence. I could even tell her the same thing twice.

Kathleen found her recovery hard to believe. In a letter to her sister describing it, she said, "It was due to a medicine used for an entirely different disorder. If someone else had told me they'd had an experience like this I would not have believed it."

About a month after Kathleen had started taking Dilantin, she and I participated in an unplanned experiment. Without consulting each other, we both stopped taking Dilantin for three days. We had gone to Hobeau Farm in Ocala, Florida, a thoroughbred breeding farm managed by Elmer Heubeck, my good friend and partner in the farm. It was pure vacation for Kathleen. Except for the horse business it was vacation for me too.

At that time I thought Dilantin only helped me with stress and problems. By problems I really meant areas of interest. They were not always problems; when they went well they could be pleasures. But the negative mood that I had been in made me think of them as problems. I had five such interests, some of a business nature, some personal. I went over them; they were all in good shape. So it seemed to me that in the nice relaxed atmosphere of the farm, I wouldn't need Dilantin. I stopped taking it.

The third day off Dilantin I felt a certain tingling in my nerves. I remember a funny expression entering my mind, that I had "worry gnats." I thought maybe I'd feel better if I went to Miami, played some tennis and swam in the salt water. So I made arrangements to take a plane to Miami at eleven o'clock that night.

That afternoon I said something to Kathleen. It might not have been as tactful as it should have been, but it couldn't possibly have called for the response that it got. Kathleen burst out crying. I was astonished. Then something occurred to me, and I asked, "Kathleen, have you stopped taking Dilantin?" She said she had; she'd thought it would be so nice on the farm she hadn't brought any. "Why didn't you take some of mine?" I asked. She said she hadn't because she'd noticed I had only a few capsules left. Before I left for Miami, Elmer told me he would arrange for Kathleen to get Dilantin.

At 11 P.M. I got on the plane to Miami. Now I was quite conscious of the "worry gnats," and I thought of Dilantin. I figured it wouldn't help since I didn't have any stress or problems. But something inside me said, Well, you're research-minded. Why don't you take some anyway and see if anything happens. My bags were accessible on the plane and I went forward and got a capsule of Dilantin. I took it and looked at my watch. In a little while I thought I felt better, but I wasn't sure. I checked the time; it was twenty-eight minutes since I'd taken the medicine. When the plane arrived in Miami it was an hour since I'd taken the Dilantin. The "worry gnats" were gone. As I walked through the airport I had the nicest feeling that peace had descended on me.

The next morning I called Kathleen. Even before I could ask how she felt, her cheerful voice gave the answer.

Kathleen's experience and my own, in stopping Dilantin and recontinuing it, confirmed our need for the medicine, and seemed to indicate this need was not based on realistic problems, but on something in our nervous systems at the time.

Now I was in Miami again. I had gone there for the last few years on doctor's orders. These trips were meant to be vacations, but there had been no fun in them. When a vacation is not in you, you don't have one. But now I was on vacation and in a frame of mind to enjoy it. I still stayed at the lovely, dilapidated old Roney Plaza. Everything was beautiful—the air, the sea, just walking to breakfast. I was happy. And I know why. As Mark Twain said in "Captain Stormfield's Visit to Heaven," "Happiness ain't a thing in itself—it's only a *contrast* with something that ain't pleasant." I had the contrast.

Tennis was a pleasure again. I had taken up tennis about eight years earlier, mostly for the exercise. Golf had been my game since childhood and I'd loved it. I'd been almost a fine golfer, won lots of club championships, and at my best had a one handicap. But in recent years golf had started to bore me. Maybe it was my perfectionism. More likely it was the long walks between shots when all that was going on was the windmills of my mind.

I had started playing tennis with the local pros at the Roney Plaza. At this time Marse Fink was pro of record. Sol Goldman was pro emeritus. I didn't play with the pros to get lessons. I'd had barrels of lessons in golf and I looked forward to doing everything wrong in tennis.

We got up all sorts of games and bet on them all. They gave me large handicaps. Sometimes Marse and Sol played doubles against me and some bum they got as my partner. Sol and Marse were good friends, but if the match got close, they were not loath to comment on each other's play. They called each other names their mothers hadn't taught them. I'd get so interested in their descriptions of each other that I would lose my concentration—and they'd usually win. On the rare occasions they lost, Marse would go to his desk in the tennis shop and mutter to himself, so we could all hear, "I'll never play with that son-of-a-bitch [Sol] again." And he never did until three o'clock the next afternoon.

Sol, a remarkable character (the world's leading authority on everything), was the second person I saw benefit from Dilantin. In his youth Sol had been a great athlete, acknowledged to be the best one-wall handball player in the world. When he was thirty he took up tennis and became an outstanding player. In a different field, Sol had ambitions to be an opera singer. He had a fine singing voice and might have made it to the Met if he hadn't damaged a vocal cord.

One morning Sol and I had breakfast at Wolfie's on Collins Avenue. The waitress brought mushroom omelettes and Sol ignored his. He seemed in a fog and was staring into the distance. I'd heard that you could pass your hand in front of someone's face and they wouldn't notice, but I'd never believed this. I passed my hand a few inches in front of Sol's face and didn't get any reaction at all.

I asked Sol what was bothering him. He said that a couple of weeks ago a wealthy friend of his, whom I knew well, had bought six pairs of tennis shoes from Marse. Sol thought it terrible that Marse had charged his friend retail prices for the shoes. This was of such monumental inconsequence that I had a hard time believing the thought was stuck in Sol's brain. But after listening to him I realized that it was almost an obsession. Then it occurred to me that Sol's tennis game had been off, and he'd been uncharacteristically quiet on the court.

I asked Sol how he'd been feeling. He told me he had constant headaches, that he slept badly and was having nightmares. His worst complaint was that he would wake up at four o'clock in the morning hearing himself shouting. His only relief was to get in his car and drive around for an hour or so. He told me he'd seen a doctor. But the medicines he'd been given hadn't helped and made him feel dopey. It seemed that Dilantin might be worth trying. I telephoned Dr. Silbermann about it, and he arranged for Sol to get a prescription.

The next day we were at Wolfie's again. Sol had eaten earlier and was keeping me company at breakfast. He had his Dilantin with him and took the first 100 mg at that time. I had found Dilantin effective in myself within an hour, and this was a chance to observe its effects in someone else. I wanted an objective reading but didn't know how to go about it. By chance I asked Sol, "What about Fink and Russell this afternoon?" We had a doubles game with them for fifty dollars a team. Sol said, "They're awful tough." This answer startled me—it was so unlike Sol, a fierce competitor. I thought, "Fink and Russell" will be a good test question. I looked at my watch.

We left Wolfie's and walked to the beach at the Roney Plaza, a couple of blocks away, and I went in swimming. When I came back it was thirty-five minutes since Sol had taken his Dilantin. I said, "Sol, do you think we've got a chance with Fink and Russell this afternoon?" Sol said, "We've *always* got a chance." With emphasis on the always. That was more like him.

Twenty-five minutes later, an hour after Sol had taken the Dilantin, I asked again, "What about Fink and Russell?" Sol said, "We'll knock the crap out of them." Sol was back to normal.

That night Sol slept soundly and straight through. He started taking Dilantin daily and continued to sleep well—no more waking up at four in the morning. His daily headaches disappeared. The monumental matter of the retail shoes shrunk back to size. And once again Sol became his usual objectionable self on the tennis court.

■ ■ ■

In that first year I saw four more people benefit from Dilantin. Each was depressed and each had symptoms of an overbusy brain occupied with emotions related to fear and anger.

Each additional case had a parlaying effect on the probability factor. A year earlier it had seemed almost impossible that important uses for Dilantin could have been overlooked. Now it seemed highly probable that they had been overlooked.

Which brings up the subject of probabilities.

THE SUBJECT OF PROBABILITIES

As I look back, I realize that it was a good instinct for probabilities that pulled me through that early period of my pursuit of Dilantin. Without this instinct I could never have survived the negative inferences drawn from the fact that the medicine had been around for over twenty years. I used to think that everyone had a pretty good sense of probabilities. But I don't now, and I've heard some strange comments about probabilities in the medical field.

Probabilities are an important underlying theme of this book and, partly to qualify myself on the subject, I will depart from the narrative and discuss them.

In some fields a sense of probabilities is much more important than in others. An insurance actuary would feel naked without a sense of probabilities. A painter, on the other hand, might swap his sense of probabilities for a two percent improvement in color sense. In medicine a sense of probabilities is more important than generally realized. Sometimes weighing the probabilities—the use of a potentially dangerous procedure against the dangerous condition a patient is in—is the whole medical question. In the FDA the weighing of risk vs. gain looms large in the question of whether a drug should be approved for listing.

I've always had a good sense of probabilities—born with it I believe—and I used to think of it as a form of intelligence. But as I began to assess some of my other "forms of intelligence" and found them lacking, I decided I'd better think of them all as aptitudes.

The word aptitude itself suggests wide variances. It seems that aptitudes come with the baby. We're not all born with a good sense of direction, and a good sense of probabilities is not standard equipment either. On the way to the subject of probabilities, let's discuss aptitudes. If the reader doesn't have a good sense of probability this should make him feel better.

Some of the genetic blanks I drew when aptitudes were being handed out were in mechanics, in remembering names, and in sense of direction.

Things mechanical are a mystery to me. In World War II, I took an exam to qualify for Officers Training School in the U.S. Coast Guard. My aptitude for mechanics helped me get a grade of 29 out of a possible 100. After looking at this score the Coast Guard decided it had enough officers, and awarded me the post of apprentice seaman.

I can't remember people's names no matter how hard I try. I seem to have a scrambling device in my head. If two strangers come into the office, my secretary discreetly writes their names on the side of a paper coffee cup and I have to refer to it constantly.

My most conspicuous aptitude—in absentia—is my sense of direction. For that reason, and because there is evidence of genetic origin, I will discuss it more fully.

My sense of direction is fine—but it's in backwards. This is not easy to explain to a person with a good sense of direction. I believe such a person has a tug he's not conscious of that pulls him in the right direction. I have such a tug, but it pulls me in the wrong direction. For example, when I leave a washroom in a strange airport, without hesitation I turn the wrong way.

Apparently my aptitude for going the wrong way is not only lateral but vertical. For fifteen years my office was on the twenty-ninth floor of 2 Broadway and our boardroom was on the thirtieth. When I was in a hurry to get to the thirtieth floor I would invariably walk down to the twenty-eighth.

I don't have to climb the family tree very high to see where I got my sense of direction. It was bequeathed me by my father. His sense of direction was in backwards too—and was even stronger than mine. He got lost all the time but it never occurred to him to blame his sense of direction, he just thought it was bad luck. It's a good thing Dad didn't have to make his living as a wagon scout in the old days. He'd have set out for California with his train of covered wagons and, if things had gone well, in a few months he'd have discovered Plymouth Rock.

It's not surprising that the family hero is the homing pigeon. You can put this rascal in a dark bag, take him 500 miles from home, and without consulting a road map or following the railroad tracks he will fly directly to his coop. Scientists may say he takes radar soundings or something. But what of it? Could Shakespeare do it, could Beethoven? The pigeon has quite an aptitude.

Without realizing it, we gravitate in the direction of our aptitudes. We bounce from one field to another, being repelled or attracted, and if we're lucky we come to rest where our aptitudes are at a premium. When I got out of college, I bounced around for a few years and wound up as assistant to a customer's broker in the stock exchange. The stock market appealed to my sense of probabilities and to another aptitude, gambling (speculation as it's called in the market).

An aptitude for gambling by itself is a dubious asset; it's fortunate for me that this aptitude came in a package with my sense of probability. This steered me into games of skill and away from casino games, such as dice and roulette, where the odds against you are slight but inexorable.

My first gambling game was marbles for keeps. I remember bankrupting a kid from down the block when I was six. When I gave up marbles, I took up other games—contract bridge, gin rummy, and handicapping the races. In these games a good sense of probabilities is an asset.

There are two kinds of probabilities. There is the mathematical kind that can be arrived at precisely. As a simple example, the chance of calling the toss of a coin correctly (provided it's not weighted) is exactly one in two. The chance of calling it correctly twice in a row is one-half of one-half of a chance, or one in four, and so forth. If you wish to determine the exact probability that a coin tossed a hundred times will come up heads thirty-one times, there's a formula for it. I don't know it.

Another kind of probability cannot be arrived at by mathematical formula. It's an estimate—exact figures can't be placed on it. Let's call it free-form probability. We use it all the time, some of us more consciously than others. For example, when I make a phone call I start to assess the probability that the person I'm calling is at home. With adjustments for the individual, I might figure it's three-to-one against his or her being home after the third ring, eight-to-one after the fourth ring, etc. After the fifth ring I usually hang up. (When I call my former wife, if the phone is answered before the fourth ring, I know I've got the wrong number.)

One who makes a living by the application of free-form probabilities is the racetrack handicapper. After studying the many variables, he comes up with the probable odds for each horse in a particular race—the morning line. Over a period of time the handicapper's "line" should be close to the odds made by the betting public, or as my friend Dingy Weiss says, "He can tell his story walking."

Free-form probability also deals with odds of a larger magnitude. Some examples. The odds against five horses, in a ten-horse race, finishing in a dead heat. The odds against finding a lion in your backyard in Manhattan. The odds against the next person you meet having a wooden leg and offering you a banana. Or, for a pertinent example, the odds against thousands of physicians, working independently, finding a drug useful for over fifty symptoms and disorders, and that drug being useful for only a single disorder.

When the odds are this large, it's easy to be approximately right. Whether you estimate one chance in a million or one chance in a billion, the estimates are almost the same—the difference between these figures is less than one in a million. (If the reader's sense of probability is like my sense of direction, his feelers will tell him this is wrong.)

A feel for probabilities is essential in two of the card games I've played, bridge and gin rummy. Although I haven't played gin in fifteen years, the *Encyclopedia of Bridge* is still kind enough to say, "Dreyfus...is reputed to be the best American player of gin rummy." This compliment, no longer deserved, is based on a system of play I discovered many years ago that relies heavily on probabilities.

Gin rummy deals mostly with exact probabilities. Another game I've played, the stock market, deals largely with inexact probabilities.

■ ■ ■

October. This is one of the peculiarly dangerous months to speculate in stocks. The others are July, January, September, April, November, May, March, June, December, August, and February.

—MARK TWAIN, *Pudd'nhead Wilson.*

With this cautionary note the reader will be given instructions on how to buy a stock.

Take the five-year earnings record of a company, its current earnings and your estimate for the near future, its book value, its net quick assets, the prospect for new products, the competitive position of the company in its own industry, the merits of the industry relative to other industries, your opinion of management, your opinion of the stock market as a whole, and the chart position of the individual stock. Put all this where you think your brains are, circulate it through your sense of probabilities, and arrive at your conclusion. Be prepared to take a quick loss; your conclusion may be wrong even though you approached it the right way.

My introduction to Wall Street was in 1941. I got a job as an assistant to a customer's broker in the garment district branch of Cohen, Simondson & Company, at a salary of $25 a week. One of my duties in this job was the posting of hundreds of weekly charts. This early experience with charts influenced my Wall Street career.

Skipping the intervening travail—fascinating as it would be to nobody—I found myself, in the early fifties, responsible for the management of a small mutual fund, The Dreyfus Fund. The fund was so small that the management fees were only $2,500 a year. Perforce, the fund could not afford a large research staff. Actually our staff consisted of a fine young man, Alex Rudnicki, and myself. Alex was a fundamentalist, a student of the Graham Dodd school. I was a student of charts and market technique. We were at the opposite extremes of investment approach, but we worked together as friends.

Alex had a wonderful memory for the earnings of companies and other statistical information; my contribution was six hundred large-scale, weekly line charts. From my experience, monthly charts were too "slow" to be of much use, and daily charts were too volatile to be reliable. I split the difference with weekly charts, posted daily. I developed my own theories about the charts, and read no books on the subject. It seemed best to make my own mistakes—at least then I'd know whom to blame.

In those early days, our statistical information was no more up-to-date than the latest quarterly reports. Alex and I were too chicken to call a company and ask a vice-president how things were going. Of necessity we put more emphasis on the technical side of the market than did most funds.

When you study the technical side of the stock market you deal with two components. One component is major market trends—bull or bear market. The other is the timing of the purchase or sale of individual securities.

In those days, more than now, the market tended to move as a whole—being right about the major trend was more than half the game. We focused a good deal of our attention on this. With three- and four-million-share days, the trading of the speculator was a key factor in market moves. Speculators tended to move in concert. Excessive optimism, with the parlayed purchasing power of their margin accounts, caused the market to get out of hand on the upside; forced selling in these same margin accounts caused the market to get out of hand on the downside.

The more money a speculator had, the healthier the technical side of the market—he had purchasing power. The more stock the speculator had, the weaker the technical side—he had selling power. Human nature being what it is, when a speculator owned stock he talked bullish. When he had cash, or was short of stock, he talked bearish. In estimating whether we were in a major uptrend or downtrend, the speculator's chatter was taken into consideration, along with changes in the short interest and the condition of the margin accounts. And of course our charts were helpful.

Objectivity—difficult to come by—is important in any field. It didn't take us long to learn that stubbornness, ego, and wishful thinking could mess up the best of market techniques; so we tried to keep our emotions separate from our decision-making. When we bought a security we didn't pound the table to emphasize how sure we were that we were right. Instead, we tried to prepare ourselves for the possibility that we might be wrong so that when the unexpected happened, which it frequently did, we were psychologically in a position to take a loss.

Our sense of probabilities was always in play. We wouldn't buy a high-risk stock, one that could go down 50 to 60 percent, unless we felt we had a chance of at least doubling our money. If we bought a conservative stock, one not likely to go down more than 20 percent, a 30 percent profit was worth shooting for.

Since our methods differed from those of most other funds, it was likely that our performance would vary considerably from the average. Fortunately for our stockholders this variance was in the right direction—it could have been the other way. At the time of my retirement, our ten-year performance was the best of any mutual fund—nearly 100 percentage points better than the second-best fund.*

That was a long time ago. Recently, my good friend Bill Rogers, of two-Cabinet-post renown, said, "Jack, I guess you're doing well in the market as usual." I said, "No, Bill, to tell you the truth I've been in a long stupid streak." It's nice to see a friend have a good laugh.

■ ■ ■

Back to medical probabilities. Including my own case, I had seen seven consecutive persons benefit from Dilantin. If each case had been the flip of a coin, 50-50, the odds against seven in a row would have been 127-to-1. But the response to Dilantin had been so prompt and the symptoms that responded so similar, that each case deserved a weight far exceeding 50-50.

Of course my objectivity could be questioned. But that didn't

---

* 326 percent to 232 percent, Arthur Wiesenberger, Inc.

bother me; it's only other people's objectivity that bothers me. Even at that early date I placed a high probability figure on the chance that Dilantin was more than an anticonvulsant.

■ ■ ■

During the first year of my experience with Dilantin I had gathered some helpful information on the subject of electricity in the body. This will be discussed in the next chapter.

BODY ELECTRICITY

For the first few months that I took Dilantin (PHT) I gave little thought to how the medicine worked. How it worked was a lot less important to me than that it did work. But one day I noticed that the flat, metallic taste in my mouth, which I'd associated with electricity, was gone. As I thought back about it, I realized that it had been gone since I'd started taking PHT.

A hypothesis about electricity had led me to ask for PHT. Was this a coincidence? It seemed unlikely. When a hypothesis precedes and leads to a finding, the hypothesis is apt to be correct. My thinking went back to electricity in the body.

Recently I found some notes to myself, made in 1963. These notes help me remember what my thoughts were at that time.

[From my notes] "I noticed figures of speech that described human emotions in electrical terms. Before then I'd thought of these terms as imaginative inventions of writers. But perhaps they weren't. Maybe sensitive people had used them instinctively because they were near the truth. There are enough of these electrical expressions to make a parlor game. Some follow:

state of tension
room charged with tension
get a charge out of something
electrifying experience
the touchdown electrified
  the crowd
dynamic personality
magnetic personality
galvanized into action

shocking experience
state of shock
it gave me a jolt
blow your fuse
blow your top
sparks flew
explosive temper
explode with anger

"This list, with its references to anger and fear, led to other thoughts. I knew that an electric goad was used in rodeos to frighten animals into rambunctious performances, and that batteries had been used to make race horses run faster. I'd read that an electric jolt causes the hair to stand on end.

"Could electricity be the mechanism that makes the fur on a dog rise when he is angry or when he is frightened? Could it account for the spectacular bristling of a cat in the act of welcoming a dog? How about our own fur? When we're scared the hair on the nape of our neck rises and we have 'hair-raising' experiences. And don't we bristle with anger? Didn't these things seem to connect anger and fear with electricity in the body?" [End of the notes]

I had gone as far as I could as an amateur. I needed a professional to tell me whether my ideas about electricity in the body made sense. But where could I find such a person?

Whenever I'm stumped as to how to find someone or locate something, I have a simple method. I ask Howard Stein. I don't know how he does it but he never lets me down. I asked Howard, "Do you know how I can meet with somebody who's an expert on electricity in the body?" Howard said he thought so. He went to Yura Arkus-Duntov, head of the Dreyfus Fund's science research. Within a week Yura had made arrangements for me to meet with Dr. Peter Suckling, a neurobiophysicist from Downstate Medical Center.

Dr. Suckling, with his nice Australian accent, had good vibes for me (a modern electrical term?). He was an expert on bio-electrical activity and had been an associate of Sir John Eccles, an authority in the field and a Nobel Prize winner.

Dr. Suckling and I had three long meetings in my office at 2 Broadway. It was a nice office, facing New York Harbor, and Peter liked it. He said he thought the moving scenery of boats helped with thinking. I hoped so.

The first question I asked Peter was, "Can you weigh the electricity in a cat?" I thought cats had an extra share of electricity, because of their hair-raising act. Peter disappointed me by saying electricity can't be measured that way. It's inside the body, but the whole animal itself is grounded. I didn't know what that meant but I took his word for it.

For the first time, I heard about the excitatory nervous system, the inhibitory nervous system, membranes, axons, synapses, negative potentials, sodium and potassium, and how a disproportionate amount of chemicals inside and outside the cell made for the electrical potential across the membrane.

Peter labored hard to explain the working of bioelectrical activity to me. By using simple illustrations, he got into me, shoehorn fashion, a rudimentary idea of how electricity works in the body. I won't burden the reader with the whole discussion, but I will summarize some of what Peter said.

The cell is a complicated entity in which thousands of activities take place. Peter said most of them were not relevant to our discussion. What was relevant was the electrical potential of the cell. He explained that the body of a cell is enclosed by a membrane, and in a nerve cell the electrical potential is minus 90 millivolts, relative to the outside of the cell. Peter said the reason there is this negative potential is because of a dispro-portionate amount of substances inside the cell relative to outside the cell—particularly sodium and potassium. Peter spoke of the membrane with obvious admiration: "This very thin membrane can sustain an electrical tension better than most insulators. The insulation strength is high. It has to be strong; it's so very thin." Then, in considerable detail, he explained the electrochemical mechanisms involved in the discharge of electrical activity. I won't go into that here.

Peter said that there are about 10 billion* cells in the brain—each with an electrical potential. He said that even a slight imbalance in individual cells, because of the proliferative possi-bilities, could cause a problem in a large area of the brain. He told me that cells vary in length in the human. In nerve cells the speed of impulse transmission varies from one hundred meters a second to three meters a second.

All the cells in the human body, although they do not have the same amount of electrical potential, work on the same principle. Peter said this was true in other animals and, for that matter, all living things. Apparently when the Lord came up with a good thing like the cell he used it over and over again.

At the beginning I didn't tell Peter what my interest was. I didn't want to influence him one way or the other. I realized later that this had been a needless precaution because we were dealing with a pretty exact science. In the meantime, Peter had been trying to figure out why the president of a mutual fund and partner of a brokerage firm was asking all these questions. He'd assumed my interest was in business. On the third day, when I told him about PHT, Peter astonished me by saying, "Oh, my goodness, I thought you were considering giving testosterone to the customer's brokers to make them produce better." Perhaps like making hens lay eggs faster (Merrill Lynch—consider).

---

* This figure was imprecise. The latest census has it considerably higher.

Then I explained to Peter what my experiences with PHT had been. Apologizing for the unscientific sound of it, and speaking allegorically, I said I felt that the brain of a person who needed PHT was like a bunch of dry twigs. It seemed that a thought of fear or anger would light the dry twigs, the fire would spread out of control, and the thoughts couldn't be turned off. PHT seemed to act like a gentle rain on the twigs, and the fire (and thoughts) could be kept under control.

I asked Peter if these impressions made sense. Peter said he had not done specific work with PHT, but my impressions were not inconsistent with the known fact that PHT prevented the spread of excessive electrical discharge. That was good news.

■ ■ ■

A few weeks after our last meeting, Peter performed an invaluable service. He sent me a copy of Goodman & Gilman's *Pharmacological Basis of Therapeutics,* considered to be the bible of pharmaceuticals by the medical profession, and said he thought I would find it useful.

I hadn't known there was such a book. In the section on PHT I found this:

> Coincident with the decrease in seizures there occurs improvement in intellectual performance. Salutary effects of the drug PHT on personality, memory, mood, cooperativeness, emotional stability, amenability to discipline, etc., are also observed, sometimes independently of seizure control.

I read and reread this paragraph. I could hardly believe it. Salutary effects in mood, emotional stability, etc. Here it was— in a medical book of high repute. Yet none of the doctors I'd met had ever heard of these uses. How could this be?

A SOFT VOICE IN A DEAF EAR

The time had come to tell the story to the medical profession. I had seen seven persons benefit from PHT, the electrical thoughts had been checked out and were not implausible, and there was the medical support of the Goodman & Gilman excerpt.

Now that the time had come, I didn't know how to proceed. I had always assumed that if I had enough evidence I would just "turn it over to the medical profession." That would be no problem, I thought. Now, faced with turning it over, I realized there was no "receiving department" in the medical profession—and I didn't know where to go. Dr. Silbermann and I discussed this problem at length and finally came up with what seemed a sensible plan.

Max, an associate professor at Columbia Presbyterian, was a personal friend of Dean H. Houston Merritt. This was the Merritt of Putnam and Merritt who had discovered that PHT was useful for epilepsy. What could be more logical than to bring the story to Dr. Merritt and Presbyterian Hospital?

At Max's suggestion we invited Dr. Merritt to have dinner at my home. Dr. Merritt accepted and brought with him Dr.

Lawrence C. Kolb, chief of Psychiatric Research at Presbyterian.

Since this was the first opportunity I'd had to present the PHT story in some detail, I was anxious to have other physicians present, and I invited my family physician, Dr. Alfred Steiner, and Dr. Ernest Klarch, a psychiatrist, whom Max had consulted in one of the seven cases. Also at dinner was my friend Sol. He had come from Miami so that the physicians could hear about PHT from a person other than myself.

Sol and I related our experiences with PHT. Then I told the physicians about the other five cases, and reported my observations of the medicine's effects on anger, fear, and the turned-on mind. They didn't express skepticism, but I think that the story, coming from a layman, was hard for them to believe. I was glad I could conclude with the quote from the respected medical source, Goodman & Gilman. To repeat:

> Salutary effects of PHT on personality, memory, mood, cooperativeness, emotional stability, amenability to discipline, etc., are also observed, sometimes independently of seizure control.

Dr. Merritt appeared surprised by this excerpt from Goodman & Gilman. He said he hadn't heard of it but hoped it was true. Then he suggested that maybe Presbyterian could do a study. Dr. Kolb agreed and said it could be arranged.

I couldn't let Dr. Merritt get away without asking him about possible side effects of PHT. He said that PHT had been in use for about twenty years, and a good record of safety had been established. There were side effects but they were rarely serious. He said PHT was nonhabit-forming, and unlike many other substances it was not sedative in therapeutic doses. This was good news and I thanked Dr. Merritt. At the end of the meeting Dr. Kolb said he would be in touch with me.

Postscript to the dinner. When I'd invited Dr. Steiner and Dr. Klarch, appreciating their time was valuable, I said they could bill me for it. Dr. Steiner didn't send a bill. Dr. Klarch (fictitious name) sent a bill for $500. This seemed high. His only contribution to the meeting had been "Please pass the butter."

A few days after the meeting, Dr. Kolb phoned and told me he had arranged for Dr. Sidney Malitz to conduct the study. Dr. Malitz and I had dinner, and I repeated the PHT story. He said he was surprised to hear such a plausible story from a layman; he hadn't expected it. Apparently Dr. Kolb hadn't told him much about our discussion.

Dr. Malitz told me that he would set up two studies and I could fund them for $5,000 each. I said the matter was so urgent that I'd prefer to give $10,000 for each study, and this was agreed upon. I told Dr. Malitz I would appreciate it if he would keep me in close touch with how things were going. I didn't ask how the studies would be conducted; it didn't seem proper. But I had the feeling that much of my responsibility to PHT was now in the hands of professionals.

Alas. Week after week went by without my hearing from Dr. Malitz and a head of steam built up in me. When I finally called him after three months, I regret that I said, "Why the hell haven't I heard from you? You know how important this is." I don't think Sidney liked this opening remark and I can't say I blame him. He explained that the patients he had selected for the study were used to getting medicine three times a day, and since I'd only suggested 100 mg of Dilantin (one capsule) he was wondering if Parke-Davis could make it in smaller dosages, so it could be given three times a day. This excuse was so lame it needed crutches. Apparently Sidney had so little faith in PHT that he didn't think it could help unless the patients were psychologically influenced, and he hadn't even tried it. Further, if he'd looked into it, he would have found that Parke-Davis already made it in smaller dosages—a breakable 50 mg Infatab, a 30 mg capsule, and a liquid. After explaining to Dr.

Malitz the different forms Dilantin came in, I expressed the hope that the study would now move forward.

Four more long months went by. I called Dr. Malitz again and this time, in the quietest way, asked him how things were going. He told me the study hadn't gotten started yet because he hadn't been able to get a placebo from Parke-Davis. I thanked him politely, and hung up with a heavy heart. Maybe Dr. Malitz couldn't get a placebo from Parke-Davis in seven months, but in those days most drugstores could supply a placebo in forty-eight hours.

In a last futile attempt I met with Dr. Kolb. He defended Dr. Malitz and said it was better to proceed slowly and carefully than the other way around. I didn't even argue with this platitude—it was such nonsense. Seven months had been wasted and I was discouraged. I'd taken what I thought was my best shot and hadn't got any results at all—not even negative.

Occasionally it may seem to the reader that I'm being critical of others. This is the opposite of my intention; I have too many motes in my own eye. But sometimes things have to be spelled out—otherwise this story would be too hard to believe. Looking back, it's easy to understand the position Dr. Malitz was in. He had been taught to think of PHT as an anticonvulsant. The idea that it had other uses came from an implausible source, a layman, and that didn't make it any easier for him. He undoubtedly had other research projects to which he gave priority—and PHT got on a back burner.

On other fronts things had not stood still. I had continued to send friends and acquaintances to doctors for trials with PHT. The effects were prompt and similar to those of the earlier cases. The numbers were mounting up. By now there were about twenty-five cases. In addition, I had a new source of information.

Dr. A. Lester Stepner, of Miami, had treated one of the first six people I'd seen take PHT. He had been so impressed with the results that he tried PHT with other patients. In a letter of April 1965, he summarized the cases of twelve patients he'd treated with PHT. In eleven of the twelve (he was unable to follow up the twelfth) he found PHT effective in treating anxiety, depression, anger, impulsiveness, temper outbursts, and incoherent thinking.

Coming at this time, Dr. Stepner's observations were a big psychological help to me, but they didn't seem to mean much to Dr. Silbermann and others I spoke to. I was beginning to understand the French phrase *ideé fixe*.

The evidence was growing, but my confidence that I could convey it to others was shrinking. For months I had been buttonholing any doctor I ran into and informally talking about PHT. I must have spoken to a dozen of them during this period. None of them had heard of PHT being used for anything other than epilepsy. They were all (with one exception) polite, even kind, but they didn't give me any encouragement. That one doctor looked at me the way a Great Dane looks at a cricket and explained: "Medicine is a complicated matter, and I'd advise you to stick to Wall Street." Bless his heart.

I called a council of peace with my friends who knew of my interest in PHT. These friends were Dr. Max Silbermann, Dr. Peter Suckling, Yura Arkus-Duntov, and Howard Stein. We met in my office in early 1965 to decide the best way to get our information to the medical profession. For the first half of the meeting, we went over many cases in detail. By this time both Howard and Yura had each seen persons benefit from PHT, and we discussed how consistent our observations were with those reported in Goodman & Gilman.

We tape-recorded the meeting. Reading the transcript brings back those days in a lively way—I can still feel the warmth of my frustrations. There wasn't a suggestion I would make that Peter, Max, or Yura couldn't find an objection to. Toward the end I must have worn through my daily supply of PHT because I was hopping up and down with frustration.

The transcript of the meeting remembers better than I do. Here are a few excerpts:

> JACK: The problem before us is to awaken the doctors in the country to the potential of Dilantin. We're not in this for financial reasons, and we're not in it for glory. It's almost a crime not to try to get this information to the doctors....We've got a lot of cases and we could do a thorough job of writing them up. If Dr. Silbermann would be willing...
>
> DR. MAX S: Jack, that would not be accepted by any medical journal. You could publish that at your own expense, there's no law against it.
>
> JACK: Why wouldn't this be accepted by a medical journal?
>
> DR. MAX S: Because. You know the old story. There is no blind control, and no medical journal would accept any drug study unless...
>
> DR. PETER S: Unless you have had a computer in on it.
>
> JACK: Max, are you serious? This can't be so.
>
> YURA and DR. MAX S: Oh, yes this is so.
>
> JACK: Yura, we are talking about research, right? Please listen before you say no. None of these people who took PHT knew each other. As far as they were concerned the study was blind. I asked them to write me letters that included details of their experiences. The same results from PHT are reported over and over again. This reinforces the evidence.
>
> DR. PETER S: It is not accepted as proof and there's a devastating

word that is applied to it, called anecdotal evidence. It doesn't go.

YURA: It's indirect proof.

JACK: Sorry fellows. Nobody in the room is thinking. These individuals wouldn't know which way to lie if they wanted to. They didn't know each other.

DR. PETER S: No, no. It's not that. This is the way...

JACK: Please. Let's not move the medical people all the way down to diapers. At least keep them in rompers, okay? I'm saying that if we added the Goodman & Gilman to Dr. Stepner's observations and the evidence of our twenty-five cases, write it up carefully, it's got to be received. We won't say we discovered America or anything like that. You, Dr. Silbermann, have got to make the effort.

DR. MAX S: Well, if we write it up and I publish it under my name and I send it in, no medical journal will accept it.

JACK: All right, Max, then no medical journal will accept it. At least we can send the information to the heads of the hospitals and say, "It would be a sin if we didn't tell you what we've found. Evaluate it on the basis of your own experience and do what you want." Once we've told the heads of fifty hospitals, at least part of it should be off our conscience. Let the nonuse of it rest on other people's consciences...

I don't care if machines are not involved. I can get machines that will lie like anybody else. Will that help? [I wouldn't have done that—in those days I was over 80 percent honest.]

YURA: No, Jack. We are talking about the best means to achieve this.

This discussion seems funny now, but it was very real then. I was too near my own suffering and I was impatient to get PHT to others. This impatience stayed with me, but after bumping into enough brick walls and closed minds, I realized it got in the way, and tabled it—with the help of PHT. Without PHT I'd have had an implosion.

For several weeks after the meeting, I thought about what was said. I had argued with my friends at the top of my lungs. But I knew they had my best interests at heart, and I had to pay attention to them because they had experience where I had none.

In the course of business I saw Howard Stein almost every day. Every once in a while Howard would say, "If you want to get anything done, you've got to do it yourself." I didn't even respond to this remark at first. But about the fourth time I heard it, I said, "Why are you persecuting me with that cliché?" He said, "I'm not using it as a cliché; I mean it." "How can I do this myself?" I asked. "I don't have any medical background, and besides I have other dishes to wash, like the Dreyfus Fund and Dreyfus & Co."

But Howard said, "You'll see."

ESTABLISHING
A MEDICAL FOUNDATION—
and the Story of My Life
(the Best Parts Left Out)

When I started to do well in business, I established a small foundation, the Dreyfus Charitable Foundation, for the purpose of giving money to what seemed good causes. It was my hope to be generally helpful, and the foundation gave money to numerous organizations and contributed equally to Protestant, Catholic, and Jewish charities. The responsibility of how to spend the money was left to these organizations.

But now I wanted to take over the responsibility of spending this money—I felt it should be spent on PHT research. PHT would need all the money I had been contributing and more, so I had to discontinue my usual contributions. And I could do this with a clear conscience—if the work on PHT was successful there would be many sources of charitable inquiry that would be helped by it. Consistent with this thinking, in 1965 the Dreyfus Charitable Foundation was changed to the Dreyfus Medical Foundation.

A medical foundation needs a medical director—but such a person can be difficult to obtain. Good physicians are fully occupied with their own matters and not easily sidetracked by what might seem a will-o'-the-wisp. After several months of search, Dr. Suckling introduced me to Dr. William J. Turner, a neuropsychiatrist at Central Islip Hospital on Long Island.

At the first meeting with Dr. Turner I got a fine impression of him, and it's never changed. He said he had been anxious to meet with me because he had seen a number of persons, with disorders other than epilepsy, respond to Dilantin. We had several long discussions. After thinking about it for a few weeks Dr. Turner decided to join the Foundation as Medical Director.

At that time I thought that the Foundation would be able to achieve its goals within two or three years. It seemed unwise for Dr. Turner to break his connections with Central Islip Hospital and move to New York City, so he joined us as Director on a part-time basis. Bill took a small office near his home in Huntington, Long Island, hired a secretary and medical assistant, and we were in business. (Jumping ahead a few years—when it became apparent that my timetable was optimistic, I was fortunate in being able to persuade Dr. Samuel Bogoch, a professor at the Boston University School of Medicine and chairman of the International Institute for the Brain Sciences, to join the Foundation on a full-time basis as General Director; Dr. Turner continued as Director.)

At the outset, Dr. Turner and I had the objective of proving— or disproving—that PHT was more than an anticonvulsant. We were as open to negative possibilities as to positive ones. I had my ideas as to what we would find: but if they were wrong, I didn't want to spend my time trying to prove something that wasn't so—there are pleasanter ways of making a fool of oneself.

Our plan was simple. The Foundation would sponsor a few studies at medical institutions. My guess was that this might take $150,000 to $200,000 a year for the next two or three years. If these studies were successful, the facts about PHT would then be in the hands of professionals. Once this happened I thought the word would spread like wildfire throughout the medical profession, and the job would be done. If I had been told, then, that in the next fifteen years the Foundation was going to spend over $15 million* (and the job not completed), I wouldn't have believed it. One reason is that $15 million was three times as much money as I had at that time.

Talking about money in connection with this work is awkward for me. I don't want to sound like I think I'm a Boy Scout. But there is a point to be made here. If I hadn't been lucky enough to have the money, I wouldn't have gotten to first base.

When I think back to my first job, at $15 a week, I realize what an implausible person I was to have a lot of money. Implausible is too weak a word. I'll tell how it happened. If you believe in fate, or whatever, you're entitled to believe the money was given to me to spend on PHT.

When I was a boy my parents were not poor, nor were they rich. Once, my father, who sold candy wholesale, was out of a job and down to his last two weeks of spending money for the family. But that was his low point, and I wasn't even aware of it at the time.

When I was ten years old, I learned what money was for. The laws of Montgomery, Alabama, permitted me to go to the movies by myself at that age. My parents would give me a dime on Saturday mornings, and the Strand Theater was assured of an early customer. I would see the Pathé News, the "To Be Continued Next Saturday" serial, and a movie—sometimes twice.

The first time the thought of making a living came up was when I was fifteen. At that time I played golf in Montgomery with a boy of my age, Alan Rice. We were both good golfers; I played a little better than he did but he didn't think so—this miscalculation kept me in quarters. One day, while at the seventh-hole water fountain, Alan, a serious boy, said that someday he was going to make $100,000. When that happened, that was going to

---

* By now, 1996, over $80 million.

be it! He was going to retire and live on the income, $5,000 a year. Alan's father was a storekeeper, and I figured Alan must have heard this from him. I was impressed, or I wouldn't have remembered it to this day. I knew I'd never make that much money. But if a miracle happened and I made $100,000, there'd be two retirees.

When I was sixteen, my father had enough money to send me to college, Lehigh University. I studied the minimum and got a C average—my only A was in Music Appreciation, and my only distinction was that I was captain of the golf team. At college my brain didn't come to grips with the problem of how I would earn a living; it didn't occur to me to study something practical. It's just as well. Lehigh is a fine engineering school; if I'd fooled with that, I would have flunked out. Even as it was, for a year after graduation I had nightmares that they took my diploma back.

When I got out of college I didn't know what I wanted to do. Well really, I guess I did, but I didn't discuss it with my father. What I wanted to do was to not work. Sometimes I had this nice fantasy. I thought if I had the courage (I wasn't even close) I'd ask John D. Rockefeller for $1 million. My reason was that he was too old to thoroughly enjoy his money, and I wasn't too old to thoroughly enjoy his money. I could play golf, travel, and be happy in every way, and he could enjoy this—secondhand.

If the reader has gotten the impression that I lacked enthusiasm for work he is on the right track. However, I had to get a job. I tried selling insurance and couldn't stand it. Everybody I said hello to was a prospect. I worked on my first potential customer for two months and must have played golf with him a dozen times (he couldn't hit the ball out of his own shadow) and finally got up enough courage to try to sell him an annuity. He turned me down. I went out to the street and cried—and retired from the insurance business. Money earned in insurance: zero.

My next effort was in the candy business. My father thought that maybe I could help him in sales. By then we had moved to

New York. He was concentrating on selling candy to just a few large customers, the chain stores—Woolworth's, Kress, McCrory, and others. To help me learn the business, he got me a job in a candy factory, Edgar P. Lewis, of Malden, Massachusetts. I liked making candy, and for six months worked on the marmalade slab, making imitation orange slices, and barely lifting 100-pound bags of sugar into a boiling cauldron. In the late afternoon I'd go back to my boarding house and take a nap before dinner. Those were solid naps. When I woke up I didn't know where I was or what I was.

My salary at Edgar P. Lewis was $15 a week—and I lived on it. No hardship, but not luxurious either. Room and board was $10.50 (lunch excluded). Both breakfast and dinner had the advantage of baked beans. I had one luxury (a necessity in getting to work), an old Buick my father had given me. Garage used up a buck a week. That didn't leave much out of the $15. When I was on double dates with Matt Suvalsky, an old college friend, Matt was encouraged to split the gas with me. A happy period in my life. But I wasn't any closer to my fortune—the Alan Rice $100,000.

After six months my father felt that I had eaten enough candy and I was ready for sales training with him. My specific chores were to drive the car and carry the samples; and I would listen while my father talked to the candy buyers.

Well, we struggled along for a few months, but you know how it is with father and son, they don't always work well together. Besides, I guess selling wasn't my racket. My father had always impressed on me how important the other man's time was, and I think he overdid it. So I retired from the candy business and still needed a job.

We hear about those people who, while still playing with their rattles, know exactly what they want to do in life. Well, I was twenty-two and I'd never had any idea what I wanted to do. Naturally I got in the doldrums. My parents were patient and didn't push me. I lay around the apartment on West 88th Street, played bridge in the afternoon and evening, and fell asleep around 3 A.M.

listening to Clyde McCoy playing *Sugar Blues*. My father thought I should see a psychiatrist. And I did, twice a week.

During this period an uncle got me a job with an industrial designer. Salary, $18 a week. The designer insisted I wear a hat, a Homburg no less; this purchase ate up my excess profits. I accompanied my employer to different stores he represented, with the thought that sooner or later I would catch on to the business. But I wasn't a quick learner. However, before I could get fired the designer offered to raise my salary from $18 a week to $50 a week, if I stopped seeing the psychiatrist, and he proposed we take a trip to Florida together. I was just bright enough to sense an ulterior motive, and resigned.

Insurance, candy, and industrial design—three strikes. Back to bridge, Clyde McCoy, and the psychiatrist. My parents were discouraged but they weren't surprised. My father always expected I'd have trouble making a living. I had no discernible useful aptitude, and my father had a suspicion that I was lazy (which suspicion he didn't keep from me).

Anyway, lazy or not, I didn't have a job. One night at the bridge club one of the players, who knew I was indigent, said I might like the brokerage business. Wall Street was the last place I'd have thought of trying, and with reluctance kept an appointment he made. My father went with me to the garment district branch of Cohen, Simondson & Co., members of the New York Stock Exchange. I was interviewed by a customer's broker who needed an assistant to answer his phones and keep his charts. I got the job, $25 a week. Years later I learned that my father had paid the customer's broker twenty weeks' salary in advance.

This time I took an interest in a job. The fluctuating prices and the gamble of the stock market struck one of my aptitudes. And it wasn't hard looking at the pretty models in the garment district. In a week I felt so much better that I tendered my resignation to the psychiatrist. Six months later I passed a stock exchange test, and became a junior customer's broker.

Although I liked the stock market, I was no threat to make a fortune; part of the job was approaching people for business and I didn't like that, it was selling again. After several years with Cohen, Simondson, I applied for a job as a full customer's broker at Bache & Co., and got turned down. Then E. A. Pierce & Co., later Merrill Lynch, Pierce, Fenner & Bean, took a chance and gave me a job at $75 a week—which I didn't quite earn.

While at Merrill Lynch I met a spry, eighty-year-old partner of the firm, Almar Shatford. In those days I got the flu and colds a lot and, being from Alabama, bundled up in cold weather. Mr. Shatford advised me to cut out that nonsense and wear less clothing. The first year I just wore a topcoat and there was improvement. The next year I discarded the topcoat and didn't get a single cold. And there was a serendipitous effect. Till then, when I was late to work, Victor Cook, our managing partner, would give me a friendly unfriendly look. But now I had the edge on Victor. When I arrived late, without a topcoat, Victor couldn't be sure I wasn't returning from the men's room.

I wasn't what you'd call a hard worker. There was usually an hour for lunch at Wilfred's across the street, and when the market closed at three o'clock I was on my way to my real enjoyment, bridge at the Cavendish Club. At my peak I was no more than a mediocre customer's broker. In market judgment I was probably above average—my charts were a big help here—but in commissions for the firm I was a dud. My career high was a salary of $1,000 a month—and this was more than my friend Victor Cook ever expected of me.

Making a thousand a month must have unsettled my brain because, although classified 4-F, I volunteered for the Coast Guard. At Sheepshead Bay I worked my way steadily up through the ranks, to Seaman 2nd Class. The Coast Guard sifted through my talents, and put me in a high position on top of a garbage wagon where I was third in charge. But enough of my wartime exploits.

From the Coast Guard I returned to Merrill Lynch and my job as a customer's broker. One afternoon, after playing gin at the City Athletic Club, Chester Gaines, a specialist on the floor of the New York Stock Exchange, said that judging by the way I played gin I'd do well trading on the floor, and should buy a seat. It was a good idea but the funds I had were a little short of the purchase price—about 97 percent short.

In those days I used to play golf with a friend, Jerry Ohrbach, at Metropolis Country Club (let me brag and say I won the club championship seven years in a row). One day, when we were in the same foursome, I got a seven on the first hole, an easy par-five. I was steaming, and asked Jerry what odds he would give against my getting a thirty-three on that nine. Par was thirty-five, so that meant I would have to be four under for the next eight holes. Jerry said 1,000-to-1. I said I'll take a hundred dollars worth of that if you like, and he said okay. He could afford the hundred thousand and I could afford the hundred dollars. Jerry had the best of the odds and I had a shot at my Alan Rice fortune. I made him sweat to the last hole. I needed a birdie there for the thirty-three, but didn't come close.

When Chester Gaines suggested the stock exchange seat, I spoke to Jerry about it. He told me that the golf bet had scared him so much he would like to be partners with me. By borrowing from my father, one of my uncles, my wife, and adding my own few dollars, I got up 25 percent of the necessary capital. Jerry and his father, Nathan, put up the rest and became limited partners in the small firm, Dreyfus & Co., members of the New York Stock Exchange. And we lived happily ever after. Well, not quite.

Our back-office work was done by Bache & Co., the firm that had turned me down as a customer's broker. A friend of mine, John Behrens, handled my accounts in the office, and I went to the floor of the Exchange where I did two-dollar brokerage and traded for the firm's account. I liked the floor. It was a lot of walking—with a little thinking thrown in—and the hours of ten to three fitted well with my lazy bones.

In the first year, 1946, with capital of $100,000, we made $14,000 trading. Not as bad as you'd think—1946 was a bear market. A floor joke describes it, "The market was so bad that not even the liars made money." I don't think Nathan Ohrbach realized how well we did not to have lost our shirts. Nathan, who had the misfortune to walk into a brokerage office for the first time in 1929, had the indestructible opinion that you couldn't beat the market and was restless for Dreyfus & Co. to become a commission firm.

One day Jerry introduced me to one of the partners of the firm of Lewisohn & Sons. The capital partners wanted to retire, and Jerry and Nathan thought we should take over this old firm, stop clearing through Bache, and do our own back-office work. I mildly resisted—it didn't look like that good a deal, and besides it sounded like work. But I was told that three of the Lewisohn partners would remain and run the business, and I could stay on the floor. So I agreed.

Well, we bought this turkey, with trimmings. The Ohrbachs and I got the trimmings.

Without going into the reasons, it wasn't long before I had to leave the floor, where I was reasonably competent, and take on managing a brokerage firm, where I wasn't competent at all. Nathan Ohrbach soon found there were more ways of losing money on Wall Street than trading in the market. Our capital went down rapidly—mine vanished. We couldn't even go out of business easily, and decided to try to stick it out. The Ohrbachs were good about it and drew no interest on their money. I cut my salary to zero, and we struggled along.

After a while business got so good we broke even. The Ohrbachs and I thought we should advertise, and we set aside $20,000 of hard (unearned) money for the purpose. In those days one agency handled all the Wall Street advertising, and it was dreary. I thought we should try another agency.

At that time the firm of Doyle, Dane, and Bernbach was in swaddling clothes. The partners were friends of the Ohrbachs and agreed to handle our account. But for our budget they couldn't afford to write the copy. So I had to. To my great surprise I loved it; it was an aptitude that had been hidden from me. Our account executive, Freddie Dossenbach, and I used to have lunch at a corner table next to a window at Schwartz's on Broad Street. Inspired by Swiss cheese and liverwurst, with iced tea, I'd write copy to fit Freddie's cartoons. The ads were so different from what was being done on Wall Street that we got a lot of attention for the money being spent. Business got better and the firm started to grow. Soon we had enough partners to always have a quorum for an argument.

One day the Dreyfus Fund walked through the front door and we didn't know it. A fine gentleman, John Nesbett, applied for a position. John was the sole proprietor of a $500,000 mutual fund, the Nesbett Fund. He had struggled with it for several years, but with a management fee of $2,500 a year it had become impractical for him to continue. When John joined Dreyfus & Co. the name of his fund was changed to the Dreyfus Fund, and we took over the struggle. In the next five years Dreyfus & Co. lost about a million and a half dollars of its earnings on the Fund. During that period I got looks from some of my partners that at best could be called askance. But one day the Fund started to break even. From then on it became a winner.

I made money in the stock market, a great deal of it in Polaroid stock. Did I carefully screen the list to select this stock? No. I wouldn't even have known there was such a company if I hadn't had a brother-in-law who worked there. I bought the stock initially for the wrong reason—Polaroid's 3-D glasses— and made money because of the camera.

It would appear I had some luck. The Ohrbachs pushed me into the commission business, the Dreyfus Fund walked into the office, and I bought the right stock for the wrong reason. As I said earlier I was an implausible person to have made a lot of money.

In the late 1960s I retired from my businesses. Since then I have worked full time with the Dreyfus Medical Foundation.

■ ■ ■

The newly established Dreyfus Medical Foundation funded its first study in 1966—with hope, and $57,000. It was a dud. It could be called a waste of time and money. But that wouldn't be quite right—it was part of education. I was learning how difficult it was to develop anyone's interest in PHT. As to the study, I'll make it brief. And I'll skip names. As explained earlier, complaining is not one of the purposes of this book.

Dr. Turner introduced me to members of the staff of a large hospital in the metropolitan area. They said they were interested in PHT and had a good patient population for conducting a study. I explained what had happened in the previous study—I didn't want to make that sort of mistake again—and said I'd like to be present in the early stages of the work. My experience, unsophisticated as it was, might be useful. They agreed to this and asked for $57,000 for the study.

I'd been given the impression that the study would start without delay, but it wasn't for several months that I was invited to attend the first interview with patients, conducted by Dr. Blank.

Four patients were interviewed in my presence. To my dismay, I was not allowed to say a word to these patients, although I sat just a few feet from them. If I wanted to ask a question, I had to write it on a slip of paper and hand it to Dr. Blank. Using "local mail" didn't improve my ability to communicate with these patients. One case is worth mentioning, a man who said he jackknifed in bed at night. Dr. Blank didn't ask for particulars, but I did—by note—and learned that several times each night, before he fell asleep, the patient's legs would jerk up almost to his head. I was surprised that PHT had not already been tried with him—these involuntary movements seemed a form of convulsion. After the session I expressed the opinion to Dr. Blank that three of the four patients were good candidates for PHT. I was never told whether they were given it—there was an air of mystery about everything—but I don't think they were.

The upshot of this study was that, two years later, the physician in charge of the study made the vapid statement at a medical meeting that "more work was needed in this field." Well, you couldn't argue with that.

It's hard to realize how frustrating this was. Here I was, eager to give money for studies on an established medicine, and I couldn't find the right people to give it to.

■ ■ ■

One fine day, in 1966, Dr. Turner asked me if I'd like to participate in conducting a study. I told him I'd like to, but I didn't know it was possible. Bill said he thought it could be arranged. A few weeks later Bill made arrangements through a friend of his, Dr. Oscar Resnick of the Worcester Foundation, for that foundation and ours to conduct a joint study at the Worcester County Jail.

Bill and I visited Dr. Resnick at his home in Worcester, Massachusetts, the following Sunday. On both sides of a nice lunch we discussed the proposed study. Until Bill had brought up the subject, I'd never thought about a study in a prison. After all a prison is not a hospital and doesn't necessarily have sick people. But now that I thought about it, it seemed that nervous conditions could be a contributing cause in many criminal acts, particularly those of anger and violence. I discussed this with Dr. Resnick, who had done many studies at this jail. He agreed and said he thought we'd find an ample number of people who had problems with their nerves.

When we discussed how the interview with the prisoners

should be conducted, Oscar won a lifelong friendship with me when he said, "Look, Jack, you know what you're looking for. It'll be a lot easier if you ask the questions. I'll chime in when I think it's necessary."

This jail study was to be an unusual experience for me—in some ways the most fruitful of my life.

ELEVEN ANGRY MEN

In 1966 Dr. Resnick and I conducted a study on the effects of PHT with prisoners at the Worcester County Jail in Massachusetts. It was done on a double-blind crossover basis. Helping us with the study was Ms. Barbara Homan, medical assistant to Dr. Turner.

The Worcester County Jail was a "short-term" jail. Although some of the inmates had committed serious crimes, no one sentenced to more than eighteen months was sent there.

From the outside the jail looked like an ordinary building. On the inside, except in the cell area, it resembled an old high school. For our work we were assigned a small room with a nice window on the second floor. This room was plainly furnished but comfortable, with a long table and some chairs. Liaison with the prisoners was handled by Lt. William D'Orsay, a kind and well-liked man.

Drug studies were not uncommon at the jail.* It was the custom for these studies to be done with volunteers, paid a dollar a

---

*Clearance for the study was given by the warden, Sheriff Joseph Smith, and Dr. Cyrus Paskevitch, the prison physician.

day. We followed custom. Ms. Homan did preliminary screening of forty-two volunteers, and eliminated twenty of the least likely candidates. This left twenty-two volunteers for Dr. Resnick and me to interview.

These twenty-two volunteers were interviewed carefully. This was a study of individuals, not prisoners; we had no intention of giving PHT to anyone just because he was in prison. We were looking for individuals who had symptoms we thought would respond to PHT. Among the most important of these symptoms were: excessive anger, excessive fear, and an overbusy mind that was difficult to turn off.

After two days of interviews, eleven prisoners were selected. Most of them had participated in other drug studies and didn't expect to get a medicine that would actually help them. They thought we were doing the study for our own purposes and they had volunteered mainly to ease their boredom. When we told them that we wanted only the truth about what the medicine did, they expressed skepticism that it would do anything. This attitude was good—it minimized the possibility of their being psychologically influenced.

In the initial interviews I was glad I was not alone in the room with a few of the prisoners. There was an animalistic bristle about them you could feel. One man had eyes with a yellowish glow that reminded me of an ocelot I'd seen. After a few interviews, whether because of PHT or getting to know them better, I felt comfortable with all the prisoners.

Dr. Resnick left most of the questioning of the prisoners to me. I tried to keep the interviews comfortable and friendly. This seemed to help the subjects relax, and they spoke freely. Some of them were more expressive than others, but communication was good with all of them.

Procedure. The eleven prisoners chosen for the study were interviewed for a second time, this time intensively. As specifically as we could, we got an inventory of their symptoms and complaints. Then they were placed on PHT (100 mg in the morning and 50 mg in the afternoon) and were not told what to expect of the medicine. They were interviewed several hours after the initial dose, the next day, and again at the end of a week.

Remarkable improvement in symptoms was observed. To see if similar results would be obtained under the most objective circumstances, we decided to do a double-blind, crossover to single-blind, study.

To do such a study it was desirable to approximate the original conditions. We thought this could be achieved by taking the prisoners off PHT for a week. However, when they were interviewed at the end of the week, their general condition was better than when we had first met them. It was as though the week on PHT had been a vacation from their nerves and the benefits had carried forward. We had to wait a second week before the original conditions were approximated.

Before starting the double-blind study we explained the procedure to the prisoners. Some of them would receive PHT, others an inert substance called a placebo. The capsules would be identical in appearance—the prisoners wouldn't know what they contained and we wouldn't know, thus "double-blind." Then they would be interviewed as before: a few hours after the first pill, after a night's sleep, and a week later. At that time we would make our decision as to which of them had received PHT, and which placebo.

What we did not tell the prisoners was that when this decision had been made, those subjects we thought had been on placebo would be placed on "single-blind." They would be given PHT without being told it was PHT. In that way, further nonsubjective evidence would be obtained.

Summary

We were correct in our assessment of ten of the prisoners on the double-blind. We were incorrect in one. The unusual circumstances in this case explain why.*

In the study it was observed that the eleven prisoners had many symptoms in common that responded to PHT. Among these symptoms in common were restlessness, irritability, fear, anger, inability to concentrate, poor mood, lack of energy, sleeping problems, and an overactive brain.

Symptoms not common to all prisoners, such as headache, stomach distress, chest pain, muscular pain, skin rash, and dizziness, disappeared while the subjects were on PHT and reappeared when it was withdrawn.

This study was recorded on tape with the prisoners' permission. Transcribed, there are 605 pages covering 130 interviews.**

The results were exceptional. Brief summaries of the eleven cases are included in this book. Only four are included here. Please see the other seven in Appendix.

JAMES L.

Before PHT:

I feel miserable, a bunch of nerves.

I have a grudge on me I can't get rid of...I take it out on everyone. It's so bad that sometimes I have myself locked in so I won't cause any trouble.

---

* In the early part of the study, Danny R.'s response to PHT was similar to that of the other prisoners. During the control part of the study, Danny R. got news that made him think his daughter was going blind. He didn't tell us, and we misassessed his realistic nervousness and decided he was on placebo. (For details, see the Appendix, pp. 314-315.)

** An 80-page condensation is available in limited number for those interested. The 605-page transcript is on file at the Dreyfus Medical Foundation.

I can't work or nothing. When you're down-and-out there isn't much you can do.

I can't digest my food right…I don't feel like eating nothing.

My thinking is bad, there are quite a few thoughts in my mind, I can't concentrate at all. It takes me a day-and-a-half to write one letter.

I get them phantom limb pains [he had a wooden leg] quite a bit, at least three times a week. The pain, I can just take so much of it. I can't sleep and I can't sit still or nothing

Sometimes I have them headaches in the afternoon and at night I get them right back again.

With PHT (Non-Blind):

I feel a lot better. All the guys down there say I ain't the same guy…because I let them all out of their cells. [James L. was a trusty.] I didn't lock nobody up.

Now I'm eating like a fool, before I couldn't eat.

I get them headaches once in a while but not too often. That's why I stopped taking those aspirins.

After Being Off PHT (Two Weeks):

I never get to sleep…I sleep about an hour, that's all.

I get weak but I can't seem to hold my weight. The guys put me on the bed and I come out of it after a while.

I get them headaches quite often now. I'm getting phantom limb pains again…I had it again yesterday. I couldn't even lay down on the bed. I kept twisting and turning.

I'll read a story and, as a matter of fact, I won't even know what I read.

With Placebo (Double-Blind):

I'm down and out right now. My mind's all bunched up now. I passed out Wednesday. I get headaches.

Anger, about the same as it was before the pills.

I had those phantom limb pains Wednesday.

With PHT (Single-Blind):

I feel good right now...I feel altogether different...I feel much better since I got them pills.

I've been kidding around with everybody...For the last two days the fellows have been saying I'm not the same guy. No headaches. No phantom limb pains.

DAVID H.

Before PHT:

I have a temper that shouldn't be...I shake when I'm angry and can't stop. I have stomach trouble...I think it's from nerves.

If something happens, I twist and turn it in my mind until I've made a problem out of nothing...I can't turn my mind off. I can't go to sleep.

Quite often I'll get depressed and start worrying about home and what's going on outside these lovely walls. I lose all hope and energy.

With PHT (Non-Blind):

Well, I feel I'm a lot calmer...I can sit still, without jumping up.

For the past five or six days I've been sure of myself in the things I say and what I do. I get angry just as fast but I can control it...it doesn't keep poppin' back into my mind.

I used to read three or four chapters without knowing what I read. Now I can lie there and remember what I've read.

I've been eating my meals and enjoying them.

After Being Off PHT (Two Weeks):

I feel very tired, irritable and grouchy. I'm not getting along well...People are getting on my nerves to the extent where I'm ready to assassinate them.

I don't eat hardly anything...I'm not sleeping very well...I feel just terrible.

I got a few problems and I just can't get them out of my mind. I'm worrying about them all the time...I've tried my case a thousand times.

With PHT (Double-Blind):

I think I'm on the Dilantin right now. I'm not nervous...I'm not tense or ready to jump at anyone.

I'm not grouchy...I seem to still have a temper, but I go into a situation with a little more confidence. I don't just jump off the handle.

I seem able to push my thoughts aside...read a couple of stories and know what I read.

I feel fine as far as my stomach goes...My appetite has picked up...I been sleeping better...able to go right to sleep.

CLIFFORD S.

Before PHT:

I'm very high-strung...I let everything build up inside...Then I just explode. I do a lot of thinking.

I get these wicked headaches...I'll take six or seven aspirin...and the headache won't go away. I'll have it all day.

I don't sleep well. Between twelve and two in the morning I usually get these nightmares...scare a guy right out of his head.

With PHT (Non-Blind):

I just feel wonderful...You know how I can feel my nerves are relaxed? I've done four paintings; I don't paint when I'm nervous because I can't concentrate...If I can sit down and do a painting a day it makes me happy.

I'm in a good mood. I don't feel angry at anybody...I've only really got mad once since the last time I seen you. It went right away.

I've been sleeping a lot. I ain't jumpy all the time. I ain't looking behind me anymore.

After Being Off PHT (Two Weeks):

I'm tense inside, I can't stay in one place too long, I get up and move around...I just pick a book up, look at it and throw it back down.

I feel that anger...Whenever I get in a fight I can't control myself.

I wake up about five or six times during the night.

With Placebo (Double-Blind):

My nerves are jittery inside...I can't sit in one place too long.

This week when I was lifting, I got dizzy three or four times and I was only working out with light weights.

I know my mind's always been going on. Actually, I don't feel these pills have done anything for me.

With PHT (Single-Blind):

I just feel good. I am completely relaxed...I ain't nervous, tense or nothing.

There's no anger at all.

Sleep better...ain't tired...all kinds of energy; washing windows, floors. I can concentrate better.

PHILIP B.

Before PHT:

I am quite nervous now. I've been more or less nervous all my life. And shake a lot, you just feel it, that you're shaking.

If I get nervous my hands break out in a little rash. I get tightness in my chest quite often. It's a pain, it takes your breath away sometimes.

I think a lot, there is too much on my mind. I try to put it out of my mind and it just stays there. The mind wanders and it doesn't focus on what I'm doing. Sometimes it's 3:00 o'clock in the morning before I get to sleep.

With PH (Non-Blind):

I feel good all over now. I seem to relax a lot more. Since I've been taking the pills I haven't been walking around, pacing back and forth so much. These past few nights I've been going right to sleep.

I haven't been so depressed. I've been eating better. And I haven't had those pains in my chest. And I can concentrate better on my work. And I'm not making as many mistakes.

After Being Off PHT (Two Weeks):

Well, I feel I'm right back where I was before I started taking the pills. I don't sleep well. I walk around all the time. Nervous all the time—agitated, quick-tempered, get shook up.

I'm always thinking—wandering away—always thinking of different things. I've been very depressed.

With PHT (Double-Blind):

I feel good, very good, feel a lot better, honestly. And I haven't had those chest pains this week at all. The rash it cleared right up. I'm more relaxed.

I can just forget about things now. I've been able to do my work better. The last few days I've been goin' to sleep right off. I feel much better than I have for the last three years.

Suggestions from the Prisoners for the use of PHT in Prisons

When the study was over we met with the inmates as a group for the first time. Each of the prisoners had told us he wanted to continue taking PHT. But I learned this was not going to be permitted, and there was nothing I could do about that. But I could tell the prisoners what I knew about the medicine—it might be useful to them later on.

We had a long, friendly discussion. As we were saying good-bye, John G. volunteered:

JOHN G: If this pill was ever put on the market it would be a godsend to both Walpole and Concord prisons. Judging by this group here, it'd work miracles up there. You have men doing ten, fifteen, twenty, and life. And that's where I'd like to see them back up a whole truckload of the stuff and—

JACK D: You mean Dilantin?

JOHN G: Dilantin is right. Those guys are walkin' on edge all the time. There's where the trouble starts, more so than here. These fellows are all going fairly short. Up there you got a bunch of fellows that got nothing to lose and, well, they're all packed in together.

JACK D: You think that in those prisons...

JOHN G: I think they need it even worse than the fellows do here. You can ask Jim and Spike.

JACK D: Do you agree with that, Spike?

Victor M: Oh, yes, I agree with that very much.

JACK D: What would you say, Jim?

JAMES L: The same thing. I was there for a while myself and I know. It would help a lot of them guys. You walk around there and if you say the wrong thing, you're liable to go bouncing off the wall.

JOHN G: Those guys are so on edge they gotta take yellow jackets and bennies once in a while to relieve that. What if they didn't have this tension built up? They wouldn't have the trouble they do now.

Jack D: Well, John, thank you for the thought.

The prisoners' suggestion that the use of PHT, on a voluntary basis, be permitted inside a prison should be considered. Some prisoners are in jail because of problems in their nervous systems, and these problems are exacerbated by their confinement. With too much time to think and brood, it's no wonder that some prisoners live in a sort of hell and can't help imposing it on those around them. Allowing PHT to be taken on a voluntary basis could make an important difference to those individuals who need it—and to others who are endangered by their potential for violence. When one realizes that PHT is not habit-forming, withholding it from prisoners is the opposite of protection of their rights.

■ ■ ■

As stated earlier, this study was not of prisoners as such but a study of individuals with problems of their nervous sytems. The objective was to see if, in a double-blind study, the effects of PHT that had been observed on an uncontrolled basis would be confirmed. They were, and additional effects of PHT were observed.*

I felt the time had come to go to the federal government.

---

* I participated in two further studies in institutions, one with Dr. Resnick at the Lyman Reformatory for Boys in Lyman, Massachusetts, the other at the Patuxent Institution in Maryland, with Dr. Joel Elkes, head of psychiatry at Johns Hopkins, and Dr. Joseph Stephens and Dr. Lino S. Covi, also of Hopkins. Although not controlled studies, the results were similar to those of the Worcester study. (See the Appendix, p. 316.)

TRAVELS WITH THE GOVERNMENT

Few of us have a clear picture of the federal government and how it operates. With millions of people in it, government has to be run by regulations. This leads to routine. Where there's routine, innovation doesn't thrive. I'm not being critical, government means well. But I'll tell you this, if you want the government to do something outside of routine—and expect to see it happen in your lifetime—you'd better arrange for reincarnation.

I didn't know this in 1966, and with the optimism of a Boy Scout I approached the federal government. I would have gone to the government sooner but had felt the evidence was too informal. Now, with the jail study done, the time was right. I had two thoughts in mind. The first was that the government might take the matter off my hands. I hoped for this, but wasn't counting on it. My second thought was that I didn't want to do anything contrary to government policy. Their objectives and mine were the same. If I was to proceed on my own, I needed official advice.

There were two logical places to go: the Department of Health, Education and Welfare, and the Food and Drug Administration. Since I was a layman, the Department of

Health seemed the appropriate place. At that time John W. Gardner was Secretary of HEW. It took me about a month to get an appointment with the Secretary. That seemed like a long time. When I got to know the government better I realized that a month was instantaneous.

I met with Secretary Gardner in Washington in May 1966. We talked for fifty minutes. That is, I talked for the first forty minutes and he talked for the last ten. In those forty minutes I summarized my experience with Dilantin and my observations of its benefits in others. I told him of my disappointment in the two hospital studies I'd sponsored, of setting up the Dreyfus Medical Foundation, and of the double-blind study at the Worcester County Jail.

Secretary Gardner listened. From the experience I'd had it wouldn't have surprised me if he had been skeptical. But he wasn't. The Secretary seemed to sense that I was on the right track. Although he didn't suggest that the government take a hand, he gave me three helpful suggestions.

The first suggestion had to do with my unmedical terminology. The Secretary laughed when I made my "dry twigs" analogy. He said he liked it but thought more sophisticated language would stand me in good stead in talking with physicians. Of course he was right, and now I talk of "post-tetanic potentiation" and "post-tetanic afterdischarge" as if they were old friends. His second suggestion was that I should tell Parke-Davis about my findings. I followed this suggestion, too, as will be explained later.

The third suggestion came as a surprise, but I welcomed it. The Secretary said I should seek national publicity for the story. He understood my disappointment with the lack of results from the two hospitals. However, he was sure that somewhere in the United States there were hospitals and physicians who would be interested in the story.

I told Secretary Gardner I could try *Life* magazine. A few

months earlier *Life* had done a kind article about me by Marshall Smith with the understated title, "Maverick Wizard Behind the Wall Street Lion." Marshall and I had become good friends, and I thought he might introduce me to *Life's* science department. The Secretary said that *Life* would be an excellent place for this story, if they would do it.

The meeting with Secretary Gardner was most helpful. His suggestions were good and I followed them all.

■ ■ ■

It wasn't easy to get *Life* magazine to do a medical article recommended by a layman. Albert Rosenfeld, *Life's* science editor, was understandably cautious. He had several sessions with me in which he listened carefully to the evidence. Then Al said he would like to do the story, but *Life* would require a medical event as a peg. He said a medical meeting would serve the purpose. Before making a firm commitment, however, Al wanted to get the reactions of a good friend, Dr. Joel Elkes, director of psychiatry at Johns Hopkins.

Before I met Dr. Elkes I thought of him as a hurdle. But after a discussion with him, I found I had a friend. Dr. Elkes said the subject was of particular interest since ten years earlier he had planned to do research on PHT with other physicians. But just at that time an exciting new medicine, thorazine, had appeared, and their interest had been sidetracked. Dr. Elkes was helpful in setting up the meeting that *Life* required, and in 1966 a symposium on PHT was held at the annual meeting of the American College of Neuropsychopharmacology.

In September 1967 *Life* published an article by Albert Rosenfeld—"10,000-to-1 Payoff." The article was a turning point. The response to it, and to the *Reader's Digest* condensation of it printed in thirteen languages, forced us to increase our small staff to keep up with phone calls and to answer letters. Many physicians wrote that they were using PHT for a variety of purposes.

We received thousands of letters from the public. The best side of human nature showed up. The writers expressed deep appreciation for benefits they got from PHT as a result of the articles. Many described their experiences in detail in the hope that by so doing they might help others. We selected a hundred of these letters and made a booklet for physicians. But readership was poor; doctors consider letters "anecdotal."

The *Life* and *Reader's Digest* articles opened things up. Now there were institutions and individual physicians with genuine interest in doing work on PHT. Soon the Foundation was sponsoring over a dozen studies. We got as far from home base as Chichester, England. There, Dr. Lionel Haward, in a series of double-blind studies with normal volunteers, demonstrated that PHT improved cognitive function. In the United States, perhaps the most significant of these early studies was by Stephens and Shaffer at Johns Hopkins. In a double-blind crossover study, they found PHT to be markedly effective in reducing symptoms related to fear and anger.

During this period Dr. Turner was searching the medical literature to see if previous work had been done on PHT. To my surprise he and his staff found hundreds of studies, published over the previous twenty years. These studies, in addition to confirming our observations in thought and mood, reported PHT to be useful for a variety of other disorders. Among them were cardiac disorders, trigeminal neuralgia, migraine, diabetes, pruritis ani, ulcers, and asthma.

■ ■ ■

Three years after I had met with Secretary Gardner, I was ready to go back to the government. When I had seen the Secretary I didn't have a lot of evidence. But now I was loaded for bear.

This was a mistake. I should have brought an elephant gun. Republicans were in.

In the sequence of events we come to President Richard M. Nixon. By chance I had known Mr. Nixon before he became president. I'd seen his interview on the David Susskind Show, and as a result, without being asked, had contributed to his presidential campaign. When Mr. Nixon was defeated I got to know him. When he lost the race for Governor of California I knew he had no chance to become President. If you can't win your own state, you can't win the United States.

That's what I thought, but Mr. Nixon was nominated for President in 1968. Again I contributed to his campaign; I also contributed to the campaign of Senator Hubert Humphrey. And I did what I suppose was an unusual thing—I told each I was contributing to the campaign of the other. In this matter of public health, it was important for me to be known by whichever one became President. I was able to talk to both before the election. With Mr. Nixon, I had a long conversation about PHT at Key Biscayne.

My discussion with Senator Humphrey about PHT took place at his headquarters in New York. When we finished he said, "Listen, son [that nearly got my vote], whether I win or lose, I want you to get back to me on this." I couldn't have hoped for anything nicer than that. After the election I was anxious to get back to the Senator but it took three months to get an appointment. We had coffee in his suite at the Waldorf-Astoria. He showed up from a bedroom in shirt sleeves, and I had the feeling we were going to get down to work. I started off enthusiastically. Then I noticed there was no response in his face, and his gaze was fixed on a picture on the wall in back of me. In about fifteen minutes my enthusiasm started to run down. When I left soon after, I had the feeling that Senator Humphrey was relieved. I was too, but deeply disappointed.

■ ■ ■

After Mr. Nixon became President I waited a few months for him to settle into position, so to speak, and then called Rose Mary Woods, his nice and well-known secretary. I spoke to her for quite a while, explaining what an urgent medical matter this was, and told her I would send her some written information. I asked her to please not talk to the President about it, just give it some thought and advise me on the best way to approach him on the matter. I'm really dumber than the law allows. Of course Rose Mary, as any good secretary would, told President Nixon about it. A few days later she called to tell me the material had been sent to Secretary of Health Finch and I would hear from him shortly. I had hoped to see the President himself, but this was fine. I waited to hear from Secretary Finch.

Days went by without my hearing from the Secretary and I started to get restless. By the time three months had elapsed I was beside myself (not easy). I didn't have sense enough, or guts enough, to pick up the phone and call Secretary Finch, so I spoke to a friend who had a friend who knew the Secretary. This worked. Apparently the material Miss Woods had sent three months earlier hadn't reached Secretary Finch on the conveyor belt that carries things to the desk of a Secretary of Health. I got a call from Secretary Finch's secretary and an appointment was made.

Dr. Bogoch and I met with Secretary Finch in his office in December 1969. The Secretary didn't say whether he had discussed the matter with President Nixon, but he'd had a chance to look at the material I had sent the President, the *Life* and *Reader's Digest* articles, excerpts from letters from physicians, and a condensed version of the Worcester Jail Study. I hadn't wanted to burden the President with medical studies. But for the Secretary of Health I brought, in a bulging briefcase, hundreds of medical studies on the use of PHT for a variety of disorders. The Secretary was impressed.

After we'd been with Secretary Finch a short while, he asked

Dr. Jesse L. Steinfeld, who had been appointed Surgeon General the previous day, to join us. Then, with both present, Dr. Bogoch and I briefly summarized the clinical evidence and basic mechanisms of action of PHT.

When we finished I told Secretary Finch about my meeting with Secretary Gardner three years earlier, and the advice he'd given me. Since that time so much new information had come into the possession of the Dreyfus Medical Foundation, facts not generally known, there was no question that this was now a matter for the government. To convey the information to the government, Dr. Bogoch and I proposed that we have a two-day conference with a broadly representative group of government physicians, including members of the FDA. At such a conference we would present the medical information, and the government would be able to take it from there.

After we had made our proposal, Secretary Finch turned to the Surgeon General and said, "Let's get moving on this. How long will it take you to get a group together to meet with the Dreyfus Medical Foundation? How soon can you get a conference set up?"

"Probably in a couple of weeks," Dr. Steinfeld said.

"Well, do it faster if you can, but do it within two weeks," Secretary Finch told him. Apparently my sense of urgency had been picked up by the Secretary. We thanked him, and after exchanging telephone numbers with Dr. Steinfeld, Dr. Bogoch and I left with the feeling that the government would soon play its part.

When we got back to New York, Dr. Bogoch and I started the hard work of getting the data organized for the conference in two weeks. Four days went by before it occurred to me that we hadn't heard from the Surgeon General. Although Secretary Finch had given him explicit instructions to hold this meeting without delay, I thought it possible Dr. Steinfeld might be waiting for a call from me. I phoned him. His secretary said he was in conference and would call back. He didn't call back and I called again the next day. He was still in conference. This was the beginning of my awareness that phoning the Surgeon General and getting to speak to him were not exactly the same thing.

Several days later the Surgeon General called to say that he had been thinking about the conference; he thought we should have a meeting to discuss it and would like to have Dr. Bert Brown, head of the National Institutes of Mental Health, with him. We were prepared to meet without delay, but he said he would be tied up for a week and suggested that the four of us meet in Washington on January 14. I could see that things were not going as smoothly as I'd hoped; the meeting to discuss the meeting that was supposed to have taken place in two weeks wouldn't take place for three weeks.

On the fourteenth Dr. Bogoch and I arrived in Washington to have dinner with Dr. Steinfeld and Bert Brown. Dr. Brown was not present. The Surgeon General explained that his secretary had forgotten to invite him. Without Dr. Brown the Surgeon General felt we didn't have a "quorum" and would have to have another meeting. We were taken aback. Still, we felt the time could be put to good use if we enlarged on Dr. Steinfeld's sketchy background on PHT. We did our best, but we didn't seem to have the Surgeon General's full attention because he would frequently interject, "I don't know how my secretary forgot to call Dr. Brown."

Before we left Washington we discussed our next meeting with Dr. Steinfeld. Where we should meet seemed a problem to him. He said maybe we should meet in a motel. I didn't know what that meant, but to get things moving I would have met in the men's room. We left Washington with no definite date. I began to have the feeling that I was looking at the "Finch medical conference" through the wrong end of a telescope.

I was not born with an oversupply of patience. Even with Dilantin I am short of perfection. This is to explain to the reader that the next six months were about as frustrating and exasperating a period of time as one could hope not to enjoy. It was that long before we had another meeting with the Surgeon General, this time with Dr. Brown. Both before and after this meeting, with a skill unequaled in my experience, Jesse Steinfeld ducked and dodged, retreated and sidestepped, and left me so off balance that I felt something was going to happen any day. Each time I managed to catch the Surgeon General on the telephone, a new subject would come up for consideration, such as, what physicians we should bring with us, where the meeting should take place, how many people should attend, what medical disciplines should be represented, and who should chair the meeting. (It was finally decided that Jesse should chair it.) It could have been chaired by Little Orphan Annie because the meeting never took place.

We kept contact with the Surgeon General, and this mirage of a meeting, for well over a year. His superb talent for keeping our interest alive, without doing anything other than that, explains why we did not think of going back to Secretary Finch until it was too late. (He left office six months after we met.)

The end came in the following way. We had gotten the Surgeon General pinned down to a meeting, the date made well in advance and its importance emphasized. Dr. Bogoch and I were going to review the medical data at length, feeling that this would motivate Dr. Steinfeld to set up the conference without further delay. And I was determined at this meeting to lay it on the line—either get results, or not.

A few days before the scheduled meeting I got a telephone call from Dr. Steinfeld's secretary saying she was sorry but we'd have to cancel the meeting for the coming Monday. I said, "But we had things all arranged for a full presentation. Why can't he make it?"

"He has to go out West on Monday to investigate the earthquake," she said. (An earthquake had occurred in California a week earlier.) If Jesse had been going to California to prevent the earthquake, well, good luck. But to cancel a medical meeting of this importance to visit an earthquake that had already happened, and not even propose a new date for the meeting, was too much. I said to myself, The heck with it, and Jesse didn't have any more of my phone calls to dodge.

I never did find out what a Surgeon General was supposed to do. He didn't do surgery, and he didn't command troops. Maybe the government couldn't find out either because when Dr. Steinfeld left, the office was retired.*

At the time Dr. Steinfeld left government, the *New York Times* reported him to have said that federal health affairs were in a "kind of chaos." He was "frustrated seeing how much good I might have achieved and how much was actually accomplished."

In a nutshell.

■ ■ ■

I had placed a lot of hope on the government's taking over PHT. I admit that part of this was because I wanted to be relieved of the responsibility and the work. But there was a more important reason. With its medical institutions, and its enormous resources and authority, the government could do a far better job than a single foundation. However, it wasn't long after the Finch conference that I began to get the idea that government lacked enthusiasm about taking over its responsibilities.

Maybe I should sum up my thoughts during this period. At the outset, when I became convinced that PHT had been overlooked, I knew that medical studies would be necessary to persuade others. After the initial unsuccessful attempts, the Foundation had sponsored numerous successful studies on PHT and was continuing in

---

* The Office of Surgeon General has been resurrected. We wish the new Surgeon General the best of luck.

this effort. But by far the most important source of evidence was already in the medical literature. This evidence had been there for the picking, like good apples under a tree.

I don't know exactly when we passed the equator of ample evidence, but at some point our goal changed, and we decided that communicating already existing evidence was more important than finding new evidence. You know that old philosophical question about the tree falling in the forest—if nobody hears it, was there a sound? I'm not sure about that, but here was a practical question. If a great amount of evidence exists for the usefulness of a medicine, and the physician doesn't know about it, does it do any good? The answer is obvious. So communication became our number one objective.

Something other than trying to tell the story to the government had to be done. By this time we had collected so many published studies on PHT they would have filled a barrel. I would like to have Xeroxed the studies and sent each physician a barrelful saying, "You'll find this useful." But it wasn't practical. We had to attack the barrel ourselves, organize the studies, and condense them for the physicians. And that is what we did.

When we finished we had a bibliography and review of PHT, the clinical section arranged chronologically, the contents fairly evenly divided between clinical and basic mechanism of action studies. It was exhausting work for our group, and just the writing of it took over a year and a half. To keep our spirits up we worked on the theory that if a doctor matched a thousand hours of our effort with ten minutes of his own (aye, there's the rub) we'd show a profit—with 350,000 doctors in the U.S.A. The bibliography, *The Broad Range of Use of Phenytoin,* was the first of two that the Foundation published. About 400,000 copies were sent to physicians and basic scientists in the United States in 1970. The response was excellent, and we had letters of thanks from nearly a thousand physicians. Still, the facts about PHT did not spread as fast as I had hoped.

■ ■ ■

One Sunday morning in July 1971, my brain was playing with the communication problem. The Foundation was sponsoring studies of PHT, mostly in new fields, but we had no other immediate plans. The thought that government had the key responsibility for PHT was always in my mind. But I had taken my best shot with the government—President, Secretary of Health, and Surgeon General. Something else had to be done; I couldn't figure out what, and it bugged me.

It's funny how we remember unimportant things if they are associated with something important. That Sunday, my housekeeper Ida Thomas, whom I love and who has a feeling for me, sensed my mood and said, "Let me fix you something for breakfast instead of those old eggs and tomatoes you eat every day." I thanked her, and went back to thinking about the government. Interesting smells started coming out of the kitchen. Soon a delicious-looking pancake arrived, with powdered sugar and hot blueberry sauce. The first bite was on my fork when the phone rang.

A voice said, "This is Walter Tkach at the White House. I'm President Nixon's doctor, and I was just telling the President and Mrs. Nixon what a wonderful piece of work I thought you'd done." If an ancestor had called I couldn't have been more surprised. Just when I was wondering how to get back to the government, here was a spontaneous recommendation to the President, from his own doctor. I steadied my voice and thanked Dr. Tkach. Dr. Tkach went on to say, "The President suggested that I invite you to visit me in Washington and I hope you can make it soon." I said I could. We made a date for the following Tuesday. Then I ate Ida's pancake and two more.

Tuesday I took a sensible morning plane to Washington that got me there at 9:45. Dr. Tkach met me and drove me to the White House in his car. During the drive he told me that after a personal

loss he had benefited from PHT, and had the *Life* article to thank
for it. I was glad he had first-hand experience with PHT; there's
nothing like it to get an understanding of the medicine.

When we got to the White House, Dr. Tkach walked me past
the gendarmes, and for a moment I had the feeling I was infil-
trating the place. But when we got to his office Walter made me
feel like a dignitary. He put me in a comfortable chair, got me a
jug of coffee, and became a voluntary and patient listener for several hours. In that sympathetic atmosphere I did a good job of
summarizing the PHT story.

At about 12:30 Dr. Tkach suggested lunch would be appropriate. He didn't have to drag me—I've always noticed that mental
effort uses more calories than physical effort—and we went to the
White House cafeteria. Walter hadn't told me we would have company for lunch, but he had invited Kenneth R. Cole, Jr., and James
H. Cavanaugh, two members of the President's staff, to join us. I
didn't get to eat as well as I'd hoped because I had to give a forty-
five-minute summary of PHT. I emphasized the government's
responsibility. Ken and Jim ate well and listened well.

When lunch was over Ken Cole, who outranked Jim
Cavanaugh on the President's staff, said they would both try to
be helpful in getting the story to the FDA. He said I could call
him whenever necessary, but Jim would work with me on a regular basis. In the past I had been treated with courtesy by the
government, but I'd felt a little like a salesman, carrying samples
in his briefcase. Now I was being offered help without soliciting
it and it put me in a different posture. When lunch was over I
thanked them all.

Dr. Tkach drove me back to the airport. He said there wasn't
any question that the government should do something about
the PHT matter. But he cautioned me against being too optimistic. He said the problem wouldn't be with people I would
meet but with the nature of bureaucracy. It was so big, and so
besieged on all sides by people clamoring for its attention, that it

was distracted from important matters—even if it could figure out which they were. A few years earlier I would have argued with Walter. Now I just kept my fingers crossed.

That same week Jim Cavanaugh came to New York and spent a day with Dr. Bogoch and me. It was one of those calorie-consuming days. I spent at least four hours going over clinical evidence, and Sam spent nearly half that time on the basic mechanisms. When he left, Jim had a good grasp of the facts. He said the next move would be for us to talk to Dr. Charles Edwards, Commissioner of the FDA.

Jim Cavanaugh made the appointment with Commissioner Edwards, and Dr. Bogoch and I spent a morning in the offices of the FDA. After a long talk with the Commissioner, he said he'd like us to explain this matter to senior members of his staff. I don't remember their names, I saw them only once, but they were sympathetic and tried to be helpful. After we outlined the story, they told us that the Foundation itself might be able to apply for new listings of PHT. They suggested that Dr. Herbert Ley, the previous Commissioner of the FDA, would be a good person to consult about procedure.* I didn't understand why the Foundation should apply to the FDA in a matter of health for the American public when that health was a direct responsibility of the FDA itself.

Still, I would have considered following the suggestion except for two reasons. One was that PHT appeared to be useful for so many disorders that to get them through the FDA in the routine way, single-file so to speak, would have taken forever. The second reason was that if the Foundation did make applications for new uses of PHT, we might be required to be silent on the subject while applications were pending. We couldn't risk that.

*We got in touch with Dr. Herbert Ley. Dr. Ley said he would like to review the summaries of the PHT studies in our bibliography; they seemed almost too good to be true. After spot-checking the summaries for a day and a half, he was satisfied. Subsequently, Dr. Ley became a member of the Foundation's Advisory Board.

Dr. Edwards visited the Foundation a few weeks later. When he had spent most of a day absorbing the medical information, he agreed that a conference with medical officials would be appropriate and said he would help set up such a conference.

Dr. Edwards made the arrangements and a two-day conference was held in our offices in February 1972. Since Dr. Edwards had already spent a day with us on PHT, he attended only the first day of the meeting. Others in attendance were Dr. Theodore Cooper (director, the National Heart and Lung Institute), Dr. John Jennings, Dr. James Pittman, Dr. Samuel Kaim, James Cavanaugh, Dr. Samuel Bogoch, and myself.

This conference was hard work. There were four two-hour sessions in the two days. Dr. Bogoch and I conducted them and, except during the discussion periods, we did all the talking. I assure you I looked forward to lunch and coffee breaks (see Agenda, pp. 222-223).

By the time we got to the last discussion period, on the afternoon of the second day, the clinical effects of PHT and its basic mechanisms of action had been outlined, and we got down to cases—what the government could do. But none of our visitors could think of a handle for the FDA to grab PHT by; nothing like this had happened before. The only suggestion I remember was that perhaps the government could give the Foundation a grant. I appreciated this, but I didn't want us to lose any freedom of action.

As the meeting was breaking up, Dr. Kaim said to me, "Well, the ball is in your court." This struck my unfunny bone. "In my court?" I said. "Where the devil do you think it's been all these years and when should it get in your court?" As many of us do, I make the mistake of thinking that an individual in the government is the government itself. Dr. Kaim meant no harm by his comment, but I repeat it because it is typical of a thousand I've heard from people in a position to do something about PHT themselves. They seem to clear their consciences by giving me advice as to what I should do. I've got enough of this advice. It's

DREYFUS MEDICAL FOUNDATION
CONFERENCE ON PHT WITH FDA

February 22 and 23, 1972

Tuesday, February 22

10:00 A.M.	Background
	Early evidence
	Institutional studies (with reference to both
	crime and problems within the institutions):
	Worcester County Jail Study (double-blind)
	Lyman School for Boys (Juvenile Delinquents)
	Patuxent Institution
1:00 P.M.	Lunch
2:00 P.M.	Basic mechanisms of action of PHT:
	Effect on hyperexcitable nerve cell
	Suppression of post-tetanic potentiation
	Stabilization of membrane
	Regulatory effect on sodium and potassium
	Resistance to anoxia
	Increase of energy compounds in brain
	(glucose, ATP, and creatine phosphate)
	Stabilizing effects on labile diabetes
	Cerebral and coronary vessel dilatation
	Protection against digitalis toxicity
	Protection against cortisone toxicity
	Other antitoxic effects of interest: DDT,
	cyanide, alloxan, radiation, etc.
3:15 P.M.	Coffee and Discussion
3:30 P.M.	"The Broad Range of Use of PHT"
	Review of thought, mood, and behavior disorders
	(1938-1971)
	Discussion
5:00 P.M.	Recess
7:30 P.M.	Dinner

Wednesday, February 23

9:00 A.M.	Review of "The Broad Range of Use of PHT"
	Symptoms and disorders for which PHT effectiveness has been reported
	Discussion of cardiac uses
	Brief review of other somatic disorders
	Alcoholism and drug addiction
	Safety and toxicology
10:15 A.M.	Coffee
10:30 A.M.	The effects of PHT on overthinking, anger, fear, and related emotions
	The One-Hour test
11:30 A.M.	Recent work reporting therapeutic benefits of PHT in glaucoma, steroid myopathy, hostility in chronic psychotics, violence, radiation, shock lung, asthma, digitalis toxicity, and hypertension
12:30 P.M.	Lunch
1:30 P.M.	PHT's value is based on the combination of many factors:
	Broad range of effectiveness
	Rapidity of action
	Beneficial "side effects"
	Not addictive
	Not a sedative at therapeutic doses
	Safety established by long period of use
	How PHT has been overlooked
	Discussion
4:00 P.M.	Conference ends

saved up in a hermetically sealed tank and I plan to sell to a util-ity—when fuel prices rise a bit more.

Although nothing specific came of the meeting, at least some members of the government had a better understanding of PHT. Jim Cavanaugh kept in touch with me regularly. Jim had a way of saying, "I'll get back to you next week." And he always did. I appreciated his efforts so much that I never pressed him as to when he would call. It was usually about 4:45—on Friday.

Occasionally I was able to get Commissioner Edwards on the phone. Charlie, who told me he was trying to work out some-thing with members of the department, finally came up with a suggestion. He said that if we could get a political figure to write a letter of inquiry about PHT to Secretary of Health Richardson, the reply—which would be an official statement and could be made public—might shed light on the matter. By that time I was so worn out I would have settled for an old shoe. But Dr. Edwards' idea seemed constructive.

Since the Foundation was located in New York, I asked Dr. Edwards if a letter from Governor Rockefeller would serve the purpose. He said it would. When I asked Governor Rockefeller, to whom I had spoken previously about PHT, he said he would write such a letter. And he did.

Secretary Richardson's response* meant more to me than it

---

*From Secretary Richardson's letter:

"Conversations with health officials within the Department have revealed that phenytoin (PHT) was introduced in 1938 as the first essentially nonsedating anticon-vulsant drug...

"A review of the literature reveals that phenytoin has been reported to be useful in a wide range of disorders. Among its reported therapeutic actions are its stabiliz-ing effect on the nervous system, its antiarrhythmic effect on certain cardiac disor-ders, and its therapeutic effect on emotional disorders.

"The fact that such broad therapeutic effects have been reported by many inde-pendent scientists and physicians over a long period of time would seem to indicate that the therapeutic effects of phenytoin are more than that of an anticonvulsant.

"The FDA encourages the submission of formal applications...."

(For the full text, see Appendix, p. 318.)

would to someone unfamiliar with the background. It showed that the Foundation's efforts had had some effect. The Secretary's comment: "Conversations with health officials in the Department..." indicated the letter had FDA approval.

■ ■ ■

I invaded the U.S. government only once more. About two months into President Nixon's second term, I made one more try. I called Rose Mary Woods and told her the PHT matter was just too important to hang in limbo any longer. I had done the best I could with government for the last four years and now I needed presidential advice. Rose Mary understood, and a few days later called back to say a date had been set up for lunch with the President—I should come at 11:30 so we would have more time to talk about PHT. Perfect.

I couldn't be late for such an appointment and planned to go to Washington the day before. But when I found the chance for rain approached zero, I made a reservation for a flight scheduled to get to Washington at 9:15, which gave me almost two hours leeway. That darn plane ("Doing What We Do Best") managed to be two-and-a-half hours late, and I was thirty-five minutes late for my appointment. If that wasn't embarrassing. But no one other than I appeared ruffled. The President set me at ease and listened closely to my experiences with the government. I told him the situation was incredible. Everyone had tried to be helpful, but they were so busy with problems they didn't have time for a solution. I said I couldn't get it out of my head that if someone with authority had the facts he'd see to it that something got done in this matter so urgent to public health.

The PHT story was not new to the President, having heard it from me on three occasions. He agreed that something should be done and asked for my suggestion. I had anticipated the possibility that he might ask. I told him that political jokes for at least a

In the Oval Room — thirty-five minutes late

century suggested that vice-presidents of the United States were not overworked. I said that if this applied to Vice President Agnew, he might be able to help. This suggestion got a prompt presidential veto (I lacked the two-thirds majority to overrule).

The President said he thought Secretary of Health Caspar Weinberger would be the man for me to see. I told him I had already seen two Secretaries of HEW and found them pretty busy; on average I'd spent an hour apiece with them. This time I had to have enough time to tell the whole story. He asked how long this would take. I said at least two days, at a quiet place away from the telephone. I thought this was shooting for the moon, but the President saw the sense in it. He said he'd make arrangements, that at the moment the Secretary was up to his elbows in some matter, but I would hear from him within thirty days. I thanked the President and took a plane back to New York. Of course it got there two minutes early.

Back home I waited for Secretary Weinberger's call. After four weeks had gone by I began to have Finch flashbacks. But, on the twenty-ninth day, Secretary Weinberger called and made a date to spend the following weekend at Hobeau Farm. Mrs. Weinberger came to the farm with the Secretary and Dr. Bogoch was with me. Over the two days we had four long sessions, during which Dr. Bogoch and I poured information about PHT into the Secretary. Mrs. Weinberger was an interested listener.

Late Sunday we went our separate ways, the Weinbergers to Washington, Dr. Bogoch and I to New York. Caspar said he wanted to cogitate on the matter and would get in touch with me soon. Time went by, more than I'd expected, and I was afraid I had struck a black hole (a semi-anachronism—they were around in those days but who knew). But after two months Secretary Weinberger called and invited me to come to Washington to meet the newly appointed Commissioner of the FDA, Dr. Alexander Mackay Schmidt.

Our meeting was in the office of our friend, Charlie Edwards, who had become assistant head of HEW. Secretary Weinberger was present, but I got the feeling that, not being a physician, he was reluctant to make suggestions of a medical nature to the FDA, and he had asked Dr. Edwards, who knew the subject well, to introduce Dr. Bogoch and me to Dr. Schmidt.

After the introductions we all chatted for a few minutes in Dr. Edwards' office about nothing I can remember. Then Dr. Schmidt and Dr. Bogoch and I went off to another room to have a talk. I assumed, of course, that Dr. Edwards or the Secretary had given Dr. Schmidt the bibliography of the Dreyfus Medical Foundation and a thorough briefing on the nature of our interest in PHT. I was totally unprepared for Dr. Schmidt's opening words, "My number one objective in my new position is to see that the FDA is run in an honest and honorable fashion."

Son-of-a-gun!

After all the years of work with the government it was apparent Dr. Schmidt hadn't even been briefed. I was back at the starting line, with a new Commissioner of the FDA, and the baton hadn't even been passed on.

I considered getting up and going home. But I wasn't delighted with the implications of Dr. Schmidt's opening remark, and I wanted to get that straightened out. I told Dr. Schmidt we were a charitable medical foundation, had no private interest of any sort, but a damned important public one, and that trying to be helpful with our government was getting to be a tiresome job.

Dr. Schmidt's response was a lot nicer than I expected. He said, "Take your time and tell me about it." For the umpteenth time I started telling the story of PHT.

After about an hour Dr. Schmidt said he had an appointment that he couldn't get out of, but he saw how important this was and he intended to pursue it personally. He said of course he knew PHT was more than an anticonvulsant. In fact he had been teaching its use in cardiac arrhythmia since 1969. I said that's just one example of what I'm talking about. "As you know, PHT does not have a listed indication-of-use for arrhythmias." Dr. Schmidt said, "You're mistaken. I'm sure PHT has such a listing." I didn't argue, this not being an opinion but a fact that could be checked. But I said I thought I was right.*

Just before we left, Dr. Schmidt mentioned that he was a specialist in communication. I said, "I've come to believe that communication is just a word in the dictionary, but if there is such a thing, you sure have a good spot to use your specialty."

---

* A week later Dr. Schmidt called to say that it was hard to believe, but PHT did not have a listed indication-of-use for arrhythmias. The head of the Heart and Lung Institute, Dr. Theodore Cooper, had made the same mistake. At our medical conference, he had said, "There is no question of the usefulness of PHT as an antiarrhythmic, and this is an approved indication-of-use in the package insert."

That was years ago. PHT still doesn't have such a listing.

Well, it turned out that Commissioner Schmidt was a gentleman of the old school (an endangered species). Even with the pressures of his new office he kept his promise to look into PHT himself and visited the Foundation twice in the following month. The second time, he spent a full day getting the facts about PHT from Dr. Bogoch and me and even stayed into the evening so we could finish our discussion at dinner. By that time I had a feeling of empathy with Mack, and with the help of a glass of wine, I emptied myself of my feelings on the subject of the great sin of neglect of PHT. Dr. Schmidt understood. Then he said something I'd been hoping to hear from a government official but had given up on. "You've done what you can. Now the ball is in our court."

Well, that was it; there was no more to do. I had been trying to turn the responsibility for PHT over to the U.S. government for ten years. Finally a Commissioner of the FDA had accepted it.

■ ■ ■

Epilogue: Of course I should have figured that a man as sensitive as Mack Schmidt wouldn't last long in government. Five months later he was back at the University of Illinois, and there was a new Commissioner of the FDA.

I have not visited the government since and have no ambition to. That's one reason this book is written. It's for members of the staff and government officials in health, all at the same time. I hope it will make it easier for them to do whatever they think is right.

TRAVELS ABROAD
(England—Italy—Russia)

It's said that the further you get from where they know you the more respect you get. And so it seems.

Before discussing the "flaw in the system," in the next chapter, I would like to tell you of some experiences I've had with PHT abroad, and of an unusual relationship that developed between the Dreyfus Medical Foundation and the Institute for Experimental Medicine in Leningrad.

England

My first trip abroad, on the subject of PHT, was to England in 1965. Soon after Dr. Turner joined the Foundation, he and I went to Chichester, England, to visit a friend of his, Dr. Lionel Haward. At the Graylingwell Hospital in Chichester, Dr. Haward introduced us to a group of his colleagues. We all sat at a large round table and for an hour I described my experiences with PHT. When I finished, to my surprise, they applauded. I know it was just English good manners but it gave me a nice feeling.

As a result of our trip, Dr. Haward did a series of five controlled studies on PHT.* They were excellent studies, three of them unusual in that they were influenced by his background as a pilot. In simulated air control tests, he demonstrated with students and experienced pilots that PHT was significantly effective in delaying fatigue and accompanying errors. Haward made the point that it's an unusual substance that can calm without sedation and also effect a return of energy and improvement in concentration.

Italy

Dr. Rodolfo Paoletti, scientific director of the Institute of Pharmacology at the University of Milan, a friend of Dr. Bogoch's, frequently visited our office when in New York. On several occasions I talked to him about PHT. During one of the times Dr. Paoletti said, "Why don't you come over to Milan and talk about PHT at a meeting of the Giovanni Lorenzini Foundation?" He suggested a date four months in the future and I accepted.

A week before the meeting I found out what I had let myself in for. I was not to be one of many speakers, but the only speaker, before a large group of physicians. I had talked at formal medical meetings before, but only as one of the speakers. This was different.

At the meeting in Milan there were about 120 physicians. Dr. Paoletti gave me a kind introduction, put me on the podium with a microphone attached to me, and told me to speak in my normal way—a UN-type device would see that it came out in Italian. I was close to stage fright, but after I got started it was all right. I talked for an hour and twenty minutes, and apparently it went well because I got a letter from Dr. Paoletti saying, "From the comments I heard afterward you certainly caught everyone's attention," and he invited me to come back the next year.

* See *The Broad Range of Clinical Use of PHT.*

After the meeting a number of physicians came up to say hello, and I learned that PHT was already being used for purposes other than epilepsy. One physician, G. A. Bozza, who seemed an especially kind man, talked to me about his use of PHT with retarded children, a use I was not familiar with. A few months later he sent me his paper, "Normalization of intellectual development in the slightly brain-damaged, retarded child."*

Russia

One day in October 1972, Dr. Bogoch phoned and said he was coming to the office with a Russian doctor he thought I'd like to meet, and that we might have lunch. The doctor was in New York for an International Brain Sciences Conference, of which Dr. Bogoch was chairman. At eleven o'clock that morning Dr. Bogoch arrived in the office with Dr. Natasha Bechtereva. Sam had not overdescribed Dr. Bechtereva when he referred to her as a Russian doctor. Dr. Bechtereva had the most impressive credentials of anyone I've met in the medical profession.

At that time Dr. Bechtereva was chairman of the Commission on Public Health of the USSR. She was also Director of the Institute for Experimental Medicine, formerly the Pavlov Institute, a group of seven large hospitals in Leningrad. Dr. Bechtereva was the first woman to become Director of the Institute and she was Chief of its neurophysiological branch.

I remember our meeting clearly. Dr. Bechtereva, Dr. Bogoch, and I sat in chairs at a window overlooking New York Harbor. I had intended to talk about PHT for half an hour or so and, if Dr. Bechtereva showed interest, give her a copy of *The Broad Range of Use of Phenytoin*. When lunch arrived at one o'clock I was surprised to find that I'd been talking for two hours. Dr. Bechtereva hadn't said a thing, but the patience with which she

* Presented at the Italian National Conference of Child Neuropsychology, 1971.

had listened and something in her remarkable eyes had kept me going.

When I had finished Dr. Bechtereva spoke for the first time. She said, "What you say seems too good to be true but it's not illogical, and I can find out to my own satisfaction. In our Institute we have sensitive electrical equipment that can test PHT. Would you be kind enough to send us a supply of your brand of phenytoin? If our tests should disagree with what you say I wouldn't want you to think it's because our brand is different from yours." That made sense, and I said we would send the Dilantin.

After many difficulties, the Dilantin arrived in Leningrad. Several months later I received a letter from Dr. Bechtereva (mail in those days took about a month—now it's not so rapid). Dr. Bechtereva's electrical instruments had not been disappointed. From the letter:

> Thank you very much for the prospect of Dilantin and the Dilantin itself. The Dilantin—really a most peculiar medicine.
>
> I am advising it to more and more people. I simply can't resist doing it—you know how one feels. And so, step by step, Dilantin is used for nonepileptic purposes, not only in Leningrad but in Moscow and Kiev as well.

Dr. Bechtereva has a refreshing way of putting things. In a later letter she said, "People use Dilantin much more, though it met the normal prejudice determined by the engram fixed in each doctor's memory: Dilantin → epilepsy." Apparently we don't have a monopoly on this engram.

A few months after Dr. Bechtereva started work with PHT, she invited Dr. Bogoch and me to visit the Institute in Leningrad, at our convenience. We accepted. Having heard too much about the Russian winters we selected June for the visit. Four of us made the trip—Dr. Bogoch and his wife Dr. Elenore Bogoch, and Joan Personette, my former wife, and I.

We stayed in Leningrad for a week at the Hotel Astoria, a very old hotel, like the Ritz in Paris, but otherwise dissimilar. But the people were nice, which is the most important thing. When we had time we saw the sights, the beautiful cathedrals and the extraordinary Hermitage, and we walked around Leningrad as we pleased. The days were long. We were near the land of the midnight sun, and it got dark at 11 P.M. and light at 2 A.M. It seemed strange reading by daylight at 10 P.M. in a park across from the Astoria.

Dr. Bechtereva's hospitality was reminiscent of our best Southern hospitality. We had a delicious dinner at her home with her family, were taken out to dinner by her, and thought-fully left to ourselves. The food in the restaurants was good, if you like garlic, which I don't. On one occasion, out to dinner with Dr. Bechtereva, I was trying to finesse my way around the meat and Natasha said, "My dear Jack, you suffer so much." A keen observer.

The first day we were in Leningrad, Dr. Bechtereva took the Drs. Bogoch and me to one of the seven hospitals and intro-duced us to key members of her staff. Later we went through other hospitals, getting to meet many doctors. I was surprised that so many of the doctors were women until I was told that 70 percent of physicians in Russia are women.

The second day we were there, Dr. Bechtereva introduced us to three patients who'd had dramatic benefits from PHT. Each had a different disorder. The patient I remember best was a woman who'd had severe headaches for many years and had to be hospitalized periodically. This time she had taken Dilantin for a few days and was on her way home. She explained, through an interpreter, that the pain in her head would get so bad she'd sit absolutely still and if anyone came near her it would make her furious. While she was explaining this in Russian, she was smil-ing happily, as though she were talking about someone else.

The next day Dr. Bechtereva called a meeting and Dr. Bogoch

and I had the opportunity to talk about PHT to eighty physicians. I talked for about two hours. That was like talking one hour because translation was not simultaneous. Then Dr. Bogoch discussed the basic mechanisms of action. Several of the Institute's physicians also addressed the group. I was told that they had given favorable reports on PHT.

The day before we left, Dr. Bechtereva and I were alone for a few moments and I brought up what I considered a delicate subject. I told her that I was most impressed with the work the Institute had done. I said our Foundation had funded numerous studies on PHT, some outside the U.S.A., and, if proper, we would be happy to do it here. Natasha set me at ease. She said she appreciated my asking but that her Institute was well financed by the government. However, we might consider a "joint cooperative effort." She said such a possibility was provided for in the recent meeting between President Nixon and Premier Brezhnev.

I thought this a fine idea and asked how we should proceed. Dr. Bechtereva said since we had introduced the PHT idea it would be best if we initiated the matter through our Department of Health to their Ministry of Health. We discussed it. Our thought was that we'd exchange ideas and information by mail, and would periodically visit each other. It was agreed that when I got back to New York I would introduce the matter to our Department of Health.

I won't bore you with details. The mills of government grind slowly all over the world. But in 1976, a formal approval was given for a "joint cooperative effort" between the Institute for Experimental Medicine and the Dreyfus Medical Foundation. I have been told that this is the only venture of its sort between a Russian and an American institution.

Before closing I'd like to say that Natasha Bechtereva is one of the most remarkable persons I've ever met, and I thank her for her help.

A FLAW IN THE SYSTEM
Parke-Davis—the Physician—the FDA

A medicine can get overlooked for a million years if no one discovers it. But can the benefits of a discovered medicine get overlooked for decades when thousands of studies have demonstrated its usefulness? The answer is it can.

We have a flaw in our system of bringing prescription medicines to the public. That there's a flaw is no surprise. We're human and all our systems have flaws. But this particular flaw should be explained. It has acted like a barrier between the American public and a great medicine.

■ ■ ■

From drug company, through FDA, to physician—that's the route a prescription medicine takes to get to the public. That's our system. It was not set up by anyone, it just evolved. But we're used to it; it has become custom. And as Mark Twain said, custom is like iron.

Years ago doctors concocted their own medicines—and leeches outsold aspirins. But for the last century the business of pharmaceuticals has been in the hands of the drug companies.

Drug companies, formed for the purpose of making money for shareholders, are not charged with a responsibility to the public that is not consistent with making money. That is not to suggest that drug companies are not interested in public welfare but they are not charged with a responsibility for it.

In 1938 the FDA was empowered to protect us against medical substances more dangerous than therapeutic. Since that time drug companies have been required to get approval as to safety of a new chemical entity and, since 1962, approval as to its effectiveness. Although the neglect of a great drug can be far more deadly than the use of a bad one, correcting such neglect does not appear to be a function of the FDA.

When a drug company synthesizes a compound which it believes to be therapeutic, it's brought to the FDA. If the drug satisfies that agency's requirements, the company is awarded a "listed indication-of-use," which permits it to market the drug. Getting FDA approval is time-consuming and expensive; it has been estimated, on average, to take seven years and to cost $11 million. (Today, the estimate of cost is far greater.)

Drug companies patent their new compounds. Patents give the company exclusive rights for seventeen years. If the FDA approves a drug and it becomes popular, the drug company has a winner since the drug will sell at a high price for the life of the patent.* However, when the patent expires, competition enters the picture and the price of the drug drops dramatically. At that point there is more financial incentive for the drug company to look for a new drug to patent than to look for new uses of an old drug.

FDA approval is the second of the three steps in our system. The third step is to introduce of the drug to the physician. This is a function of the drug company and is done through

---

*This is reasonable; a drug that is a winner has to pay for the research that went into it, the expense of getting FDA approval, and for money spent on the many drugs that are not successful.

advertisements in trade journals and by visits of their salesmen to physicians.

That is the system—and physicians have come to depend on it. If a doctor doesn't hear from a drug company about new uses for an old medicine, the doctor infers there aren't such uses. This is a reasonable inference. But in the case of PHT it's wrong.

So this is the flaw in the system. When a drug company doesn't do what is expected of it, and the FDA can't or doesn't do anything about it, the physician doesn't get vital information. And, as in this case, a great drug can get overlooked.

Parke-Davis

Parke-Davis's research did not discover PHT. The company bought the compound from a chemist in 1909. For twenty-nine years this remarkable drug sat on the shelf doing nobody any good. Then Putnam and Merritt, two physicians outside the company, discovered its first therapeutic use. Parke-Davis paid almost nothing in money for PHT. They paid less in brains for PHT.

Still, were it not for Parke-Davis we might not have PHT today. Someone in the company did buy the compound, and someone else in the company did give it to Putnam and Merritt for trial. It should also be said, to its credit, that Parke-Davis has been consistent in manufacturing a good product.

■ ■ ■

It is not easy to understand how a drug company can overlook its own product. An outline of my own experience with Parke-Davis may help.

In 1966, as Secretary Gardner had recommended, I made contact with Parke-Davis. I phoned the company and spoke to the president, Mr. H. W. Burrows. I told him of Secretary Gardner's recommendation that I speak to Parke-Davis, and supposed that would arouse his interest. But as I talked I didn't hear the noises one expects from an interested listener. To get his attention I said, "Look, I've spent $400,000 on your medicine and I don't want anything for myself, I just want to tell Parke-Davis about it." That got Mr. Burrows' attention. He said, "I wouldn't know anything about this, I'm just a bookkeeper."

That startling statement was my introduction to Parke-Davis. President Burrows said he would have someone get in touch with me. Two months later I got a call from Dr. Leon Sweet of Parke-Davis's research department. He was calling at Mr. Burrows' suggestion and made a date to meet with me in New York.

We met at my home. Dr. Sweet brought Dr. E. C. Vonder Heide with him. Dr. Turner was with me. Dr. Sweet said that Parke-Davis's recent head of research, Dr. Alain Sanseigne, had left the company a few months earlier to go to Squibb, and Dr. Vonder Heide, a former head of research now retired, had come along to be helpful.

Dr. Turner and I talked at length about the overlooked uses of PHT. Dr. Vonder Heide said it didn't surprise him that PHT was more than an anticonvulsant. In fact Parke-Davis had had numerous reports that Dilantin helped with alcohol and drug addiction. He said that he had tried to get doctors to conduct studies in this field without success. He was rather critical of the doctors. I remember thinking, What's going on here? The doctors depend on Parke-Davis to do something, and Parke-Davis depends on the doctors to do something. This is an interesting game of tag, and the public is "it."

I didn't realize till years later what a poor excuse Dr. Vonder Heide had given. Many research-minded doctors had already done a great deal, and at that time, 1966, Parke-Davis's files were stocked with a variety of clinical studies on PHT. Yet apparently neither Dr. Vonder Heide nor Dr. Sweet had heard of them. It seemed Parke-Davis's research department and its filing department were not acquainted with each other.

Our next contact with Parke-Davis came a few weeks later when we had a visit from a friendly gentleman, Dr. Charles F. Weiss. Dr. Weiss explained that he was a pediatrician and didn't know anything about PHT, but had come to see us because he'd been asked to. He offered the opinion that Parke-Davis was a little disorganized. He said he wished some company would take them over. Well, he got his wish—but not for six years. Today the company is a subsidiary of Warner Lambert.

When Warner Lambert took over in 1971, Mr. J. D. Williams became president of the Parke-Davis division. I felt I should bring the matter of PHT to the attention of the new management, and had several discussions on the telephone with Mr. Williams. The talks were friendly but not useful in furthering the PHT cause. On one occasion Mr. Williams expressed a thought I'd heard from Parke-Davis before, that since we were working on their product, it might be better if we stayed apart—some notion that the FDA might like it better. I couldn't understand this—I was sure the FDA would want a drug company to know all it could about its own product.

But such is life. An item in the *Arizona Republic* (at the time I retired from Wall Street in 1970) will give the picture. The paper reported Dr. Joseph Sadusk, vice-president for Medical and Scientific Research of Parke-Davis, to have said that the Dreyfus Medical Foundation is doing "an excellent job" in investigating PHT. As a result he said Parke-Davis has made only "a minimal effort" in this area of research. "Results from an unbiased third party like Dreyfus," he said, "would mean more to the Food and Drug Administration."

I appreciate compliments. But the division of labor seemed uneven. The Dreyfus Medical Foundation should do the research, influence the FDA—and Parke-Davis should make the profits.

There appears to have been only one person who, while passing through Parke-Davis, got a good grasp of PHT. That was Dr.

Alain Sanseigne, head of research before Dr. Sweet. Dr. Turner brought PHT to Dr. Sanseigne's attention. Dr. Sanseigne graciously acknowledged this in a letter to Dr. Turner in which he said, "Your very thorough knowledge of Dilantin put me to shame."

Once his attention had been directed to PHT, Dr. Sanseigne, in 1965, reviewed its pharmacology, site of activity, and therapeutic activity.* It's an impressive review, and it refers only to information on PHT available over twenty years ago. There are no signs that this review stirred Parke-Davis.

When Dr. Joseph Sadusk said Parke-Davis's efforts had been "minimal" he selected the right word. I know this from first-hand experience. A few years ago Mr. Williams changed his mind about Parke-Davis staying apart from our Foundation and graciously arranged for three members of the research staff to meet with us on the subject of Parke-Davis's Dilantin package insert. (This package insert will be discussed later.)

At this meeting, I met the senior research officer of Parke-

---

* From Dr. Sanseigne's review:
  The Parke-Davis Medical Brochure includes as indications of Dilantin the following:

Epilepsy	Migraine
Chorea	Trigeminal neuralgia
Parkinson syndrome	Psychosis

The following indications...have been studied and seem to show considerable therapeutic response to treatment with PHT:

Cardiac arrhythmia	Wound-healing acceleration
Neurosis	Polyneuritis of pregnancy
Behavioral disorders in adolescents	Tabetic lancinating pain
Myotonia	Pruritus ani
Diabetes insipidus	Asthma

The following are indications on which the possibility of favorable response to PHT should be investigated:

Prophylaxis and treatment of cerebral anoxia (carbon monoxide poisoning and other asphyxiation, precardiac and pulmonary surgery)	Wilson's disease
	Poorly controlled diabetes
	Cicatrization of oral surgery
	Osteogenesis imperfecta
	Conditions related to hypothalamus

Davis. When we finished our discussion he mentioned that the FDA had not approved Parke-Davis's application for the use of PHT in cardiac arrhythmias. The reason, he said, was that the company did not supply cardiograms requested by an individual in the FDA. The research officer said, "We could get them for $100,000 but why spend the money, all the cardiologists are using PHT anyway." I won't take sides in this hassle between the FDA and Parke-Davis. There was foolishness to spare.* But you'd think Parke-Davis would have considered it a privilege to spend the $100,000.

A few weeks after this, a physician applied to our Foundation for a modest grant ($6,000). He had done interesting preliminary work on the use of PHT as a protection against brain damage after cardiac arrest. We intended to make the grant, but it occurred to me that the new Parke-Davis management might appreciate the opportunity. I called my new acquaintance, the research officer, and asked him about it. It didn't surprise me that I was told no. It did surprise me how quickly I got the answer, on the phone, without consideration of the matter. The senior officer explained that Parke-Davis was spending its research moneys on a new medicine the company hoped to patent. I thought there will be snow on the Devil's roof before they came up with as good a medicine as Dilantin. But I got the point—patents on Dilantin had expired.

Well, to sum up, Parke-Davis got Dilantin by luck. They didn't understand their own product, have done little to try to understand it, and haven't spent a bean in furthering its understanding. This has contributed to the overlooking of PHT.

But let's see Parke-Davis in perspective. There's no Mr. Parke, no Mr. Davis—just an entity with those names. Since Parke-Davis did not get PHT by the sweat of its research there was none of the interest in the drug that would be found in a com-

---

* PHT is so widely used for cardiac arrhythmias that AMA Drug Evaluations has it in the category of antiarrhythmic agents.

pany that had developed its own product. As a result, new uses for PHT was a job never assigned to anyone and no one took it upon himself. It has been easy to cuss Parke-Davis, the entity, but not the people. In fact I've never met anyone at the company I didn't like.

■ ■ ■

About Parke-Davis's Dilantin package insert.

I was weaned on the Securities Exchange Commission. The SEC is a fiend for full disclosure—the positive as well as the negative. If Parke-Davis operated under SEC regulations the SEC would have the company in court for the rest of the century because of the great amount of positive data that's not disclosed in its package insert.

But Parke-Davis operates under FDA regulations. Apparently full disclosure is required on the negative side, but no disclosure is permitted when the evidence is positive, unless it has an FDA listed indication-of-use. No matter how flimsy the evidence for the negative, it must be disclosed. No matter how solid the positive evidence, it may not be mentioned. It seems a poor way to run a railroad.

An example of inexplicable illogic. For some years prior to 1972, Parke-Davis's package insert made reference to a number of the uses of PHT other than epilepsy. In 1971 the insert stated: "Dilantin is also useful in the treatment of conditions such as chorea and Parkinson's syndrome and is employed in the treatment of migraine, trigeminal neuralgia and certain psychoses." In 1972 reference to these uses was deleted, although the evidence for their use had been substantially increased.

Unfathomable. I don't know whether this was the fault of Parke-Davis or the FDA. But an innocent public has suffered.

The Physician

A physician's remedy of the eighteenth century from *A Majestic Literary Fossil* by Mark Twain.

> **Aqua Limacum.** Take a great Peck of Garden-snails, and wash them in a great deal of Beer, and make your Chimney very clean, and set a Bushel of Charcoal on Fire; and when they are thoroughly kindled, make a Hole in the Middle of the Fire, and put the Snails in, and scatter more Fire amongst them, and let them roast till they make a Noise; then take them out, and, with a Knife and coarse Cloth, pick and wipe away all the green froth: Then break them, Shells and all, in a Stone Mortar. Take also a Quart of Earthworms, and scour them with Salt, divers times over. Then take two Handfuls of Angelica and lay them in the Bottom of the Still; next lay two Handfuls of Celandine; next a Quart of Rosemary-flowers; then two Handfuls of Bearsfoot and Agrimony; then Fenugreek, then Turmerick; of each one Ounce: Red Dock-root, Bark of Barberry-trees, Wood-sorrel, Betony, of each two Handfuls. Then lay the Snails and Worms on top of the Herbs; and then two Handfuls of Goose Dung, and two Handfuls of Sheep Dung. Then put in three Gallons of Strong Ale, and place the pot where you mean to set Fire under it: Let it stand all Night, or longer; in the Morning put in three ounces of Cloves well beaten, and a small Quantity of Saffron, dry'd to Powder; then six Ounces of Shavings of Hartshorn, which must be uppermost. Fix on the Head and Refrigeratory, and distil according to Art.

Serve with a shovel, no doubt—Mark T.

I had taken PHT for about a year when I started talking to doctors about it. These were informal talks and occurred when chance brought me together with physicians, as at a dinner or in a locker room. I must have spoken to more than twenty doctors during that early period. None of them had heard of PHT being used for anything other than epilepsy. The discussions were friendly, but it was almost impossible to get a physician interested in the subject of PHT. I thought this was because, as a Wall Street man, I was an improbable source of medical fact.

But my lack of credentials was the smallest part of the communication problem. In the physicians' minds there was the fixed notion that PHT was just an anticonvulsant. They had been taught this in school, the "knowledge" had been in their heads for a long time, and had calcified. Don't pick on the physician. Calcification of ideas is a human trait not special to him.

There was an even bigger obstacle—the sure knowledge the physician had that if Dilantin had as many uses as I said it had, they would have heard about them from Parke-Davis. After all, Dilantin was their product, wasn't it? And they wanted to make money, didn't they? This "irrefutable logic" always defeated me. If I tried to explain, time would run out before we could get back to PHT.

There's been a recent trend to knock the doctor. I think it's a reaction to the pedestal position we had him in a decade ago. We learned from "Dr. Kildare" and "Marcus Welby, M.D." that there are two physicians to every patient. In real life this isn't so. Doctors rarely make house calls anymore. They can see three patients in the office for one in the home—and still it's hard to get an appointment. Don't blame the doctor. It's the ecologists' fault—they've allowed the spread of *Homo sapiens* to get out of hand.

When you are giving a member of the medical profession a hard time (in your head of course—who would dare do it in person), consider that the doctor's day never ends. Sick people don't care what time it is, and the doctor has to go around with a beeper attached to him or be in constant touch with his telephone service. This means twenty-four hours' tension. We complain about what the doctor doesn't do. But do we appreciate the things he does that we wouldn't do?

■ ■ ■

We come to an important subject: medical literature. Medical studies are called literature (Shakespeare might demur) when they're published in a medical journal or as part of the record of a medical conference.

There is a great deal of this literature. You could wallpaper the world with it and have enough left over to do your kitchen. The notion that physicians know what's contained in the literature is bizarre. But some of them sound like they half believe they do. If you ask a physician a question he can't answer, don't be surprised if he responds, "Nobody knows." Which seems to suggest he has read all the literature and has total recall.

It's estimated that there are 3,300 medical journals in the world. A poll in seventeen counties of upstate New York (not exactly the boondocks) showed that the average physician subscribed to 4.1 of these journals. Double this figure if you like. Even if he read the 8.2 journals cover to cover, he would still be 3,291.8 journals short. You can see it's impossible to expect the physician to read the medical literature to determine which drugs he should use. That's why, in this day of specialization, this is left to the drug companies and the FDA.

However, when a physician gets a new idea about an approved drug, he may apply it.* But the opportunity doesn't come up often. Usually new uses of a drug are well explored by the drug company that introduced it. PHT has been a marked exception, and a rare opportunity was presented to the physicians.

The medical profession did not fail us. The work of thousands of physicians has given us a rich literature on PHT. This literature, international in scope, covers a wide variety of medical disciplines. Published in many languages over a period of years, it is spread far and wide. But intermingled with millions

---

* Former FDA Commissioner Charles C. Edwards states: "Once the new drug is in a local pharmacy, the physician may, as part of the practice of medicine...vary the conditions of use from those approved in the package insert, without obtaining approval of the FDA." *The Federal Register,* Vol. 37, No. 158, Aug. 15, 1972. This was clearly restated in the April, 1982, FDA *Drug Bulletin.*

of other studies, this literature is almost lost unless someone seeks it out.

The science fiction writer Robert Heinlein calls it the Crisis of the Librarian:

> The greatest crisis facing us is not Russia, not the Atom Bomb...It is a crisis in the organization and accessibility of human knowledge. We own an enormous "encyclopedia" which isn't even arranged alphabetically. Our "file cards" are spilled on the floor, nor were they ever in order. The answers we want may be buried somewhere in the heap....

Let me give you an example of how difficult it would be, even in a single field, for a physician to be acquainted with the literature on PHT. Disorders in the field have many names. A general description of the field is uncontrolled muscle movement, or continuous muscle fiber activity.

To illustrate the point, we made up a table of twenty-one published studies on this subject in 1975.* These studies show dramatic recovery in intractable patients when given PHT. In many of the cases myogram readings (electrical muscle recordings) confirmed the clinical observations. The difficulty an individual physician would have in becoming acquainted with this work is shown by the following:

The studies were published in eight different countries, in sixteen different journals—*Journal of Neurology, Neurosurgery and Psychiatry, Lancet, The Practitioner, South African Medical Journal, Klinische Wochenschrift, Arquivos de Neuro-Psiquiatria, Acta Neurologica, Proceedings of the Australian Association of Neurologists, Ceskolovenska Neurologie, Connecticut Medicine, Neurology, Archives of Neurology, New York State Journal of Medicine, California Medicine,* and *New England Journal of Medicine.*

---

* Since then many more studies have been published, see *The Broad Range of Clinical Use of PHT.*

In only two of the twenty-one studies was the word phenytoin used in the title. The other studies were published under such dissimilar titles that Scotland Yard couldn't have found them, without the key word phenytoin.

Some members of the medical profession have prescribed PHT for a variety of purposes for many years. The breadth of its use has been more than might be imagined. IMS America Ltd. surveys the use of thousands of drugs. For their estimate of the many clinical conditions for which physicians are using PHT, see Appendix, p. 319.

One might draw the conclusion from the IMS America survey that the medical profession knows all about PHT. But this is not the case. Many physicians know of one or several uses of PHT. Few have an overall picture of the drug. Thus we have a strange situation. Dr. Jones prescribes PHT for depression. Dr. Smith uses it for migraine. Dr. Hemplewaith for trigeminal neuralgia. But, if a patient asks Dr. Snodgrass if he could try PHT for any of these purposes, he may get ushered from the office with the admonishment that PHT is only for epilepsy.

The right of a physician to prescribe whatever drug he wants is fundamental. But in making his decision he should have a reasonable amount of evidence on which to base his judgment. A reasonable amount of information has not been available to the physician, at least not from the expected source, the drug company. The information has been there, but it's been hidden in millions of medical papers, like trees in a forest.

When physicians know more about PHT they will realize they have been imposed on by the system and deprived of a remarkable therapeutic tool.

The FDA

This is not going to be a treatise on the Food and Drug Administration. I haven't the facts or the desire to write such a treatise.

The FDA is in this book because of its relation to PHT.

The FDA was established, in the best tradition of good government, to help American citizens in matters of health, in ways they can't help themselves. But it was conceived as a defensive unit. If it were a football team it would have six tackles and five guards, and no one to carry the ball. All that was expected of the FDA was defense—to protect us from dangerous substances and unwarranted claims of effectiveness.

Understandably the founding fathers of the FDA presumed that the drug companies, with their profit incentives, would furnish the offense. It could hardly have entered their minds that a drug company would leave a great medicine "lying around." Nor would they have been able to figure out how to equip the FDA against such an eventuality unless the FDA were put into the drug business, which is a far cry from the original premise—and is not being recommended here.

The FDA has done nothing about PHT. That is to be expected when a drug company doesn't play its role. Unfortunately this does not leave the FDA in a neutral position. Through no fault of the FDA's, PHT's narrow listing has a negative effect. Absence of FDA approval is thought of by many as FDA disapproval—or at the least that something is lacking. The system of drug company through FDA to physician has become such a routine that the physician, with other things on his mind, waits for the system to bring him PHT. It's been a long wait.

The real purpose in establishing the FDA was to improve the health and well-being of the citizens of the United States. The neglect of a great drug certainly falls into that category. If a man were drowning and a doctor was prepared to throw him a life preserver that had more lead than cork, the FDA would say, "Hold it! That thing might hit him and kill him, and even if it doesn't it can't help him." Nice work, FDA. But suppose the FDA knew there was a good life preserver under a tree, which the doctor didn't see. Shouldn't they say, "Try that one, Doc." Of course they should.

It is not suggested that the FDA go into the drug business. It is more than suggested, in this extraordinary case, where thousands of physicians have furnished us with many times the evidence required to get approval of a new drug (keep in mind this drug has been approved for comparative safety and has stood the test of over forty years of use), that the FDA should no longer take a hands-off policy. It's a sure thing our public shouldn't suffer any longer because Parke-Davis stayed in bed after Rip Van Winkle got up.

Let us understand the magnitude of what we're talking about. The non-use of PHT has been a catastrophe. We are not accustomed to thinking of the non-use of a medicine as a catastrophe. We think of a catastrophe as a flood, a famine, or an earthquake. Something tangible, overt, something in the positive tense. But something passive, such as the non-use of a great medicine that can prevent suffering and prolong lives, is also a catastrophe.

Something must be done. How it is done is for the government to decide. But here is a suggestion. It would seem a waste of time, and thus to the disadvantage of the American public, for the FDA to attempt to approve the many clinical uses of PHT separately. That could take forever. It would be far simpler for the FDA to address itself to the basic mechanisms of action and give PHT a listed indication-of-use as a stabilizer of bioelectrical activity, or as a membrane stabilizer. Certainly the published evidence for this is overwhelming. Such a listing would stimulate the physician to think of clinical applications of PHT and to refer to the existing medical literature.

Even a nod from the FDA to the physician would help. It could take the form of a letter to the physician, calling attention to the literature of his colleagues, and reminding him that since PHT has been approved for safety he is permitted to use it for whatever purposes his judgment suggests. Certainly the FDA would never try to tell the doctor how he should use PHT. That's always the doctor's decision. But such a letter would lift the cloud of negativism, and the physician would get an unobstructed view of PHT and the work of his colleagues.

I'm sure the problem-agriculturists will say that if the FDA takes any action in this matter it will set a precedent. Fine. Good. If this happens again, if another established drug is found useful for fifty or more disorders by thousands of physicians, then the FDA should take this as a precedent.

Every once in a while, routine or no routine, a little common sense should be permitted. This is an extraordinary matter, vital to our health. If the FDA was set up to help the American public, here's a chance to do something great for them—with no one's feelings hurt except routine's.

OBSERVATIONS ON PHT—
EXPLORATION OF POSSIBLE NEW USES

It used to be that the word drug had a solid respectable meaning. But in recent years drug and abuse have been put together in the same sentence so often, without discrimination, that the word drug has come into disrepute. It's confusing, and a shame. Today people brag, just before they ascend, "I never took a drug in my life." As if St. Peter cared.

Good drugs are a cheerful feature of our society. We should stop tarring them with the same brush we use on the bad ones and be grateful for them. With this general comment off my chest I would like to make some observations about PHT.

■ ■ ■

PHT would appear to be the most broadly useful drug in our pharmacopoeia (unless another is hidden in the literature). Paradoxically, this valuable feature, this versatility, has interfered with our understanding of the drug. The idea that one substance can have as many uses as PHT has been difficult to accept. And this is understandable. Not too long ago the thinking was a single drug for a single disorder.

A discussion of the basic mechanisms of action of PHT will help us understand how one drug can have so many uses.

A basic mechanism of action study was the first study to demonstrate that PHT might be a therapeutic substance. In 1938 Putnam and Merritt tested PHT on cats in which convulsions were induced by electricity. Of a large group of substances, including the best-known anticonvulsants, it was the most effective in controlling the convulsions. Putnam and Merritt said, Eureka! Maybe we have a superior antiepileptic drug.

They did. And not only was PHT the most effective anticonvulsant but it was found to have another remarkable property. Unlike previously used substances it achieved its therapy without sedation.

Let's go back to Putnam and Merritt's original study and apply hindsight. Suppose, instead of inferring that PHT would help the epileptic, Putnam and Merritt had drawn a broader inference from their data. Suppose they had inferred that PHT worked against inappropriate electrical activity. That also would have been a correct inference—but with far broader implications. And the properties of PHT would not have been obscured by the label "anticonvulsant." Today basic mechanism scientists use broad terminology for PHT. They refer to it as a membrane stabilizer.

From the early basic mechanisms study of Toman, in 1949, PHT has been found to correct inappropriate electrical activity in groups of cells, and in individual cells. This includes nerve cells, brain cells, muscle cells—in fact, all types of cells that exhibit marked electrical activity. Whether a cell is made hyperexcitable by electrical impulse, calcium withdrawal, oxygen withdrawal, or by poisons, PHT has been shown to counteract this excitability. Further, it has been demonstrated that, in amounts that correct abnormal cell function, PHT does not affect normal function.*

When we understand that PHT is a substance that stabilizes the

---

* See *The Broad Range of Clinical Use of PHT*—Basic Mechanisms of Action.

hyperactive cell, without affecting normal cell function, we see its therapeutic potential in the human body, a machine that runs on electrical impulse. It is estimated that there are a trillion cells in the body, tens of billions in the brain alone. Thinking is an electrical process, the rhythms of the heart are electrically regulated, the rhythms of the gut are electrically regulated, muscle movement is electrically regulated, messages of pain are electrically referred, and more.

It's important to know that after a cell has been stimulated to fire a few times it becomes potentiated, easier to fire than a normal cell. This is called post-tetanic potentiation. If the stimulation is continued, the cell starts to fire on its own, and continues to fire until its energy is depleted—post-tetanic afterdischarge. PHT has a modifying effect on post-tetanic potentiation and a correcting effect on post-tetanic afterdischarge. This may account for PHT's therapeutic effect on persistent and repetitive thinking and on unnecessary repetitive messages of pain.

■ ■ ■

PHT has a number of properties that set it apart from most substances. For ten distinctive characteristics see *The Broad Range of Clinical Use of PHT*, p. 306. For purposes here we should consider several of these properties.

PHT is a nonhabit-forming substance.* The desirability of a nonhabit-forming drug that can calm and also relieve pain is apparent—it may be particularly useful during withdrawal from habit-forming substances.

PHT, in therapeutic amounts, has a calming effect without being a sedative. This characteristic is unusual, and clinical observations, supported by basic mechanisms studies, show that

---

* This is *not* to be confused with the well-known fact that a person with epilepsy should *not* abruptly discontinue PHT.

PHT does not affect normal function. Not only does PHT not sedate but it has been shown to improve concentration and effect a return of energy. This can be attributed, at least in part, to the fact that an overactive brain (hyperexcitable cells) wastes energy compounds.* One can conjecture that when thoughts with negative emotions are diminished, the effect of these "down" emotions is eliminated, and "psychic" energy may return.

Now that preventive medicine is being given more and more consideration, PHT may be of special interest because of its general properties and its versatility.

PHT, as do other drugs, has side effects. Safety and Toxicology of PHT is reviewed in *The Broad Range of Clinical Use of PHT.* A replication of Parke-Davis's package insert is included in the *Physicians' Desk Reference.* It should be noted that PHT is not on the government's list of Controlled Drugs.

PHT can be used on a regular basis or on an occasional basis by the nonepileptic—depending on need. In the nonepileptic, effective doses tend to be lower than those used for epilepsy. The reader is reminded that PHT is a prescription drug and should be obtained from a physician.

■ ■ ■

When the Dreyfus Medical Foundation was preparing *The Broad Range of Use of Phenytoin,* in 1970, there were many published studies to draw on—1,900 by the time of publication. Seven hundred and fifty references were selected and over 300 of them were summarized. These summaries were presented

---

* PHT has been shown to increase energy compounds in the brain. See *The Broad Range of Clinical Use of PHT*—Basic Mechanisms of Action.

chronologically in order to show in sequence how the information about PHT developed.

Five years later when *PHT, 1975* was published, there were more than twice the number of studies to review, and the interrelationship between the clinical effects and basic mechanisms of action of PHT was in better perspective. In this bibliography the medical material was arranged according to subject matter for the convenience of the reader. Examples of this are found under such headings as Stabilization of Bioelectrical Activity, Anti-anoxic Effects, Antitoxic Effects, Treatment of Pain, and others.

As an instance, under Anti-anoxic Effects of PHT, ten studies are grouped.* They were published in nine different journals, over a span of twenty years. Each of them is interesting but, by itself, would not carry much weight. But when these studies are reviewed together, the evidence that PHT has an offsetting effect against oxygen lack in animals is highly significant.

These basic studies furnish rationale for the clinical findings first made by Shulman in 1942, *New England Journal of Medicine,* that PHT is effective in asthma—and other studies in asthma, by Sayer and Polvan, *Lancet* (1968), and Shah, Vora, Karkhanis, and Talwalkar, *Indian Journal of Chest Diseases* (1970).** They also furnish rationale for exploration of new uses.

■ ■ ■

Exploration of Possible New Uses

Since Putnam and Merritt's discoveries in 1938 that phenytoin was a therapeutic substance, a steadily increasing number of uses for it

---

* This was in 1975. In the present Bibliography, there are forty-one studies.
** The latter authors give an additional rationale, PHT's potential usefulness against the paroxysmal outbursts of asthma by its ability to stop post-tetanic after discharge.

have been found. The probabilities are high that there are more to come. Evidence from existing clinical and basic mechanisms of action studies furnishes clues for further exploration.

PHT has been reported effective in a wide variety of severely painful conditions. Its usefulness as a nonhabit-forming analgesic in many forms of pain has been established.*

The antianoxic effects of PHT point to its possible usefulness in stroke, emphysema, shock, and, in fact, in any condition where oxygen lack is a problem.

There are a number of references in the literature to beneficial effects of PHT on hypertension. Recently, in a study of mildly hypertensive patients, treatment with PHT was reported effective.** Further study of PHT in hypertension, both by itself and in combination with hypertensive drugs, seems indicated.

A use of PHT that has received little attention, and that may have great potential, is its use topically, for the treatment of pain and for the promotion of healing.

Systemic PHT has been reported useful in healing in a variety of disorders—in leg ulcers, stomach ulcers, scleroderma, pruritus ani, and epidermolysis bullosa.†

Since the foregoing was written, there has been substantial evidence from at least four countries that, used topically, PHT is rapidly effective against the pain of burns, ulcers, wounds and other surface conditions, and that it speeds healing time. In recent years, its effectiveness against intractable ulcers of leprosy has been established.

Other areas of investigation will suggest themselves to physicians.

---

* See *The Broad Range of Clinical Use of PHT*, Treatment of Pain.
** See de la Torre, Murgia-Suarez and Aldrete, *The Broad Range of Clinical Use of PHT*, Cardiovascular Disorders.
† See *The Broad Range of Clinical Use of PHT*, Healing.

THE ONE-HOUR TEST

When the *Life* and *Reader's Digest* articles were published in 1967, there began a steady flow of people to the Dreyfus Medical Foundation. Many were struck by the similarity of the symptoms they had to symptoms I'd had, as described in the articles, and wanted to talk to me about it. After they'd gotten a prescription I had the opportunity to talk with many of these people before they took their first PHT. These talks were beneficial to both of us—informative for them and educational for me.

I haven't kept exact count—no study as such was being done—but over the years I've talked with over two thousand persons before and after they've taken PHT. As a result of these talks, a test evolved. The test is in two parts. The first part deals with somatic conditions and is outlined at the end of this chapter. The second part deals with the effects of PHT on thoughts and emotions—in an explicit way. Because it differs from other tests, I will discuss it in some detail.

■ ■ ■

While I was in the depression, described earlier in this book, my brain was busy with thoughts I wanted to turn off but couldn't. These thoughts were invariably unhappy ones, mostly associated with fear, sometimes with anger. My brain worked on its own. It paid little attention to the landlord, I hesitate to use the word owner. When I took PHT this symptom disappeared, and I had an insight (in the literal sense) into the effects of PHT on thoughts and emotions. In those days I thought of this symptom as the "turned-on mind." It still seems an appropriate description and I will use it or the initials TOM.*

The turned-on mind is a symptom that most of us will identify with. Let me describe what I mean by it. We're told that we're always thinking about something. But "always thinking" can be misleading. There's a great difference between normal cerebration and abnormal. For example: You sit in the park relaxed, listening to the birds, enjoying the trees, and smelling the grass. Beautiful, and healthy. Or, you sit in the park and your mind is so busy you're not even aware of the birds or the trees or the grass. This might be because you have a real problem. But if you don't have a real problem, then it's the turned-on mind.

My first opportunity to observe the TOM closely was in the Worcester Jail study. Its effects were clear. The brains of the prisoners were so overactive that concentration was impaired. This interfered with reading. The subjects would see the words, but thoughts would intrude and they couldn't absorb what they read. They couldn't even remember what they'd seen on TV. The prisoners made it clear that their turned-on minds were busy with thoughts connected with the emotions of anger and fear. Obviously, with these emotions predominant, their mood was poor.

Subsequent experience showed that the TOM is a common complaint with most of the people who need PHT. For years my

* I dislike making initials out of phrases but it's been the vogue since WW II.

only way of ascertaining this was by the straightforward question, "Do you have any thoughts now, other than what we are talking about, that you can't turn off?" Answers were usually in the affirmative. I got replies such as "I can't stop thinking for a minute," "My mind is like a five-ring circus," "My brain is going around and around." And similar comments. An hour after 100 mg of PHT, the same question got a different response. It was apparent that the overthinking had quieted and the mood had improved. But the change couldn't be measured. I would have liked to have had a more objective test.

One day I was talking to a young woman before she took her first 100 mg of PHT, and asked the standard question, "Is your brain busy with thoughts you can't turn off?" She said, "Oh yes, a lot of them." Something in the way she answered made me ask, "How many?" She said about fourteen. "Fourteen?" I said, and challengingly asked if she could write them down. I gave her pencil and pad and almost without pause she wrote down twelve thoughts. I was astonished that she could locate these thoughts and write them down. It didn't occur to me to ask her questions about the thoughts.

An hour after PHT I again asked if she could write down her thoughts. She said she could—this time there were just two. One of them was, "I am angry with my mother." Earlier, she had written, "I am very, very angry with my mother." With PHT her mother was two very's better off.

The following day I met with a man I'd known for several years. Jim was thirty-five and had a lot going for him. But he said he was depressed. PHT had been prescribed and he wanted to talk with me before taking it.

These were Jim's circumstances as he related them. He was doing so well in his work that he was leaving a firm he'd been with for years to go into business for himself. The firm had been good to him and he felt badly about leaving. Also, there was a change in his private life. He had fallen in love with another woman and was leaving his wife and two children to get married again. It was a mixed bag. There were things to be happy about, and there were realistic concerns.

As with the young woman the day before, I asked Jim if he could write down the thoughts he couldn't turn off. He considered for a moment and then wrote steadily. When he finished, he said there were nine thoughts. (See column on the left, below.)

At that point I asked a question I'd never asked before. I asked Jim to think of the first thought on his list, and if any emotions came with it to write them down. He thought, and then wrote. I asked him to repeat the procedure with the second thought, and so on.

The above list of Jim's thoughts and the emotions attached to them. When he handed it to me he volunteered, "'Unfocus' is the worst problem in my life."

With his thoughts and emotions in writing, Jim took 100 mg of PHT. Not wanting my presence to have a possible effect, I left him to his own devices for an hour. When I rejoined him I gave him a fresh piece of paper and asked the same questions. This time he wrote:

When he finished Jim looked at what he'd written and had a belly laugh. He said, isn't that a typical American boy's story— JOB, GIRL, MONEY, WIFE. I report the laugh because there weren't any laughs in Jim an hour earlier.

This was the first complete one-hour test for thoughts and emotions. It is a good test for illustration purposes; it demonstrates three points:

One. A striking diminution of extraneous and unnecessary thoughts is seen within an hour after PHT. These thoughts are usually accompanied by emotions related to anger and fear.* When the thoughts disappear, the negative emotions disappear with them.

Two. The PHT needer has poor concentration and is unlikely to remember what his condition was before he took PHT. That is why it is necessary to get things down in writing. Before taking PHT, Jim said that "unfocus" was his worst problem. An

---

* Note that on Jim's first list, with the exception of love, all the emotions are related to anger and fear.

hour later I asked, "What is your worst problem?" Jim couldn't remember "unfocus."

Three. PHT does not cause realistic concerns to go away. Jim had two real problems. They were still there but in better perspective. After PHT he still felt guilt in leaving his firm, but now "guilt" was coupled with "success" (he was starting his own business). He still had realistic concern about his family, but instead of *children (guilt, remorse)* this was moderated to *wife (sadness).**

Let me re-emphasize that the test should be done in writing. People who need PHT are poor observers and are almost sure to forget how they were an hour before.

■ ■ ■

Everybody's talking at me
I don't hear a word they're saying
Only the echoes of my mind.
—"Everybody's Talking,"
Midnight Cowboy

"Only the echoes of my mind." What a beautiful and perceptive line. To a lesser or greater degree it describes the PHT needer.

---

* This was the first of many hundreds of such tests. These tests were not "controlled" by placebo or other drugs. The persons were taking PHT for therapeutic reasons and that was out of the question. However, there was an interesting element of control. Initially, I wasn't sure how long it took for PHT to become effective and I experimented with repeating the questions at different time intervals, including five and ten minutes after PHT. In these two time periods I never saw positive results. On the other hand, beneficial effects of PHT were always seen between forty-five minutes and one hour.

This was a useful control. A suggestible person (placebo responder) would be as apt to respond in ten minutes. On the other hand, for all to respond within the same narrow time frame, and it not be due to PHT, would strain the laws of coincidence.

Until this test evolved it wouldn't have occurred to me that a person could identify the thoughts alive in his brain, think of them singly, and write down the emotions that came with them. I'd always thought of "echoes of my mind" as being unconscious or subconscious. I still think they are—most of the time. But when a specific question is asked, the echoes become conscious and can be identified. Thus the same questions, asked before and after PHT, enable one to compare quantitative changes in thoughts and qualitative changes in emotions.

When you have seen the response to this test over and over again, you start to think of the thoughts as kites and the emotions that come with them as the tails of the kites. When the thoughts disappear, the tail (the negative emotions) disappears with them. Deeper consideration of this point makes one realize that sometimes the negative emotion (the tail) may come first. When that happens the emotion (of chemical or bioelectrical origin) can always find a thought to attach itself to. But PHT does not care for these niceties. Whether the tail or the kite comes first, improvement an hour after PHT is marked.

A majority of PHT needers have persistent thoughts they can't turn off. A small minority do not have persistent thoughts, but a jumble of thoughts flashing in and out. Both conditions are corrected or improved within an hour. The effects of PHT are so consistent that it helps to remember that, in the laboratory, PHT always corrects post-tetanic afterdischarge. It makes no exceptions, regardless of the type of nerve or the cause of excitation.

The turned-on mind is not just a daytime phenomenon. It continues at night and can make it difficult to fall asleep. It can also be the cause of light sleep filled with unpleasant dreams and frequent nightmares. That is why PHT's effectiveness against the turned-on mind is helpful with sleeping problems.

Only two more tests will be discussed here. One test was with a woman who used to be seen frequently on television. You could call her an intellectual, in a nice way. Before she took PHT I asked if she had any thoughts, other than what we were talking about, alive in her head. "Oh, I always do," she said. "Doesn't everyone?" Then she wrote down seven thoughts she couldn't turn off. All of them were connected with worries and concerns. When she finished she said, "I always have music playing in my head. It's like a jukebox and I can tell you what record is on."

An hour after taking PHT, before I could ask any questions, this woman volunteered that she was trying to be objective but she didn't think PHT had any effect. Again, I asked if there were any thoughts that she couldn't turn off. She said no—in the most matter-of-fact way. I said, "What is playing in your jukebox now?" She said, "Nothing." That woke her up, and she exclaimed, "My goodness, I feel like a weight is off my chest."*

One other test. It was with a physician who was doing research on PHT. He mentioned that he had been sleeping badly and that he was a little depressed. I suggested it might be useful for him to try PHT, both for personal reasons and also for research purposes. He agreed.

After I asked him the standard questions** he started writing down the thoughts "alive" in his brain. He wrote and wrote. When he had written twenty-six, he paused for a moment and looked up. I said, "That's enough, Fred, you've already set a record. Now go back to the first thought, think of it for a moment, and write the emotion or emotions that come with it."

---

*This sort of comment is not uncommon. When negative emotions are relieved, people tend to become more lighthearted and have a return of energy.
** It can be helpful to start with the question, "Do you remember what you had for breakfast?" When the subject tells you, you explain, "You weren't thinking of that until I asked. You got it out of your memory. That is not the type of thought we're interested in. What we want to know is, are there any thoughts alive in your head going on now?"

For our purposes, and to save space, I'll leave out the thoughts and just show the last twelve emotions.

> 15. frustration — problem all my life — too many ideas at once
> 16.   (")
> 17. fear — annoyance — impatience
> 18. tension — ~~stress~~
> 19. conflict — guilt
> 20.   "   "   sorrow
> 21. expectation — impatience
> 22.   "   "
> 23. annoyance — irritation —
> 24. strong frustration — key frustration of my life
> 25 sadness
>   Depression

Fred took 100 mg of PHT. An hour later I asked the same questions. He wrote:

> 1. Lunch in sun — pleasant place to relax
> 2. Coffee ~~was~~ good this morning
> 3. no noticeable effect of PHT

When I read No. 3, "No noticeable effect of PHT," I thought he was putting me on. But I saw he was serious. I said, "Fred, get out the list you wrote an hour ago." He looked at the list— and it all came back to him. He wrote:

> no neck, shoulder, or back
> tension or pain —
>
> Feeling tone pleasant —
> anticipating sitting in sun
> at lunch.
>
> Depression seems entirely
> gone
>
> Relaxed! — not overwhelmed
> by multiple, simultaneous
> thoughts or ideas.
>
> at peace with myself —

The turned-on mind is usually occupied with the same thoughts, repeated over and over again. This last test illustrates a less frequent condition—a confusion of thoughts flashing in and out. As Fred described it, "frustration—problem all my life—too many ideas at once."

■ ■ ■

The one-hour test is in two parts. As to the somatic part of the test: No person has all of the listed symptoms, but three, four, or more are not uncommon. An hour after PHT, moderation or elimination of symptoms is usually observed.

As to the second part of the test: Unnecessary thoughts usually disappear in one hour and the negative emotions that come with them are decreased or eliminated. This is a more objective method of assessing changes in mood than asking, "How do you feel?" before PHT and again an hour later.

(Outline of the One-Hour Test is on the next two pages.)

THE ONE-HOUR TEST

PART I—SOMATIC CONDITIONS

These questions pertain to how you feel now. If you answer yes to any question, grade your symptom, on a scale of 1–10 (1, minimal; 10, most severe).

	Before PHT	*After PHT*
Do you have a headache of any sort?	_____	_____
Any pain or blurring in the eyes?	_____	_____
Any ache or pain in the neck?	_____	_____
In the shoulders, the back, or chest?	_____	_____
Shortness of breath?	_____	_____
Aches or pains in your arms or hands?	_____	_____
Aches or pains in your legs or feet?	_____	_____
Are your hands or feet hot or cold?	_____	_____
Any tingling sensations?	_____	_____
Any "knots" or "butterflies" in your stomach?	_____	_____
Are you trembling now? Hold out your hands and observe.	_____	_____
Do you feel any trembling inside?	_____	_____
Do you feel a pulse, or beat, or throb inside you?	_____	_____
Do you have any pain or discomfort not asked about?	_____	_____
How is your energy now? (use 0 for normal, and + or - figure)	_____	_____

PART II—THOUGHTS AND EMOTIONS

Begin by asking the patient what he had for breakfast. When he tells you, remind him that he got that out of his memory, it wasn't alive in his brain. Tell him what you want are thoughts that are going on now, that are difficult to turn off.

If there are such thoughts, ask the patient to write them on the left side of a piece of paper (you don't need to see them, they might be personal). Then ask the patient to think each thought separately, and write opposite it the emotion or feeling that comes with it.

An hour after 100 mg of PHT, ask the same questions.

Before PHT

THOUGHTS   EMOTIONS

_____   _____

_____   _____

_____   _____

_____   _____

_____   _____

_____   _____

_____   _____

_____   _____

_____   _____

After PHT

_____   _____

_____   _____

_____   _____

_____   _____

_____   _____

CONCLUSION AND
PERSONAL NOTE

"Truth is a precious thing and should be used sparingly."—
Mark Twain. I have squandered a good deal of this precious
commodity in writing this book—my supply is low—and it is
time to conclude.

With the completion of this book I will have done what I can to
communicate the facts about PHT. The Dreyfus Medical Foundation is going out of the communications business. It is not that we
have lost interest, but to continue to argue the case for PHT could
be counterproductive. This is a matter for others now.

Duplicates of the Foundation's extensive files on PHT are here-
with offered to the federal government. Access to these files will
continue to be available to physicians. The Foundation intends to
stay in the field of PHT and hopes, selectively, to sponsor
research in new areas.

Thank you if you have read some of this book. And the best of
everything to you. As for me, I am going to get in a rowboat and
float upstream.

For a later conclusion, see page 273.

Foundation Changes

In 1976, with mutual understanding our scientific Director, Dr. Samuel Bogoch retired and returned to his personal interests in the field of scientific research. I thanked him for his fine assistance and his invaluable help with our bibliographies. And I thank him again.

An ever-increasing amount of medical studies were being published around the world. Our excellent librarian, Vivian McDermott, and her assistants continued to collect this literature. Soon it was obvious that another bibliography was necessary.

In 1984, Dr. Barry Smith, an outstanding neurosurgeon, joined the Foundation as Scientific Director. The PHT story appealed to Barry's heart and he's been an extremely hard worker. With his help a third bibliography, *The Broad Range of Clinical Use of Phenytoin*, was written—3,100 medical references. It was sent to all the physicians in the U.S. (508,000), along with *A Remarkable Medicine Has Been Overlooked*.

ANOTHER CONCLUSION

"Conclusion and Personal Note" was written sixteen years ago. I'll try to summarize what has happened since then.

Complaining is not my game. But sometimes telling the facts is essential—and may sound like complaining. Please read Table of Contents (pp. 299-304). Then consider. Phenytoin, reported useful for over 70 symptoms and disorders by thousands of independent physicians from 38 countries, is listed with our FDA only as an anticonvulsant. This is such a detriment to the health of the American people that it is the cause of a great catastrophe.

We are used to the word catastrophe being applied to volcanoes, hurricanes and earthquakes, where hundreds or more people are killed. We can count them, they're before our eyes. These are overt catastrophes. The labeling of PHT exclusively as an anticonvulsant by our FDA is the cause of a covert catastrophe. Millions of people suffer and die because of it. We just can't count them.

■ ■ ■

This has been discussed before, so I'll be brief. In 1908 a German chemist, Heinrich Biltz, synthesized a substance, diphenylhydantoin (now called phenytoin—PHT). He sold it to a drug company named Parke-Davis. It sat, unused, on their shelves for 29 years.

In 1938 Drs. Putnam and Merritt, looking for a better anticonvulsant drug than phenobarbital, jolted cats with electricity until the cats had convulsions. PHT was the most effective medicine tried in preventing these convulsions. Putnam and Merritt had an anticonvulsant, and it was approved as such by the FDA. However, Putnam and Merritt also had a drug that was effective against inappropriate electrical activity. It was not well known at that time that most of the body's functions are bioelectrically activated, so the great potential of the drug was not envisioned.

Shortly after PHT was used in epileptic patients, physicians published studies saying that those who'd received it had improvements in personality, mood, memory, concentration, and amenability to discipline. That was the beginning of physicians around the world starting to report, in medical journals, PHT's use for an ever-increasing number of symptoms and disorders.

There are almost thirty-four hundred medical journals. The average physician receives seven or eight. Thus he has less than 1/2 of 1% of the world's medical literature. It follows therefore that the studies on PHT are independent and objective, and the volume of them makes them evidential to the greatest degree.

In our system, a physician is made aware of drugs that are therapeutic by the drug companies, through advertisements and salesmen. If the physician doesn't learn about a drug this way, he's apt to be skeptical.

In recent years, there's been a game called "sue the doctor" in which lawyers sue for valid reasons and for no reason except to make money. It's understandable that physicians and hospital committees try to do things in a conventional way, and the lack of an FDA listing has more influence than was ever intended.

■ ■ ■

As related, in some detail, in the chapter, "A Flaw in the System," Parke-Davis has done little or nothing to get PHT listed for its many uses with the FDA. Management has felt that to spend the time and hundreds of millions of dollars to get the uses of an inexpensive, nonpatented, medicine through the FDA would not be worth their while. Since *A Remarkable Medicine* was written there is much more evidence of this. I'll give just one example.

Dr. Stephen Preston, former Head of Research at Parke-Davis, visited our offices, on two occasions, to discuss phenytoin. After he left Parke-Davis he wrote me a heart-warming letter:

> PHT is now a daily part of my life since I have developed a familial type of Chorea. After suffering through several experimental drugs I finally demanded that my neurologist put me on PHT and I found that Dr. Dreyfus knew what he was talking about. Except for you...I would not be leading the happy and productive life which I presently am.
>
> In closing I would like to state that neither the Food and Drug Administration nor Parke-Davis could ever have done such a magnificent job of making the medical profession aware of the therapeutic value of DPH as you have.— (excerpt)

I appreciate this compliment. I think the FDA can do a more important job.

■ ■ ■

Let us go to the FDA. I realize they don't know better. Nothing like this had ever happened. Physicians around the world had published thousands of studies about a remarkable drug, and its parenting drug company had not brought the facts to the FDA. When a Charitable Foundation organized a vast amount of this published information into bibliographies to help the FDA, it didn't occur to the FDA that they should do anything about it. It was not custom. They don't seem to be aware that they were established to help with the health of the American public, custom or no custom.

You have read my travail with the U.S. Government in the chapter, "Travels with the Government." There has been much more travail since then. I'll relate just two experiences.

In 1982, Senator Paul Laxalt, a friend from Nevada, introduced me to Secretary of HEW, Richard Schweiker, and Commissioner of the FDA, Dr. Arthur Hull Hayes. It was agreed by all that a committee of ten should be set up to study this matter. Dr. Hayes wiggled on this agreement, and put the matter in the hands of Dr. Marion Finkel, Director of Orphan Products Development. I told Dr. Hayes this was not an orphan drug, this was an orphanage. However...

Dr. Finkel studied the literature conscientiously, even went to Mexico with Dr. Smith and me and saw a variety of uses of PHT, including topical. After three months Dr. Finkel was convinced. At a meeting, at which I was present, Dr. Finkel recommended to the Senator, the Secretary, and the Commissioner, that five or six uses of PHT be published in the May *FDA Bulletin*. This was agreed upon unanimously.

About ten days before the May *Bulletin* was to be published, I was told that the five or six uses of PHT would not be published. "Someone" in the FDA had ruled against it. Imagine. A Senator, a Secretary of HEW, and a Commissioner of the FDA had been overruled by "someone" in the FDA. This was like the Joint

Chiefs of Staff being overruled by a sergeant. I was given no explanation.

■ ■ ■

About six years after my book was written, I met with President Reagan. He asked John Svahn, an assistant, to look into the matter. Mr. Svahn did the opposite of what we'd asked and went to

In the Oval Room again

the FDA and received the following comment: "The FDA knows of some anecdotal reports of the success of Dilantin for some few patients but is unaware of scientific studies supporting the claim." The President quoted this in a letter to me.

This statement upset me so much I wrote the following letter—which I didn't send.

My dear Mr. President:

Thank you for your letter. I have been trying to figure out why it's taken me so long to answer it. I've worked on it every day, including Saturdays and Sundays. But something has had me stumped. Finally I realized what it was. I have run out of hypocrisy—with Government, that is—I have plenty left for civilian life.

For over twenty years, the basis of my approach to Government has been "you can catch more flies with honey" and it's worked—we have barrels of flies. But we're out of honey—or hypocrisy in this case. So, to the truth.

The memo you received was an insult to the office of the President. It was also an insolence, an ignorance, and an arrogance.

The notion that the FDA is an authority on everything medical underlies this matter. It is a bizarre notion. But the author of the memo, note I do not say "the FDA," must believe it. With his twenty minutes of experience on the subject, you would think he would have referred you to this Foundation, which has had twenty years of experience. But no. He gives his considered opinion, "we know of anecdotal reports of some few patients." He could as sensibly have said, "we know of anecdotal reports of some few elephants in Africa."

I wrote the President a calmer letter—which I did send. He phoned, he told me, 20 minutes after he'd read it, and said he'd put the matter into the hands of James Miller, Director, Office of Management and Budget.

Mr. Miller arranged for Dr. Frank Young, Commissioner of

the FDA, to visit our offices. In three long sessions, we discussed with the Commissioner the tragically misleading listing of PHT. At the end of the third session, Commissioner Young told Dr. Smith, Ms. Raudonat and me, "Jack's been jerked around." I said, "Frank, I haven't been jerked around. The American people have been jerked around."

Well, one couldn't ask for anything better from the Commissioner of the FDA. I was sure something good would happen. Unfortunately, Dr. Young left, or was removed from office a few weeks later. However, I knew the word would be passed along, with emphasis. Would you believe it, Dr. Young wasn't even able to get me an appointment with the new Commissioner, Dr. David Kessler. Of course you wouldn't believe it. But it's a fact.

Frank Keating, now Governor of Oklahoma, who'd studied this matter thoroughly, couldn't get me an appointment with Commissioner Kessler either. Governor Keating's letter said embarrassingly nice things about me, but the letter is pertinent:

> For the past 25 years, Jack Dreyfus has selflessly devoted his energies to the health and well-being of our citizenry...Almost single-handedly and with no financial interest, Dreyfus has championed the expanded use of phenytoin...Physicians around the world have made remarkable contributions...Two FDA commissioners (Ley, Edwards) have decried the neglect of phenytoin.
>
> Like Cornwallis at Yorktown, to whom does Jack surrender his sword? Who will take this magnificent man's life treasure and apply it to the needs of suffering people?—(excerpt)

In the Commissioner's response to Governor Keating he said,

"Our scientific review staff has reviewed data on Dilantin for various uses and has concluded that effectiveness has not been shown for any of the indications."

If I knew the "scientific" word for rubbish I would use it.

But this statement requires some thought. It's so ridiculous you'd think that Dr. Kessler might be lying. But let's presume he's telling the truth. In 1970, 1975 and 1988 extensive bibliographies on PHT were sent to all the physicians in the U.S. including those on the scientific review staff of the FDA. The last bibliography contained 3,100 medical references, and hundreds of double-blind, and other controlled studies. Either of two things happened. The "scientific" review staff didn't even glance at these bibliographies, which would be a disgrace. Or, if they read a tiny amount of this literature, you could say this is not a scientific review staff, but an idiotic review staff.

Dr. Kessler's letter continued, "Our Center for Drug Evaluation and Research remains prepared to review formally any fully developed submission of organized data Mr. Dreyfus or his associates is prepared to generate in support of one or more new uses of Dilantin."

Imagine that. The government prates about the private sector helping them. I got out of two highly successful businesses, the Dreyfus Fund and Dreyfus & Co., and have spent $80 million of my own money, and 30 years of my life trying to help the government. The fact that I tried doesn't mean much, but the fact that I've been working in a gold mine of good health means a lot. And Commissioner Kessler won't even meet with me— and tells me what I should do next.

Millions of people, in this country alone, suffer because of those letters F D A. Another way of spelling FDA is **USA**. The FDA was established by our Congress with approval of our President, yet Congress doesn't even know who's in it.

To become a member of the Supreme Court a candidate is put through many weeks of grueling questioning by congressmen. Congress knows all the members of the Supreme Court, and almost none of the members of the FDA. We have a strange situation here. If the Supreme Court makes a dumb ruling, and I don't say they do, there would be a public outcry, because we would all know about it. If the FDA does something dumb, and I do say they do, the public says, "It must be so, the FDA said so."

We hear, "The FDA says this," "The FDA says that," "The FDA needs more time to study this," and we get the impression that the FDA is the second edition of *The Gideon Bible*. I assure you it's not. There are many good people in this organization and some of the other kind. But that doesn't matter, they have tenure. The listing of PHT, only as an anticonvulsant, is a crime. Perhaps I should be kind and say it's a sin.

■ ■ ■

A wise man said, "No man can be a prophet in his own country." Largely due to this Foundation's work, PHT, a drug parented in the United States, is being used widely in many countries.

The Broad Range of Clinical Use of Phenytoin and *A Remarkable Medicine Has Been Overlooked* have been translated into Russian by the Russians, and Chinese by the Chinese. In India and Ghana physicians speak excellent English, so there was no need to translate the books. Tens of thousands of our books have been circulated there, and other places as well.

There follows current uses of this American drug in Russia, China, Ghana, India and Mexico. Additional uses are constantly being reported.

China

Attention deficit disorder
Alzheimer's disease
Healing—topical use:
   Burns
   Diabetic ulcers
   Oral ulcers in leukemia
   Varicose ulcers
   Gouty ulcers
   Ulcers of leprosy
   Pressure ulcers
   Traumatic wounds
Scleroderma
Ischemia
Stroke
Cardiac arrhythmias

Enuresis
Depression (including anxiety)
Psychosis, symptoms of
   (violence and agitation)
Heroin abuse
Continuous muscle
   fiber activity
Mountain sickness
Gilles de la Tourette
   syndrome
Atherosclerosis / hyperlipidemia
Pain (stroke, burns, cancer)
Migraine
Trigeminal neuralgia
Restless legs

Russia

Anxiety
Concentration
   (uncontrolled thinking)
Alcohol withdrawal
Neurosis
Parkinson's disease
Healing—topical use:
   Burns
   Chronic skin ulcers

Hypertension
Cardiovascular disease
Atherosclerosis
Cushing's disease
Hypothalamic dysfunction
Temperature regulation
Gynecologic dysfunctions
   (infertility, menstrual
   regulation and symptoms)

Ghana

Violent behavior
Anxiety
Asthma
Sickle cell disease:
   Ulcer healing
   Pain
   Crisis

Healing—topical use:
   Burns
   Chronic skin ulcers
   Ulcers of leprosy
   Buruli ulcers
   Dental surgery
Pre-eclampsia (hypertension
   in pregnancy)

India

Healing—topical use:
    Ulcers of leprosy
    Venous stasis ulcers
    Diabetic ulcers
    Abscess cavities
    Burns
Asthma
Migraine headaches
Pain

Neuropathic pain
Cancer pain
Tetanus
Rheumatoid arthritis
Alcohol and heroin withdrawal
Mood disorders
Eclampsia and Pre-eclampsia
    (hypertension in pregnancy)

Mexico

Healing—topical use:
    Burns
    Ulcers
    Surgical wounds
    Dental surgery
Pain
Mood disorders

Excessive fear
Excessive anger
Depression
Pre-anesthesia
Sleep disturbances
Enuresis
Tetanus

PHT is being used in Brazil, Guyana, Iraq, Jordan, Nigeria, Poland, Tanzania, Zambia, and other countries for an increasing number of uses. Dr. Smith has visited many of these countries.

■ ■ ■

The FDA is different people at different times. The FDA has done some excellent things. You will recall the FDA, under Dr. Charles Edwards, in 1972, had Secretary Elliot Richardson write the following letter to Governor Rockefeller:*

*Gov. Rockefeller's and Sec. Richardson's letters are in the *Appendix,* pp. 317-318.

June 22, 1972

Dear Governor Rockefeller:

...A review of the literature reveals that phenytoin has been reported to be useful in a wide range of disorders. Among its reported therapeutic actions are its stabilizing effect on the nervous system—its antiarrhythmic effect on certain cardiac disorders—and its therapeutic effect on emotional disorders...

Your interest in encouraging the Department to provide a public clarification of the status of phenytoin is very welcome...(excerpt).

Sincerely,
Elliot L. Richardson, Secretary,
Health, Education and Welfare

In their April 1982 *FDA Bulletin*, the FDA made an excellent statement:

Once a product has been approved for marketing, a physician may prescribe it for uses...not included in approved labeling. Such 'unapproved' or, more precisely, 'unlabeled' uses may, reflect approaches to drug therapy that have been extensively reported in medical literature. (excerpt)

▪ ▪ ▪

To the President and to Congress

Although this matter is not your conventional work, please don't think it's not one of the most important matters ever to come before you. Look at it this way. This is not a problem. This is a solution for some of our most serious problems.

The most versatile and benign medicine ever given us by God

(or luck, as you may see it) is listed with our government agency for only one use. And the reason—it's so cheap. Think of that, at a time when government is struggling with the cost of Medicare and Medicaid.

For God's sake, I do not use His name in vain, shouldn't the President and Congress set up a committee of intelligent and conscientious people to study this matter. It would only take a week or ten days. And the rewards for the American people would be inestimable.

In addition to improved health for millions of people, PHT could have a marked beneficial effect on crime and violence, one of our greatest problems.

In our present Bibliography there are twenty-nine studies reporting PHT's beneficial effects on violent behavior, and synonyms for it such as assaultive behavior, destructive behavior, and episodic dyscontrol. Eight of the studies deal with large numbers of patients (over 100 on avg.). Seven other studies are double-blind studies.

An exercise in probabilities will help. If we assess the chance of being correct to the double-blind studies of 10 in 11, the large studies of 5 in 6, and the other studies of 1 in 2, the chance of PHT being useful for violent behavior is slightly more than 275 quadrillion-to-1.

PHT's Use in Prisons.

Some of those in prison have committed crimes because of nervous disorders. Being confined gives them time to brood. This exacerbates their tensions. Fear, anger, inability to concentrate, poor mood, sleep problems, pain, and an over-busy brain are symptoms common in prisoners. Phenytoin is therapeutic for all these symptoms.

Allowing prisoners to have phenytoin, a nonhabit-forming medicine, <u>on a voluntary basis</u>, would be an act of responsibility on our part. It would also be a great kindness.

There would be tremendous collateral benefits. As prisoners become healthier, tensions in prisons would decrease. Further, when prisoners got out, if they continued to take phenytoin, as they likely would, the physiological need for violence would be reduced. And the terrible cycle of crime and drug abuse would start to be reversed.

Let me stress—it's hard to get this point across—PHT should <u>not</u> be given to prisoners to control their anger. It should be given to prisoners to improve their health. Uncontrolled anger would be one of many symptoms that would be improved. And let me stress again, it should be given on a voluntary basis.

■ ■ ■

A Temporary Solution

If the FDA tried to approve PHT, use by use, in their usual fashion, it would take forever, and a century. What they could do (without delay) is allow Secretary Richardson's letter, which he said could be made public (remember the FDA wrote that letter for him), to accompany phenytoin's package inserts.

The FDA could then remind the physicians of the April 1982 *FDA Bulletin*: "Once a product has been approved for marketing, a physician may prescribe it for uses...not included in approved labeling. Such unapproved uses may reflect approaches to drug therapy that have been extensively reported in medical literature."

Having these two simple statements accompanying phenytoin's package inserts would open up the matter for the physicians and hospital committees in this country and be of great benefit to the American public.

Mr. President and Congress and American public, it's in your hands now.

Best wishes,

Jack Dreyfus

Something Personal

This book started with an autobiography, and I'll conclude with something personal.

My life has been incredibly lucky or, as suggested by the Reporting Angel, interfered with from above.

I've had the fortune to have many happy avocations: golf, tennis, bridge, gin rummy, horse handicapping, race horses, and management in the field of racing. In business there has been advertising and marketing, Wall Street research, and making a great amount of money. And then something far more important happened.

I got out of a depression, by finding that a great drug had been overlooked. This gave me a unique privilege—to spend my money, and the last 30 years of my life, trying to get the information to the rest of humanity. I can't imagine a nicer life. I thank God for it.

To The Reader

I'd hoped to include *The Broad Range of Clinical Use of Phenytoin* in this book, but our publishers have told me that it would be impractical from the book dealers point of view. However, the first 15 pages, through the Summary of Thought, Mood and Behavior, are included.

If you would like to have this extensive Bibliography and Review, please send your address and $6.00, to the Dreyfus Medical Foundation, Lenox Hill Station, P.O. Box 965, New York, N.Y. 10021-0029. If you can't afford the $6.00, and I hope you can, we will send it at no cost.

Four articles I've written, "Rules of Evidence," "The Placebo," "Substantial Evidence," and "The Tuna Fish Story" are in the Appendix (pp. 321-328)

Dreyfus Medical Foundation

THE
BROAD RANGE
OF CLINICAL USE OF
PHENYTOIN

BIOELECTRICAL MODULATOR

The painting on the cover is by Joan Personette.

The Broad Range of
Clinical Use of Phenytoin

Biolelectrical Modulator

BIBLIOGRAPHY AND REVIEW

Barry H. Smith, M.D., PH.D .
Jack Dreyfus

THE DREYFUS MEDICAL FOUNDATION

"The greatest crisis facing us is a crisis in the organization and accessibility of human knowledge. We own an enormous 'encyclopedia' which isn't even arranged alphabetically. Our 'file cards' are spilled on the floor. The answers we want may be buried somewhere in the heap."

—*Robert Heinlein*

Photograph of over 10,000 studies from 38 countries,
published in over 250 medical journals,
that form the basis of this Bibliography and Review.

This picture was taken sixteen years ago.
Today there is much more published information.

Prefatory

If one looks at the Physicians' Desk Reference, one will find that phenytoin's only listing with the FDA is as an anticonvulsant. This is a narrow description of a drug that has been reported by thousands of physicians throughout the world to be useful for over fifty symptoms and disorders.*

The misunderstanding of the broad clinical usefulness of phenytoin amounts to a great catastrophe. Millions of people—in this country alone—suffer because of it. This is not the fault of our physicians. There is a flaw in our system of bringing prescription medicines to the public.

The purpose of this Bibliography and Review is to put together, in one place, for the convenience of the physicians and the government, a comprehensive summary of the world medical literature on phenytoin.**

* See Table of Contents, pp. 299-304.
** Other than in epilepsy.

Evidence

It is customary for a drug company to sponsor new uses for a drug. That hasn't happened in the case of phenytoin. This doesn't make the evidence less evidential.

Physicians around the world, with no interest but the scientific and a desire to help others, have reported PHT useful for a wide range of disorders. Published in more than 250* medical journals, the reports and studies have many forms of control:

1. Double-blind studies with placebo or other drugs as controls.
2. Studies in which PHT has been found effective when other drugs have failed.
3. Trials in which PHT is found effective—withdrawn and symptoms return, reinstituted and symptoms disappear.
4. Promptness of action.
5. Clinical studies in which improvements are confirmed by laboratory means.

The most important control is the fact that the evidence comes from thousands of impartial observers. So many independent reports are like strands in a rope, each adding to its strength.

. . .

Basic mechanism studies confirm the clinical observations. They demonstrate that phenytoin corrects inappropriate electrical activity at the level of the single cell—with little or no effect on normal cell function. This fundamental property makes understandable how PHT can have so many uses.

---

* Today (1996) over 300 medical journals.

Use of Approved Drugs for
Unlabeled Indications

FDA Drug Bulletin, April 1982

"The appropriateness of prescribing approved drugs for uses not included in their official labeling is sometimes a cause of confusion among practitioners.

"The Federal Food, Drug and Cosmetic Act does not limit the manner in which a physician may use an approved drug. Once a product has been approved for marketing, a physician may prescribe it for uses or in treatment regimens or patient populations that are not included in approved labeling. Such 'unapproved' or, more precisely, 'unlabeled' uses may, in fact, reflect approaches to drug therapy that have been extensively reported in medical literature." (Excerpt)

Terminology

The drug that is the subject of this book is known by two generic names, diphenylhydantoin and phenytoin. Phenytoin (PHT) is used in this book.

PHT's best known trade name in the United States is Dilantin. Other trade names, outside the United States, include Aleviaton, Dintoina, Epamin, Epanutin, Epelin, Eptoin, Hidantal, Idantoin, Phenhydan, Solantyl.

Prescription Medicine

PHT is a prescription medicine, which means it should be obtained through a physician.

Table of Contents

Clinical Uses of Phenytoin

Basic Mechanisms of Action

Clinical Uses of Phenytoin

Distinctive Characteristics of Phenytoin

Phenytoin has distinctive characteristics which, when viewed together, set it apart from other substances.

1. PHT regulates bioelectrical activity at the individual cell level. This action, at a level fundamental to all body functions, helps explain how PHT achieves its therapeutic effects in a wide range of disorders.

2. PHT corrects inappropriate electrical activity, but does not affect normal function. It has been found effective in both hyperexcitable and hypoexcitable conditions.

3. PHT has a corrective effect on post-tetanic potentiation and post-tetanic afterdischarge. This action seems to explain how repetitive and uncontrolled thinking is decreased and repetitive messages of pain are modified.

4. PHT has regulatory effects on endocrine and metabolic processes, and on stress. It has been demonstrated to have anti-anoxic effects, and anti-toxic properties, and to promote healing.

5. PHT's action is prompt. Taken orally, it is effective within an hour, intravenously within a few minutes. Used topically, it promotes healing and is effective against pain.

6. In therapeutic doses PHT has a calming effect without being a sedative, and an energizing effect without being a stimulant.

7. PHT is effective for a wide range of symptoms and disorders. In addition to being useful for a target symptom, PHT can be therapeutic for many other symptoms—in effect have beneficial "side effects."

8. PHT is not habit-forming.

9. PHT's parameters of safety have been established over a fifty-year period by extensive and intensive use.

THOUGHT, MOOD
AND BEHAVIOR DISORDERS

Summary

Phenytoin has been found useful for so many symptoms and disorders (see Table of Contents) that an overall summary is impractical.

The section on Thought, Mood and Behavior Disorders deserves special attention—not only for the benefits in these disorders themselves, but because of the resultant lessening of tension and stress, associated with many other disorders.

Soon after phenytoin's introduction, in 1938, reports started to appear in the medical literature of patients' improvement in mood, concentration, cooperativeness and sense of well-being. By now, extensive published evidence from widely separated sources has established PHT's usefulness for thought, mood and behavior disorders.

. . .

Phenytoin has been shown to have a calming effect on the overactive brain. Symptoms of this condition are preoccupation, multiple thinking, and flashes and fragments of thoughts coming and going. PHT reduces this uncontrolled activity enabling more normal thinking processes to be restored. This effect is usually achieved within an hour, without sedation.

Anger and fear and related emotions are usually found in combination with the overactive brain. Emotional states related to anger for which PHT is therapeutic are impatience, impulsiveness, irritability, aggression, hostility, rage and violence. Emotional states related to fear for which PHT is therapeutic are worry, anxiety, guilt, pessimism and depression. Although excessive anger and fear states are decreased or eliminated by PHT, realistic reactions of anger and fear are not interfered with.

Sleep disturbances found in combination with the overactive brain fall into two general categories. The first and most frequent category is symptomatized by difficulty in falling asleep because of over-thinking, light sleep accompanied by unpleasant dreams and frequent nightmares, and insufficient sleep. A less frequent category is symptomatized by excessive sleep, so-called avoidance sleep. Relief from both types of sleep disturbances is usually prompt with PHT.

PHT is effective with extremes of mood ranging from depression to the hyperexcitable state. These apparently disparate effects are observed in the overactive, impatient individual who is calmed by PHT, and the tired, energyless individual who has a return to normal energy levels.

Somatic symptoms frequently associated with thought, mood and behavior disorders are usually relieved by PHT within an hour. Among them are headaches, pain, stomach discomfort, dizziness, trembling, excessively cold or warm hands or feet, and shortness of breath.

Stress. When the brain becomes overactive and the emotions of fear and anger appear, the body goes on alert, and a state of vigilance develops. For short periods this can be normal. But, if this is a chronic condition, there is constant stimulation of the hypothalamic-pituitary-adrenal (HPA) axis, resulting in the release of the chemicals of fight and flight. A cycle is created, the chemicals keeping the brain overactive and the overactive brain stimulating release of the chemicals. A condition of stress develops. By correcting the overactive brain, PHT seems to break this cycle, causing a more normal state to return—and stress, commonly associated with a wide range of disorders, is diminished or eliminated.

Basic mechanism studies are consistent with the clinical observations of the effectiveness of PHT. Of particular relevance are the studies in the section, Stabilization of Bioelectrical Activity. They show that PHT, without affecting normal function, corrects hyperexcitability, as in post-tetanic potentiation or post-tetanic repetitive discharge. This would seem to be the mechanism by which PHT corrects the overactive brain.

APPENDIX

Transcripts of Seven Cases
Worcester County Jail Study

JOHN G.

Before PHT:

I'm nervous, irritable, and I brood a lot over things that are already over and done with. I make more of them inside which keeps me in quite a state of nervousness, anger, tension, what have you.

I magnify everything to the extent where I make myself uncomfortable...I'm never relaxed enough to take time to try to figure out what makes me move—I can't control myself and I just don't seem to give a damn one way or the other.

With PHT (Non-Blind):

I'm quite relaxed. I feel good.

I slept real good...I'm not as worked up so I stay awake...When it's bedtime, I'm ready to go.

I'm more easygoing...I'm not as short with the fellas as I usually am...I've only blown my top once...It just lasted a few seconds...I didn't brood about it afterwards.

After Being Off PHT (Two Weeks):

Before I took the medicine, I felt the same way as I do now...More or less quick to jump. In fact, a lot of times I might jump before I think it over.

I've had two good arguments since I've been off the medication.

I've had a few headaches in the morning...A lot of times I have a headache during the day when I get worked up over something.

I'm not sleeping. I wouldn't say I'm sleeping sound at all...I'm having some dreams...they are very unpleasant...and uncomfortable, tiring.

With PHT (Double-Blind):

I think I'm improved all over...An hour after I took the pill I could have told you it wasn't sugar...You could feel the engine just slowing right down.

I'm very relaxed and I'm not uncomfortable in any way...I can sort of think ahead.

I been sleeping soundly, no trouble, no lying awake thinking about things. That's more or less what kept me awake; the brain was overactive...but now I just drop right off.

I still have anger but I don't blow up...Quite a bit of restraint which I never had...The anger doesn't hang on like it did before.

VICTOR M.

Before PHT:

Well, I am nervous. I bite my fingernails. I got a nervous disorder...my hands shake...I have a lot of headaches and a pain in the stomach all the time.

I don't go to sleep till about one or two o'clock in the morning...I toss around a lot...I could put the blanket over me and sometimes find the blanket on the floor.

My mind must be busy...I can't turn it off.

With PHT (Non-Blind):

I'm sleeping better...I sleep right through and don't get up anymore like I used to.

I feel better than I did...I don't feel that nervous now...About the pain in my stomach, I don't get it as often as I used to...I don't get headaches as much.

I'm not as grouchy as I used to be...Now very often I don't get mad.

After Being Off PHT (Two Weeks):

When I was taking the pills I felt better and now, after I came off the pills, I don't feel so good...I'm restless.

I can't sleep.

I get in my cell and I won't even come out.

With PHT (Double-Blind):

I'm in a good mood...I wasn't angry all week long...I didn't have any arguments with anyone.

Right now I've been sleeping more than before...Every afternoon, pretty near, I take a nap.

The pain in my stomach went away...I haven't had a headache all week...I haven't been biting my nails.

ALTON B.

Before PHT:

I'm pretty nervous...I feel a little shaky all over.

My stomach is all tied up...It feels like it's all twisted up. Bothered me quite a lot lately.

I've been having headaches.

At the end of the day I get worn-out.

With PHT (Non-Blind):

I feel pretty good for a change...I don't feel shaky...I feel more relaxed.

I don't think too much...it seems like I have more patience...I sit down and watch television for one program. I never could do that before.

I guess I been sleepin' better...When I wake up in the morning my head feels clearer than it did before.

My stomach don't feel like it's all tied up...I can eat good.

I haven't had any headaches and I'm not so tired.

After Being Off PHT (Two Weeks):

I have been feeling nervous...I feel like I'm going right back where...like a nervous stomach and like I was before.

Right now I'm rundown and I'm tired...no pep, no nothing.

With Placebo (Double-Blind):

I feel miserable, lousy, tired, rundown...I feel shaky.

With PHT (Single-Blind):

I don't know what the pill was, but I'm pretty sure it helped me.

I feel pretty good...I feel cheerful...I feel good all over, I guess.

ALBERT M.

Before PHT:

I get depressed very easily...Nothing seems good to me...I don't care what happens...I don't care if they put me in the hole, put me in solitary confinement.

I'm quick-tempered...I hold back sometimes...the thought keeps harping, keeps harping...it stays longer than I like.

If I get excited...if I get mad...I'll start shakin'...my whole body is goin'.

With PHT (Non-Blind):

I feel more relaxed...I don't feel as much tension as I had.

I haven't got angry...don't wake up grouchy like I used to.

As far as headaches, I haven't had a headache now for about three days.

After Being Off PHT (Two Weeks):

When I come off the pills I get depressed, very depressed. Headaches, anger, not eating well, not sleeping well...Nervous, very nervous.

With Placebo (Double-Blind):

I didn't get to sleep till about three o'clock this morning and I was up about five-thirty.

I'm worried...I don't know what's going to happen, but I don't think I can do any more time. It's really got me down. It's really got me depressed.

Everything galls me. I just don't care for anything.

With PHT (Single-Blind):

I'm pretty steady, sleepin' good, my appetite has come back...I'm not angry, not a bit. I was down-and-out. Since I been back on the medicine I feel pretty good.

WILFRED S.

Before PHT:

Once in a while I just feel scared...I have a bad habit of biting my fingernails and biting my lip.

I'm quick-tempered. I always want to keep on the move. I pace the floor, it seems to make me feel better if I just keep moving.

I seem to think all the time. I have a hard time sleeping. I toss and turn for about an hour and wake up sometimes in the middle of the night from nightmares.

With PHT (Non-Blind):

I feel fine...I haven't been nervous. I don't find myself thinking like I used to...I don't think as heavy.

I haven't been scared, and I don't get in so many fights and arguments...I get along with the other fellas.

I've been sleeping good...haven't had nightmares like I did before...feel more awake...I'm just not so tired.

After Being Off PHT (Two Weeks):

Well, since I've been off the pills, I've seemed to tire more easily, I don't sleep too well at night and I'm more nervous now. And I notice myself quick-tempered.

I do a lot more thinking now.

I've noticed the last couple of days I've slacked down on my eating. I don't have too much of an appetite.

With Placebo (Double-Blind):

I'm nervous all the time, very quick-tempered, feel depressed, feel tired.

I think constantly. I try to stop but I can't...I sort of keep thinking of different things all at the same time...I tend to think of other things at the same time I'm reading...I have a hard time remembering what I read.

With PHT (Single-Blind):

Well, it seems like all of a sudden I'm coming back to life...

My mood is much better. I don't get in so many arguments...I'm not so hot-tempered.

I can understand things better and concentrate on things. I don't have that continuous thinking. I'm not so tired because my mind isn't running all over the place.

ROBERT B.

Before PHT:

I would say I'm nervous...I have my fears. I get mad fast...

My mind is turned on...I go in my cell, I sit down, and I start thinking. Many things go through my mind...and I work myself up and this can go on for a whole day...The only way I could probably turn it off is if somebody started talking to me...As soon as I stopped talking...it would just start up again.

I have a lot of trouble with sleeping...I wake up frequently.

I think I get very easily depressed...Many times a day. When anything doesn't go my way I get very depressed...I sulk. I don't talk to anybody and nobody can talk to me.

With PHT (Non-Blind):

I'm in a very good frame of mind...I just feel relaxed and comfortable...The feeling that I got now is that I can sit here and listen to you talk rather than me talk to you.

I'm much calmer...And I noticed that the days go quicker. I didn't have any run-ins with anybody. Nothing bothered me.

I seem to have a clear outlook and everything seems to be sharper for me. I seem to be able to concentrate better...My mind just doesn't seem to be wandering as much.

After Being Off PHT (Two Weeks):

I feel lousy...very edgy, constant depression most of the time...I'm just not interested in anything...I have no desire to do anything.

I tried sleeping all morning, laying down, reading a book, but I just couldn't sleep. And I'm not getting that good a night's sleep.

I go from one subject to another...I have a lot of trouble writing a letter. I guess my mind wanders so much that as I'm writing a sentence out I completely forget what I'm writing about.

With PHT (Double-Blind):

I have no nervousness, no depression, no trouble with sleep. I just feel great.

I'm in a good frame of mind...I've been pretty calm, cool, and collected. Happy.

I feel pretty lively...I have the feeling I want to do something...I don't have that tired, dragged-out feeling.

DANNY R.
ASSESSMENT OF DOUBLE-BLIND

In ten of the eleven cases, the investigators, and the subjects themselves, correctly assessed who was on PHT. The assessment of the eleventh case was complicated by a realistic problem that developed during the study which the subject did not tell us about, and the effects of PHT were masked by a realistic reaction. This was the case of Danny R.

Before the problem arose, Danny R.'s response to PHT was similar to that of the other subjects.

At the beginning of the study, on PHT, Danny R. reported that he slept sounder, that nervousness and excessive anger disappeared, energy returned, muscular pains in his shoulders went away, and his mood and concentration improved. Then a serious question of his daughter's eyesight arose and Danny R. wrote home five times and received no reply. He explains:

DANNY R: Well, you mail a letter and you don't hear nothin'. Then you mail another one. You can't find out nothin'. You get in your cell at night, you start wonderin' is the baby going to lose an eye...You toss around half the night.

JACK D: When we saw you Monday morning, you were nervous.

DANNY R: Right.

JACK D: We noticed it and assumed that you were on placebo. We put you on Dilantin, but you didn't know it. We saw you later and you had received a letter from home. Explain about the letter.

DANNY R: I got a letter from my sister. She told me that my wife had said that the baby was all right. I felt good about it.

JACK D: Dan, you've had two experiences with the pill. The first one was for about a week. Do you think it helped you then?

DANNY R: It helped me. I know it did. You see, when I went into that first week, my nerves about normal for me...That week I was sleeping good, as I told you before. My hands were steadier. And I stayed out of trouble.

JACK D: But this week, seemingly, the realistic problems overburdened the medicine. We don't know how you would have reacted without the pills.

DANNY R: If I wasn't taking them, truthfully, I think I would be in the state hospital right now. That's how bad I was.

JACK D: Okay, Dan. Thanks.

Note—At the time this study was done (1966) I didn't realize that PHT did not eliminate thoughts concerning realistic problems—a desirable feature.

Lyman and Patuxent Studies

LYMAN

The study at the Lyman Reformatory for Boys was done with six boys aged eleven to thirteen, and the results were similar to those seen at the Worcester Jail. Five of the boys were moody and belligerent. After PHT they became friendly and smiling, and their fights decreased from five or six a day to one or two. The sixth boy was obviously depressed when we first saw him. We had a hard time even getting a *yes* or *no* from him. He never got into fights and stayed apart from the other boys. After he had taken PHT, he became loquacious and started having the "normal" one or two fights a day. The disparate effects of PHT, the calming effect on the boys that needed calming, and the return of energy to the depressed boy, were interesting to observe.

PATUXENT

The Patuxent Institution was different from the Worcester County Jail. Unlike the inmates at Worcester, the prisoners at Patuxent had been convicted of the most serious crimes. But PHT made no distinction and the effects on the nervous systems of the five prisoners studied were similar to those observed at Worcester.

As a result of observations made during this study, Dr. Joseph Stephens conducted two double-blind studies with outpatients at Johns Hopkins and found PHT effective in reducing symptoms relating to fear and anger.*

---

* See Stephens and Shaffer, *Psychopharmacologia* 1970, and Stephens and Shaffer, *J. Clin. Pharmacol.*, 1973, *The Broad Range of Clinical Use of PHT.*

Exchange of Letters Between
Governor Nelson Rockefeller and Secretary of
HEW Elliot Richardson

April 19, 1972

Dear Mr. Secretarty:

It has come to my attention that a great many published reports, written over a thirty-year period by physicians and other scientists, have indicated that the substance Phenytoin has a broad range of beneficial uses. Further, it is my understanding that physicians are prescribing Phenytoin for many purposes other than its original indicated use, in 1938, as an anti-convulsant. In spite of the evidence of phenytoin's broad usefulness, I understand that today, in 1972, its only listed indication is that of an anticonvulsant.

I realize that the Food and Drug Administration is set up essentially to rectify errors of commission. This certainly does not fall into that category. However, I believe a public clarification of the status of phenytoin by the FDA would be most valuable, and timely. I enclose with this letter a publication, *The Broad Range of Use of Phenytoin—Bibliography and Review*, that extensively deals with this subject.

I hope you will give this your consideration.
With warm regard.

Sincerely,

/s/ Nelson A. Rockefeller

June 22, 1972

Dear Governor Rockefeller:

Please forgive the delay of this response to your April 19 letter concerning the current status of the drug, phenytoin.

Conversations with health officials within the Department have revealed that phenytoin (PHT) was introduced in 1938 as the first essentially nonsedating anticonvulsant drug. The dramatic effect of PHT and its widespread acceptance in the treatment of convulsive disorders may have tended to obscure a broader range of therapeutic uses.

A review of the literature reveals that phenytoin has been reported to be useful in a wide range of disorders. Among its reported therapeutic actions are its stabilizing effect on the nervous system, its antiarrhythmic effect on certain cardiac disorders, and its therapeutic effect on emotional disorders.

The fact that such broad therapeutic effects have been reported by many independent scientists and physicians over a long period of time would seem to indicate that the therapeutic effects of phenytoin are more than that of an anticonvulsant.

The FDA encourages the submission of formal applications, which, of course, would include the necessary supporting evidence for the consideration of approval for a wider range of therapeutic uses.

Your interest in encouraging the Department to provide a public clarification of the status of phenytoin is very welcome and I hope that this information is responsive to your concerns.

With warm regard,

Sincerely,

/s/ Elliot L. Richardson

Survey of Use of Phenytoin

There follows a survey by IMS America, Ltd. (year ending March 1975) of the number of prescriptions of Dilantin and desired action. For this survey, physicians in private practice are selected at random and include representatives of all specialties.

Desired Action	No. of Prescriptions in Thousands
Anticonvulsant	3,057
Prophylaxis	255
Curb Cardiac Arrhythmia	124
Anticoagulant	121
Symptomatic	64
Pain Relief	62
Sedative-Unspecific	46
Control Heart Rate	27
Relieve Headache	24
Withdrawal Symptoms	19
Analgesic	17
Psychotherapeutic	17
Control Dizziness	17
Antineuritic	16
Reduce Tension	15
Relieve Migraine	12
Anticonvulsant and Prophylaxis	12
Sedative Night and Promote Sleep	12
Stimulant	11
Calming Effect and Tranquilizer	11
Antinauseant	10
Uterine Sedative	9
Antidepressant	7
Prophylaxis and Sedative-Unspecific	6
Antispasmodic	5
Mood Elevation	5
Antiallergic and Anticonvulsant	4
Prevent Migraine	4
Control Vertigo	4
GI Antispasmodic	4
Antihemorrhagic	3
Relieve Headache and Anticonvulsant	3
Cardiotonic	3
No Reason Given	1,820
TOTAL	5,826

Over the years I've written articles with the FDA in mind. Some are included here.

The Rules of Evidence

The Rules of Evidence have something in common with the Law of Gravity. Neither can be amended by Congress nor by any branch of Government. The Rules of Evidence are simple. They are the application of common sense to probability.

Let us apply the Rules to the question of whether or not phenytoin is useful for thought, mood and behavior disorders. The material on which this exercise is based is found in the Thought, Mood and Behavior section of *The Broad Range of Clinical Use of Phenytoin*.

There are many kinds of evidence: Studies with placebo. Studies in which a drug is effective after other drugs have failed. Trials in which a drug is found effective—is withdrawn and symptoms return, reinstituted and symptoms disappear. Clinical studies in which improvements are confirmed by laboratory means. All of these methods have been used in establishing PHT's effectiveness.

Before arriving at a probability figure for thought, mood and behavior disorders, we will define them, for these purposes, to be problems of excessive anger and related symptoms such as impatience, irritability, impulsivity, hostility and violence; excessive fear and related symptoms such as worry, anxiety, apprehension, depression; also uncontrolled thinking, occupied by negative thoughts and interfering with concentration.

(In four papers PHT was not found "significantly" effective (not necessarily ineffective). For these purposes we allowed the four papers to eliminate ten positive papers that we have assessed the chance of being correct of 1 in 2.)

To arrive at an overall probability figure of PHT's usefulness for thought, mood and behavior, we assess individual probability figures to each of the studies. This is done by estimate, but since most of the authors assess the chance of their own work being correct in excess of 19-to-1 or 99-to-1, the following estimates are conservative:

	Probability that PHT is Effective
For each of the first seven reports, controlled by phenobarbital and/or bromides, we assess the probability of being correct of 1 chance in 2.	1 in 2
	1 in 2
	1 in 2
	1 in 2
	1 in 2
	1 in 2
	1 in 2

	Probability that PHT is Effective
Lindsley and Henry, the first paper in non-epileptics, in problem children	1 in 2
Brown and Solomon, in delinquent boys	1 in 2
Silverman, in a jail study, 64 prisoners, double-blind crossover, placebo—also other drugs	5 in 6
Bodkin, observations of 102 nervous patients	3 in 4
Goodwin, 20 patients out of 20 nervous patients	2 in 3
Walker and Kirkpatrick, 10 behavioral problem children out of 10, all improved	2 in 3
Zimmerman, 200 children with severe behavior disorders, 70% of cases improved	3 in 4
Chao, Sexton and Davis, 296 children, response rapid, often striking	4 in 5
Jonas, in his book, *Ictal and Subictal Neurosis* 162 patients - over 12 years	3 in 4
Lynk and Amidon, 125 delinquents	3 in 4
Dreyfus, 80 patients	1 in 2
Rossi, behavioral problem children	1 in 2
Turner, 46 of 56 adult neurotic patients	2 in 3
Tec, 15 years' experience	2 in 3
Boelhouwer, et al., 78 patients, double-blind crossover and placebo	4 in 5
Baldwin, 109 children with behavior problems	3 in 4
Stephens and Shaffer, double-blind, 30 adult outpatients	4 in 5

Goldberg and Kurland, double-blind, 47 retardates,
 ages 9 to 14   3 in 4
Daniel, aged patients   1 in 2
Bozza, 21 slightly brain damaged retarded children   1 in 2
Alvarez, in a book covering 25 years' experience   5 in 6
Stephens and Shaffer, second double-blind with
 10 patients   3 in 4
Maletsky, episodic dyscontrol, 22 adults—other
 drugs had failed.   3 in 4
Maletsky and Klotter, episodic dyscontrol,
 24 adults, double-blind with placebo   4 in 5
Solomon and Kleeman, 2 cases episodic dyscontrol   1 in 2
Bach-Y-Rita, et al., 130 adults with assaultive
 and destructive behavior   3 in 4
Kalinowsky and Putnam, 60 psychotic patients,
 improvement in over half   1 in 2
Freyhan, 40 psychiatric patients, behaviorial
 problems   2 in 3
Kubanek and Rowell, double-blind, 73 psychotic
 patients unresponsive to other drugs.   4 in 5
Haward, double-blind, 20 psychotic patients   3 in 4
Haward, three double-blind studies: 3 in 4
 concentration—last study, 59 pilots   3 in 4
Smith and Lowrey, 20 adult volunteers, double-
 blind—cognitive function   3 in 4
Smith and Lowrey, 10 aged adults, double-blind
 crossover—cognitive function   2 in 3
Stambaugh, hypoglycemia, unresponsive to dietary
 management—including 6 hour glucose test   3 in 4
Wermuth, et al., double-blind crossover, 19
 "binge eaters"   2 in 3

Based on the foregoing, the chance that PHT is useful for Thought,
Mood and Behavior disorders is:

   8,453,784,125,030,400,000-to-1, or thereabouts.

PHT's parameters of safety have been established over a 56-year period, by millions of people taking it daily, for long periods of time. It has properties which, viewed together, set it apart from other drugs. It acts promptly, calms without sedation, energizes without artificial stimulation, and has beneficial side effects. PHT is not habit-forming.

Conclusion—Having PHT listed in the Physicians' Desk Reference (PDR) only as an anticonvulsant is a grave injustice to the American public.

The Placebo

When one is trying to determine if a medicine is effective, the use of a placebo is sensible. If a doctor gives a patient a medication with the expectation of helping the patient, the patient may pick up on that expectation and rationalize that it's going to help him. Psychologically this might actually help for a while. If a medication is useful, comparing it to a placebo will demonstrate that it was not expectation that made the patient feel better, but the medication itself.

A placebo is not needed with a drug that is effective in a clear-cut fashion. But initially that might not be known, so starting with a placebo makes sense.

The Negative Placebo

Suppose a patient has a disorder and the doctor gives him a drug with the hope it will help him. Suppose the patient rationalizes that it's going to help and gets a psychological lift, which wears off after a while. Then the doctor prescribes a second drug to the patient. This time the patient is less optimistic, but a little bit of wishful thinking may be left. This drug doesn't work and the doctor gives a third one. This time the patient's wish-thinking device is depleted and he's not expecting any results. You could say he's placebo-proof. Let's say that drug doesn't work either, and a fourth drug is given. By now, there's a negative expectation by the patient. He expects the drug not to work because, if the first three didn't, why should the fourth?

There are thousands of studies on PHT in which a variety of drugs had been tried. These are well-controlled studies—the drugs that had been used had the effect of a placebo. In many, they might have been better than placebo studies—there might have been a negative placebo effect.

Substantial Evidence

In the Federal Food, Drug and Cosmetic Act the FDA is required to have "substantial evidence of effectiveness." The word substantial, in this context, cannot mean quantity. A study of 10,000 cases could be inconclusive. The evidence from a few cases can be "substantial." Let's take one example of how the evidence from just eight cases could be substantial.

For the purpose of this example, we eliminate the possibility of collusion or hoax.

Suppose there is a government station in North Carolina that is set up to receive reports of UFOs. On average they receive one call a day. Suppose that one night, between 3:00 and 3:10, eight calls come into this station all reporting similar observations, to wit, that a huge ball of fire was seen slowly floating a few hundred yards overhead, and that suddenly at tremendous speed it went upward, and disappeared from sight. Remembering our premise that collusion is eliminated, what are the probabilities that this really happened?

Since one call a day, at random times, is the average, the first call at 3:00 AM means no more than any other call received by the station. The second call could have been a coincidence. However, because it was within a ten-minute span of the first, this coincidence would occur, on average, once in 144 days (there are 144 ten-minute spans in 24 hours). The third call would be one heck of a coincidence, one hundred forty-four times one hundred forty-fourths of a chance. By the eighth call, the odds that there had been an unusual occurrence around 3 AM would be: 1/144 x 1/144 x 1/144 x 1/144 x 1/144 x 1/144 x 1/144, or 1,283,918,464,548,864–to–1.

This is "substantial evidence."

Now, in the UFO example, we took a premise that we couldn't take in real life, that collusion or hoax were impossible. The fact is that collusion would seem far more likely than anything else, and the investigators of this matter would spend a lot of time proving or disproving this.

We now come to the real life proposition, the evidence that PHT is a widely versatile medicine. Here the probability of collusion is ruled out by applying common sense to the facts.

Let's look at the facts before we apply the common sense. Physicians in at least 38 countries have reported PHT to be useful for more than 70 symptoms and disorders, in over 300 medical journals, written in seventeen different languages. This information started appearing in the literature in 1938 and has increased steadily to this date. It's obvious that the reporting physicians did not know of the work of more than a few of their colleagues. Common sense rules out collusion. Thus, the probability that PHT is a widely versatile drug is of the same order of magnitude as in the UFO example.

The Tuna Fish Story

Once upon a time some people were shipwrecked on a desert island. Their only food was tiny fish they caught daily. To get the most from the fish they constructed a machine that ground them up, including the heads and tails.

A year went by and all the food the people ate went through the machine. Five years went by, ten years, and still their food went through the machine.

One day a man caught a tuna. "Now we will all have plenty to eat," he said.

"Put it through the machine," the people told him. "It's too big," he said, "it won't fit." "Then we can't eat it," they said.

The phenytoin story is too big. It won't fit in the FDA machine.

In 1988, the Dreyfus Medical Foundation established The Health Foundation, an affiliate, headed by Dr. Barry Smith. At that time the Advisory Board of the Dreyfus Medical Foundation wrote me such nice letters that excerpts are included here.

"There is no one but you that comes to mind who has had the compassion, the common sense, the courage, the patience, the perseverance and the prescience, the greatness of heart, the gentle good humor and the generosity to try to show the entire medical profession *and* the government of the United States of America that a truly remarkable medicine was being not only overlooked, but often consciously avoided by the arrogance of science."

—THEODORE COOPER, M.D.
Former Director, National Heart & Lung Institute;
Assistant Secretary of Health, Education and Welfare

"My admiration and respect for you as an individual, and as a scientist, has grown over the years... But even more than being a scientist, you are also a humanist, and have pursued your goals despite all of the obstacles, wittingly or unwittingly, set in your path by others."

—HERBERT L. LEY, M.D.
Former Commissioner FDA;
Associate Prof., Harvard School of Public Health

"As you probably know I was something like 70-80 times abroad attending congresses, conferences, meeting people, attending talks, lectures and and delivering them myself.

Only one of the people I met was a genius—so, please my dearest genius, live as long as possible, be healthy and happy."

—NATASHA P. BECHTEREVA, M.D.,
Former Chariman of the Commission for Healthcare
and Welfare of the Supreme Soviet;
Former Director, Institute for Experimental Medicine
(formerly the Pavlovian Institute);
Member of Six Academies of Science

"Among this peculiar scenario has risen the strong personality of Mr. Jack Dreyfus, with gentle manners, the mind of a wizard, the quick wit of a bridge champion, but the kind soul of an apostle."

—ANTONIO ALDRETE, M.D.,
Former Professor, Dept. Anesthesiology,
University of Alabama Medical School;
Chairman, Dept. Anesthesiology & Critical Care,
Cook County Hospital, Chicago

"You need to know that it has been your unerring insights and guidance which have brought this work to its current state."

—PAUL L. KORNBLITH, M.D.,
Former Chief, Surgical Neurology,
National Institutes of Health;
Chairman, Dept. of Neurosurgery,
Albert Einstein College of Medicine

"You have demonstrated to the entire world—at no little expense to yourself and considerable effort in going to the far corners of this world—what a valuable medication Dilantin is for many purposes. You have also demonstrated something that Mark Twain once said, 'I have never let my schoolin' interfere with my education.'"

—JOSEPH C. ELIA, M.D.,
Most decorated Flight Surgeon in World War II;
Editor, Medical Page,
New Hampshire Union Leader

"You are a human being that is forever young, forever giving, forever caring, and forever wise. Your works will be forever young."

—EDUARDO RODRIGUEZ-NORIEGA, M.D.,
Professor of Medicine and Chief,
Dept. of Infectious Diseases,
University of Guadalajara